I Don't Want to Die All Alone

Joseph F. Henderson III

AuthorHouse™
1663 Liberty Drive, Suite 200
Bloomington, IN 47403
www.authorhouse.com
Phone: 1-800-839-8640

First published by AuthorHouse 11/6/2007

ISBN: 0-7596-1318-4 (sc)

Printed in the United States of America
Bloomington, Indiana

This book is printed on acid-free paper.

This book is dedicated to:

In Loving Memory

James D. 'PEANUT' Henderson(Son/Brother)

6-6-1979 *to* 12-11-1995

you are not alone

Jessie S. Henderson-Watkins(Moma)

5-9-43 *to* 4-15-2000

Peace to all I knew that died in the cause- *my brothers*: my lil bro James, Peter Joyner, Gilbert Guy, Trent Buckner, Peter Harris, Melvin Graham, Antonio O'Neil, Tremaine Watson, Mike Lee, Stephen Fredricks, Randy Johnson, Bay Brown, Keith Brown, Joseph White, Robert Wade Sr., Johnny Mims, Akeive Bolden, Mark Bowser, Clyde Brown, Mario Burton, Thomas Triggs, Thurman Thomas, Raymond 'suger boo' Briggs, Ronald Petus, Anthony Wilkins, Tony Copeland, Ricky Stanley, Marion Swift, Bruce 'damien' Brodus, Elmer Iron, Napolean Ware, Radeen Glass, Bryan Hadley, Leroy Jones, Ambrose Tate, William Strong, Darrin Butler, Terrell Gothard, Freddie Armstrong, Dwayne Smith, Antwon Johnson, Luther Lawrence, Chicago-Greg Jackson, MS Eddie Shaw, Rodney Thomas, Phillip 'Tyrone' McCullum, Samuel Berry, Freddie Branson, Frankie Cox, and many more that wasn't mentioned but not forgotten.

As salaam Alaikum Brothers

Peace to all I knew during the cause- my sisters: Mittie Jean Carlisle, Annette Jeanette Ware, Lisa Tucker, Ebony Lee, and many more that wasn't mentioned but not forgotten.

As salaam Alaikum Sisters

Special thanks page!

This page is for Ms. Judith Krabbe, a woman that has stood by the family's side since I can remember walking.

Ms. Judy, you are a very special woman.

Even though it's over eight-hundred thousand words in the English dictionary, not one will fit the love and caring you have shown me and the whole Henderson family for decades.

Your unselfish love and generosity could only be that of a GOD sent Angel.

You have looked and watched over us, even when we didn't know you were watching.

Even though some of us strayed off the path of your love, and mistaken your kindness as being light weight, I'm here to ask for forgiveness from all.

Our GOD sent mother that was there when disaster came upon us, and even when we were in our good times, you were still there.

A woman that never asked for anything in return, you are a true example of 'does no favor's seeking gain.'

I'm glad to have come across a human being that has been the most honest and the most trust worthy person in my life.

You're truly one of a kind.

You are so unique, and so worthy of being called my god mom.

Ms. Judy, I loved you yesterday, today, and will love you even more tomorrow.

If you ever read this book, please understand that this is not the same Joe you knew and still know, but was a lost child that is now found.

I Love you always, Joseph F. Henderson III

In the Name of Allah(God), the Beneficent, the Merciful
Praise be to Allah(God) alone. The Beneficent, the Merciful
Master of the day of requital
Thee do we serve, and Thee do we beseech for help
Guide us on the right path.
The path of those upon whom Thou have bestowed favors,
Not those upon whom wrath is brought down, nor those who go astray.
We give praise and thanks to Almighty God Allah, for sending us Moses and the Torah. We believe in Moses, and we believe in the Torah.
We thank Allah(God) for sending us Jesus and the Gospel. And we believe in Jesus, and we believe in the Gospel.
We thank Allah for sending us Muhammad, and the Holy Quran. And we believe in Muhammad, and we believe in the Holy Quran.
Peace be upon all of these worthy servants of Allah(God).
AMEN

The Beginning

Well Joe, this is it. This day has finally arrived, and you're leaving early. You were supposed to have left Battle Creek in July 1997, but circumstances prevented that latter move. It's been only two days, since you quit your job of four years, at I.I. Stanley as a team leader.

It's May 18th and moms is on the phone crying. Satan, her son, in the background saying "bitch I'll kill you." She has only been back in Mississippi for a year, since living in Michigan fourteen years.

She's trying to escape the memories of Peanut, her youngest son, since he was murdered December 11th, 1995. You worry a lot about her health, and every since you sent Satan to Mississippi, her condition is worse.

Sometimes there are thoughts, if you should have let the thugs that wanted to kill him, actually kill him. The guy that was shooting at him gun jammed and Satan got away, and now you're worried, that he may be the next one murdered. He had just broken into someone's house, and stole a five thousand-dollar stereo set, and sold it for only one hundred dollars in crack.

You tell moms that you're in the midst of moving back to Mississippi, but she tells you no of course. She doesn't want you to quit the job, but what she doesn't know is you already have.

Now you are wondering if that was the right move. With all the overtime, at the time, you were grossing a grand a week or more.

The money was good, but where was the happiness. The cars, money, jewelry, and attention were meaningless, since there was no happiness.

You still can't find the answers, as to why your little brother was murdered. Blaming yourself for his death is driving you crazy. You drive around town playing his favorite tape 'Purple Rain'. Tears start to roll when you hear the lyrics "It's such a shame our friendship had to end."

Your family is not getting along, never have, and from the looks of things, they never will.

You were always trying to satisfy everyone else. People followed, because you lead to satisfy them. That's the problem. You should never lead to satisfy anyone, lead to satisfy yourself. Rather you are satisfied with yourself or not, you can still live anyway.

You were always the center of attention, so getting what you wanted came easy. Now since your little brother is gone, everything really is meaningless.

Your life is somewhat unorthodox.

A lot of people may have had similar encounters, but they will never in their life experience the things you have experienced.

All in this is true, so no one can say or think that this could have been fabricated.

This is why it is titled; 'I don't want to die all alone'.

A lot of people may get offended by some of the things you will write about.

Some of the names have been changed, not to protect the innocent, but to escape possible legalities from your own family.

What has been written is not to anger or upset people, but some will be upset.

There are a lot of skeletons in the closet. And Joe you have enough to populate a graveyard. A lot of them will not be told.

You have been places, and done things with people that don't ever want it to be disclosed. You are real, so never betray them, as long as they don't betray you. You have never screwed anyone over, that didn't have it coming to them.

Through out this, they will be angry with you. Before this is over, they will probably understand that the things that happened were from the way you grew up, perception of life, and no spiritual upbringing.

You were a heartless person that didn't care for no one, not even yourself. You could 'kill a brick', and 'drown a drop of water'. That means Joe, you didn't care about life, nor did nor did you care about taking one.

You have been called every cruel name you can imagine, and you did some calling yourself, and most of them by your own family members.

Those of you that know or knew Joe, always stand by his side. Those of you that don't or didn't know him, continue to let it be that way.

You are a controversial thinker.

You sound as if you are a militant person. They way you think, a lot of people don't think like that. Your thoughts are not their thoughts.

You are an analytical thinker that looks at both sides of a coin instead of one. You analyze everything to get the correct understanding.

From my understanding, there has never really been any sorrow to the people you treated wrong.

You won't see everyone to tell them you are sorry, so others will pass these words from you. "As GOD is my witness, I am sorry from the bottom of my heart. I can only say sorry, for the ones that have been traumatized by me some point in life. Some of you will forgive me, and some of you won't. I can't worry about that, now that I have a new life to live. To my enemies that didn't like me, and still don't like me, I have much love for you anyway. I wish we could have called a truce a long time a go, but it's never too late. I'm glad to be here, so there can one day be some peace."

You have started a new lease on life, and people still say ill things about you. It's mainly the people in Michigan where you spent most of your life.

After being gone for over two years, people are still talking about you. Some good, some bad, and the rest, just gossip.

You should be flattered to hear that your name is still being mentioned often.

Some people will be offended, by your rhetoric and emotional tirades.

Before the book is over, you'll end up with few associates, few friends, and a few family members.

But the sad part about it is, is that the people will get mad for the truth that is being exercised. The old saying 'the truth hurts', is about to be displayed.

You don't worry or about that, because there's a lot more to think about.

People say that your truth offends people. How can that be, when you have no truth of your own, but the truth.

You think about the brother's lives that were taken during this madness, but they are not forgotten.

It's sad that you had to loose your little brother, to really wake up. GOD moves in mysterious ways, and your brother died that you may live. Peanut feels what you are going through. It's a lonely world out there, so he knows it's a lonely world down there.

He'll see you at the crossroads, and he didn't want to die all alone.

The way you grew up, you're not supposed to be here today. There must be a GOD. Remember when you were coming out of the store, and seen this guy you knew a while back. You remembered his face, but could not remember his name. It was ironic, because he knew you, and remembered your name. The bad part about it was, he said, "I see you are still living". That was a weird thing to say. This guy had not seen you in seventeen years. Why would he say something like that?

Don't pay attention to the English. I could have written this like a scholar. I'm not one, so there's no need to try and write like one.

Some of the information you are going to read, you may think of as being irrelevant. It's not. Everything in this context has a meaning behind it that made me realize 'I Don't Want to Die All Alone.'

Chapter 1

My first recollection of life is when I was around five or six. And the only remembrance of that is when my mother would have me to sleep in bed with her. She used to call me skippy dick or something like that. Can remember when she used to take her index finger and thumb and twirl my wee wee around. Guess that was to compliment the nickname. I always wondered if it was something wrong with doing that and if so when did it start, and how long did it take place before it ended. I'll probably be hated for mentioning this but I can help but to speak the truth.

Anyway, it seems like the only things that can remembered, as a little child, are the bad things.

I'm sure there are some good things out there, but just can't recall any. And let me get something straight, this is not a story designed to point out all the negative things in my life. This is a way of me knowing where I've been to understand where I'm going.

Well at six, I can remember drinking beer. I'm not talking about sips, try polishing off cans.

You know how it is, when you ask your parents for a sip of beer, and they tell you it's going to kill the worms. I must have been full of worms, because I was forever buzzing.

And you love it when your moms tell you to get them another beer, because you can sip the suds out the can they just finished.

Or, when company leaves, it's always half cups or cans of beer left over. You are quick to volunteer to clean up so you can get your buzz on.

Then after that, you get brave and start sneaking in the fridge and taking a can or two off the six pack. Then moms would give us a dollar food stamp for allowance to buy something. My sisters would get candy or chips, Mike and I couldn't wait to get us a can of brew.

You know how it was with the neighborhood store. You can buy beer as a child, with food stamps or cash. Then moms used to be able to get credit for food, beer, or cigarettes. We used to tell Dan, the storeowner; moms need a six pack of beer on credit. He would give it to us without trying to check with moms first. Don't think she ever found out either.

Moms never found out about a lot of things that were done as a little child. I mean at age seven, eight, or nine, moms didn't know what I was out doing.

When you want to hang with your older brothers, you have to prove you're not too young. The things that were done, at the expense of proving my self, were crazy.

One night one of my brothers came to me for a favor. I couldn't say no, because hanging with them, was wanted just that badly.

We went to the laundry mat around the corner from the house. They took the dryer tube from this hole, and had me to crawl through to open the door. I was just that small to crawl through the removed tube.

Didn't realize my first breaking and entering crime was being committed. The door was opened and they were let in. They had tire irons, hammers, and pillowcases. Said to myself, what are we about to do?

They took the doors off the front of the washers and started dumping quarters into a pillowcase. We went back home on Minerva Street to divide up the money. They gave me only nine dollars in quarters for doing what I did. That didn't matter because I was happy to hang, and to get the money they gave me.

They started hitting all the laundry mats around. They always took me, since the dryer tube was open wide enough, for me to fit through. Guess in my case, I was small enough to fit through.

That hustle ended, after nearly all the laundry facilities were hit.

Now I'm close to ten, and my hustling days are starting to get strong.

After the washer hook up faded out, money was needed, since it was always being in my pocket.

A car wash gig was started to keep dollars in my pocket. Washed and vacuumed cars for five dollars. That wasn't a bad price for cars that were big in those days.

Four to five cars would be washed a day, but only would have twenty or twenty-five dollars for a long days work. Now something had to give.

I started pumping gas, at the food store, across the street from the car wash, for a little extra cash. Since the cars were washed, and they went across the street to get gas, why not pump it for them, for an extra dollar or two.

One day someone's gas was pumped, and they gave me the money to go in and pay for it. An idea came to my brilliant mind. The money was held, for a little while, to see if the people that worked at the store would say anything. No one paid any attention to me.

So now every time a car was washed, they would be asked if they were getting gas. If so, they would be met across the street and the gas would be pumped for them.

They would give me the money to go in and pay for it. When they gave me the money, I would go in and talk to the workers for a few minutes, and then leave after everything looked ok. The washing cars hustled ended, and pumping gas was started full time.

I met Greg, mom's husband, by pumping his gas and keeping the money. Pumping gas was cool, since it was only done a few minutes every other hour. I didn't want the people to find out about me keeping the money.

Well the money wasn't kept every time gas was pumped. If someone only wanted two or three dollars worth of gas, that money would be turned in.

If they wanted five or more dollars worth, then the money was kept. Then greed started to set in.

When money was needed, and people would only get two and three dollars worth of gas, they would be told to get five or six dollars worth and their tank would be filled up.

It would be a line of people waiting for me to pump their gas. The people that worked there would wonder why they were getting so much business. The employees were told, the customers think I work here pumping gas, so they wouldn't have to pump it.

In the evening, we would help the workers stock the shelves and the beer coolers for a couple extra dollars. Mike, my brother, started working with me pumping gas and helping on the inside at night. He saw that it was a good hustle and didn't want to miss out.

He would control one side of the gas station and I controlled the other. When we stocked the grocery shelves and beer coolers, we would open up food and drink beer. Now we can keep the money when we pumped gas and didn't have to worry about paying for food.

Now another idea was born of and implemented. When we stocked the shelves and coolers, we would leave food and beer in the boxes. The workers would think the boxes were empty, when we took them out to the garbage dumpsters. Then later on when the store closed, we would go back to the dumpsters to get our goods and leave. The store didn't stay in business, after we went into business.

I truly believe Mike and I put York Food Store out of business.

After the store closed down, it was back to washing cars again. The way easy money was coming by; I knew washing cars was not going to last long.

I'm a true hustler, so you have to peep (recognize) game everywhere you go. Luck, well by now you can say skill, came across me again so to speak. One day while walking down Monument Street in Jackson, I crossed Jitney Jungle, a grocery store, parking lot. It was noticed, when an elderly lady was having trouble putting her grocery in the car.

Went over and helped her put the groceries in the car. Just for doing that she gave me a dollar. Now we were back in business. Everyday we were at Jitney Jungle, helping people put the groceries in their car.

Bradley McKeon, he's a store manager now; used to have us to help him bag groceries on busy days. Since he was a cashier, after we helped him, he would let us get anything we want from the store.

We would usually get things like Nyquil, cigarettes, or Goody's headache powders. Moms would send us to the store for these items everyday anyway, so why not keep a supply already on hand.

It didn't take long before Bradley's manager told him to tell us that we couldn't hang around the store anymore. That didn't stop our hustle, because we still used the store to make money. When moms would send us to the store for food or whatever, we would get a bag, go around the store and get the items, then leave like we paid for them.

This time, after that hustle was over, we didn't go back to washing cars. We started breaking into the boxcars at the nearby train yard.

That idea came across one day, when Mike and I were walking down the railroad tracks. We usually walk the tracks until a moving train come along to hitch a ride to the other end of the city.

We saw an open boxcar with cereal on it. We started throwing boxes of cereal into the bushes to come back and get them later. Now, what were we going to do with about fifty cases of cereal with about twenty boxes in each?

Since Lonny, my next to the oldest brother, worked at a store, we hipped (informed) him about the hustle. Dennis, the owner of the store, would buy several cases of cereal at a time.

Then our operations widened. We started paying more attention to the boxcars we hit. Like what each boxcar contained. Pacific Fruit Express would carry frozen goods, like pizza, turkey, beef rolls, and all kinds of cheeses. Dual Air Pack would carry the cereal.

We would stash the goods in an area we called Death Valley. We cooked, and camped out there, and when someone had an order for something, we would go to Death Valley and fix him or her up.

We had to leave a lot of the frozen goods at moms, so it wouldn't spoil. She would ask where the goods

had come from. We would tell her that Randy, Lonny's best friend, worked at Denzel's restaurant, which he did, would bring food home and give us some of it. She believed us.

My luck ran out one day. We knew this guy name James Earl, and wanted to expand the operations to another area. Mike brought him in to the organization.

We started hitting more and more boxcars. We found out which boxcars carried the beer, TV's, and

stereos. Now we were really clocking lots of dollars. (Making a lot of money)

One day we hit the beer train for at least two hundred twenty-four packs. My brother's boss took a lot of beer off our hands, plus we were drinking it like it was water.

I mean we literally stayed intoxicated everyday. I was about eleven now.

We told some Indians that lived across the street from us, about the train with the beer on it. Don't really know how many cases they took, but it must have been a good lick.

Federal officials were being seen throughout the neighborhood asking questions. We chilled out while things cooled off. Now all the money and goods had been depleted.

Now our customers needed us, and we had to start operations back up. We hit another beer train, and I'm glad we told the Indians about it.

They must have finished off the boxcar. The next day federal officials came to the house and asked if moms was home. We said no, but that didn't convince them. They said people around the neighborhood said we had stolen goods in the house.

We didn't, because the goods were stopped being brought in the house when the Fed's first started coming around. After that, everything was being taken to Death Valley warehouse for redistribution. All that we could not sell or give deals to the ones that could afford to buy, we gave it away to the low income in the neighborhood. This was a good way of giving something back.

We let the Feds look around the house, even though they didn't have a search warrant. They didn't find anything like we knew they wouldn't. We did tell them the Indians across the street be carrying a lot of beer and cereal inside their house.

We knew that they would find a lot of stuff, because every time we hit a train, we'll tell the Indians about it. The only problem was they would put the goods in their house. They arrested everyone in the house for having stolen merchandise. I didn't feel bad about telling, because we needed someone to blame to get the heat off our backs.

We slowed down on hitting the boxcars for a long time. The Feds were cracking down hard, and our names were surfacing all over the neighborhood. They mentioned my name in particular.

The Fed's called me, an eleven-year-old kid the ringleader. They knew I handled all the business transactions, and Mike would handle distribution.

One day, Mike, James Earl, and I were in need of money, so we decided to hit another boxcar.

Moms sent us to the store that night, and it was perfect timing. We saw a lot of boxcars in the train yard and decided to open one.

It was cereal in this one. We got in, pushed the cereal off the boxcar into the bushes, so we could come back, and get the goods when we returned from the store later.

When we came back to get the goods, this time the Feds were waiting on us. James Earl and I got caught and Mike was hiding.

While they were looking for Mike somewhere else, he let James Earl out of the police car. As Mike was trying to let me out, the Fed's were trying to grab him.
All this is happening like three houses from where we lived.

Anyway moms came outside, after hearing all the commotion. The police told her that they had me, and was looking for Mike, for breaking in the boxcars. She told the police how could we break in a train, and go to the store, all in less than an hour. She didn't know we had already broken in the train. When she sent us to the store, we asked Lonny's boss if he needed any cereal. Don't remember how many cases he needed, but that's what we were going to get, before getting caught.

They took me to jail anyway.

They had me sitting in a cell with murderers, robbers, and kidnappers, at eleven years old.

Juvenile detention was out of the question for me.

Police treated me as if I was on the same level, as the hard core criminals.

They kept me for a whole week. Five days at the most.

My food would be taken and they picked with me constantly.

Being only eleven at the time, I couldn't really defend my self. I saw no weapons in the cell.

They wouldn't take the food when I was awake, it always when they saw me passed out.

Would wonder why they pissed in one toilet and never flushed it.

They would have these socks to soak in piss, in the toilet for a day or two then take them out to dry.

Thought the dudes were crazy, until I found out what the purpose was.

This guy took a dry sock and asked for my food. After telling him no, the last thing remembered was this stinking sock being waved across my face. It knocked me out instantly.

Another whiff of that sock I would have probably died.

My court date finally came. The judge dropped the charges for insufficient evidence. The Feds couldn't prove how we went to the store, and broke in the boxcar, in a matter of less than an hour. We told the judge the cereal was already there, when we found it, so the charges were dropped.

That didn't stop me from breaking into anymore boxcars. We quit until one day, a boxcar that said Illinois Central Gulf PiggyBack or Piggy Bank, had to be looked into.

All I remember is the feeling was great. Mike was down with the idea.

Tell you what GOD love and that's the truth, if we would have known the value of money, we would have been millionaires after that hit.

It was nineteen-seventy nine, the year the Susan B. Anthony dollars came out. I was still eleven and becoming more and wiser on the streets.

We didn't know what the contents of the boxcar were, but when we did find out, what a gold mine we could have had.

It was barrels of Susan B. Anthony dollars.

When we opened up one of the barrels, dollar coins spilled out everywhere.

Everyone from the neighborhood was in on the action.

We were selling buckets of Susan B. Anthony dollars for only thirty dollars, not knowing what we had.

After that hit, the Feds started patrolling the train yard permanently. That was the end of my boxcar hustle.

Besides, we had moved to a different location again, and were use to hustling on every kind of occasion.

Chapter 2

Mike and I would walk around all day, trying to do this and do that to keep our bellies full.

Since we were never really at home to eat, we would scrounge and pilfer through trash for something to eat.

We would often hit garbage dumpsters to find food or go into stores and open meat, bread, and mayonnaise and make sandwiches.

That's the true life of a hustler.

Can remember living in the country in nineteen seventy-six, not eating meat for weeks. And when we did get meat, I would always say "meat cooking on the stove", "meat cooking on the stove".

We would eat corn, beans, and salads all day, everyday. We grew everything we ate. We even made our own salad dressing out of vinegar, mayonnaise, salt and pepper.

See, you have to know what it is like to have a hustle. You cherish those days of hustling money to get some real food to eat.

Don't get me wrong; when that's all you have to eat, you would act as if you were at a famous restaurant. It was seven of us then, so you know how tight food was.

I can remember eating possum and coon, as if it was a delicacy. Really don't see how such nasty looking creatures, could be eaten. It got to the point where I could no longer eat those things. It was like we were eating some of the rats that were running around.

Looking back, no one deserves to eat like that.

One night we were riding home going to the country, we must have hit a possum or a raccoon.

It was either Bro or moms driving. One of them backed the car up, put the road kill in the trunk, and went home.

The next day, it was soaking in vinegar, waiting to be cooked and eaten.

And Fran, my next to the oldest sister, would only eat the brains, tongues, and the eyes of the possum or the raccoon.

Yeah it sounds sick, but that was all she would eat.

We were the Beverly Hillbillies of Mississippi.

A lady that lived down the street from us rescued us many of times.

She always cooked, and would leave her door open, so we could go in and eat.

We never took anything, so that's why she trusted us.

Times when she didn't have her door open, we still ate somewhat well.

She had a pear tree that grew pears the size of grapefruits. We treated the pears as if they were meat and put barbecue sauce on them.

It was good, but to some it might be gross. Ask my sisters and brothers. They know the pears came in on time, a lot of days.

When you were living in the country, and in our condition, pears with barbecue sauce were a meal.

Guess that was the life of the country in those days.

It was not until after we left the country, illegal hustling was learned.

Moms had us shelling peas and beans for this man every other day.

Then the other days, we were out in the field picking the beans and peas.

It would have been cool if we received more than a dollar a bushel to pick, shell, and snap the beans.

After a while, that didn't cut it. If you knew how many peas it took to fill a bushel, you would feel me.

Mike and I would walk to Jackson from the country everyday. This was about twenty-five miles from Brandon to Jackson. Eventually, after Satan was born, we moved back to the city. That was in July nineteen seventy-six so I had just turned eight.

That was cool because the hustle had started.

We started legally hustling. Well at least I did. Lawns would be raked, then eventually saved enough money and bought a push mower.

Everywhere I went, the mower was there with me.

If people were getting their yard done for twenty dollars, they would be charged ten. If they paid ten then five was charged. You get the picture.

A lot of them would have me to do the yard once a week, since they were getting it done every two.

Mike and I became business partners again, since my workload was getting bigger. That was cool since we had a permanent schedule. We didn't have to go around asking for customers, since we did good work.

Mowing lawns was a good business. We would make about three to four hundred dollars a week. Guess that beats hitting up garbage cans for food or robbing boxcars.

Cutting grass and raking leaves became obsolete. Or one should say legal hustling became obsolete.

I think hanging with the wrong crowd seeing them do criminal work for more money opened my eyes.

Having the feeling you could do less work and make more money gave me the thought why not go do it.

We were breaking in to schools, churches, or any business that had something of value.

We would bust the front window out of the snack machines that were located around town.

Then a tire iron would be used to get the money from it. The snacks were easy to retrieve from the broken glass, since that was the only thing preventing us from getting the goods.

Now they don't leave snack machines outside, and the drink machines are harder to get into. Not that it's my desire get into them.

It was easy to put your hand where the drinks were discharged and pull pops from the chamber.

We would stick paper up in the coin return slot. When people bought something to drink, and had change coming back, the paper that was lodged in the hole prevented them from getting it.

We checked on the coins every morning, and it would be a nice pile up. I would sometimes get up a little earlier than Mike to check to see if we had any change. I didn't want to split the profits with him fifty-fifty every time. The change was a good hustle, and came in handy with the other change.

The change we received from the phone booths.

High powered firecrackers were put in the coin return chamber.

Once the firecrackers exploded all kinds of coins would be released.

We would pay for one newspaper from a machine, and then take all that were there. That brought in a few dollars everyday, and a little more on Sundays.

When we lived on Gallatin Street, around nineteen seventy eight we didn't have to worry about money.

This auto mechanic shop, Jackson Generator and Starter Service, was right across the street from where we lived.

It was like a body shop that repaired semi trucks.

You could go into the body shop to buy snacks and pop from the machines that were there.

After always having the correct amount to buy pop or candy, this time change was needed.

Someone that worked there came to the front and gave me change, then went to the back.

It was strange, because they had one of those wooden cash drawers that you pull out. When he was given me change, all could be seen was fifty's on down.

Scoped the place out the next couple of days, and noticed that all the workers went to the back of the shop after five o'clock, in the evening.

One day I went to get a pop, and no one was around. Opened the drawer and took about five hundred or more dollars.

I showed Mike and Lonny what was taken, and split it with them. We would give moms some money, and tell her we worked for Edwards Lumber Co. down the street. That was good because she never questioned anything we did.

Girls in the neighborhood loved us. We were the only kids running around with hundreds of dollars in our pockets. We kept the girls supplied with what they needed, for a kiss or two. I was into girls at an early age. Anyway, I would hit the shop every other day. This was by far the best hustle I had ever come across. Then, got greedy, and started hitting the shop up everyday.

It was Mike or Lonny's idea.

Guess the employees started to notice the money being missing, because they started locking the door after business hours.

Mike and Lonny must have talked me into doing it one last time. I can remember them telling me to take everything. I had to go around and sneak in to hit them one last time. And I took everything in sight. Even took the change.

That hustle played out, and it was time for another adventure.

You're probably thinking, was I ever in school?

Yes, but under the circumstances, I didn't want to go. Yes I was smart. And was getting good grades, but it was a waste of time, since no money was involved. And besides, I was educating myself on the streets.

The only thing was, like any other hustler, I saw no reason to go. Before age thirteen was reached, I was getting into all kinds of trouble. More than any normal eleven or twelve year old could handle.

Fighting, stealing, or doing whatever to get by everyday.

A person that knew me and didn't know me was shooting at me constantly.

Moms would tell me that my life would never live to see sixteen. Every year that passed, a year was added to it, minus sixteen. In other words, when I turned seventeen, I turned one. When I turned eighteen, I turned two. Get the point.

A child must have to be really out there, or bad as hell, for a mother to tell her son, he will never live to see sixteen.

No one was ever there to show me any other way. No fathers to play sports or, show me how to defend myself, or show me how to be a man. So I ended up turning to the streets to raise me.

Parents, especially the fathers, please take care of your sons. Spend time with them so the streets won't have them.

Every time we would speak of dad, moms would always say he wasn't this, or he wasn't that. Then she would tell us how he was a good father. Which one was it? Either you were a good father, or you were a bad one. Period.

There was no in between to choose. The only in between that can be seen, is that he took care of us after they separated.

Yeah he's paralyzed and all but, he still could have showed a little interest in us.

Was four years old when he left, and wondered, how he could have been a good father? Maybe that's one reason, for the things that were done, coming up.

I'm not making excuses, or trying to have people to feel sorry for me, but a stable father may have changed a few things. No doubt about it.

At the time, my mother was one of the seventy percent of households being headed by a single black woman. I can understand that having nine kids isn't easy to bring up. How moms did it or anyone else I have no idea. But at times it did appear she didn't like us very well.

I didn't ask to be here, so it frustrated me when moms would say that she hated us. When your moms say she wished she never had you, why have reasons to live.

We sometimes can say things out of anger on occasion, but to hear it constantly. And the sad part about it is we are taught that sticks and stones may break our bones but words never hurt us.

What kind of hurt are they referring to? It may have not hurt us physically, but mentally it did. And that's the worst kind of hurt.

And you know they mean it when you are looked in the face and the eyes gleam with anger.

Though I try to blot it out of my memory; I truly believe that has scarred me for the rest of my life.

When your moms don't have love for you, you have no one. I'm not trying to say my mother never loved me, the things she would say or do to me, would negate the thought.

There were occasions when we wouldn't see moms for days at a time. When we got up for school, she would be sleep, and when we got home, she would be gone. There was no one to help with homework, or answer questions if you needed. We were pretty much on our own. And I did a lot of bad things at my young age.

There's no one to blame for my actions, but believe me, if someone was there, a lot of the bad things that happened in my life, wouldn't have happened.

Even the sisters and brothers of mine have hate for each other. Rochelle, my oldest sister, has a lot of dislike for my mother. Maybe it's because, of the way she was also treated. Moms would sometimes have us to beat up Rochelle.

She made it appear that Rochelle was so bad she didn't deserve to be one of us.

Later to find out, Rochelle, like the rest of us, was only products of moms.

And moms see her self growing up all over again. And to add injury to insult, we all have mom's ways.

There were times when Rochelle would be accused of going with someone moms was dating.

When Rochelle, Tara, and Fran, in different eras, would get accused of a man moms was dating, that was painful to see.

Fran would have to wait in different rooms, when Greg, moms husband, came home.

If he went to the bathroom in the night, moms would wake her up so he could go to the bathroom.

And it didn't help that when Fran had her child, Tara said the baby looked like Greg, and that infuriated moms even more. It didn't help that what Tara said only added insult to injury.

When we were living in Jackson, moms and Rochelle had it out about one of the men she was dating.

And the sad part about all this is, these were grown men, and the girls were little children. And it seems as though most of the time, the blame was put on the girls, rather than the men. And the girls were the one's that suffered persecution. Why did moms wake Fran up when Greg went to the bathroom? Why she didn't just go to the bathroom with him, and let her sleep? Because it made him think that she didn't trust Fran, instead of him.

It was always animosity between moms and Rochelle, and why, who knows.

Rochelle either left at fourteen of fifteen, or moms put her out. She never came back. One day, they were arguing, and moms had us to her up. Right to this day, I can't understand why. It hurt me so bad to think of the days, when moms had us to beat up Rochelle, until I just broke down and cried to her. Begging and asking for her forgiveness.

Felt moms didn't love us, so she kept constant grief between everyone.

No love from your mother is a hell of a pill to swallow. I really believe moms took care of us, because she had to. If she really had a choice, she would have probably given us away, a long time ago.

Tara and Fran would always end up staying with mom's sisters. They would always say moms would be gone for days at a time. They talk bad about your mother, your mother talk bad about you.

Yes it was true moms would always be gone somewhere. But the way they would put it, made you wish you were dead when you may as well be.

That's another reason why there's a lot of hate in the family. No kind of unity between us, all the years of our lives.

Moms have played one sibling against the other.

She would tell one something, and then tell the other something else.

She would speak harshly against one to the other, and vice verse. No kind of unity in the family, from the start, and even to this day, it's still the same.

We are constantly at each other's throat as if we are enemies. No one have love for one another, and today, no sign of it.

Sisters living four blocks from each other and don't even speak. I can't go around Rochelle's house. Even when I apologized to her years ago, and promised there would be no more arguing, that didn't do any good. I don't get along with Mike. He's another one I won't argue with anymore.

But he and Rochelle will talk about me and lie as though I don't even exist. I guess the statement is true; birds of a feather flock together. Mike, Rochelle, do you not like me because I don't gamble. I don't drink, smoke, do drugs, or go to clubs and waist my money. I mean it's always constant grief, and animosity.

Even coming up, there was no love for one another. We would fight like enemies. Mom was gone most of the time, and no one was there to break us up. It was almost like when the slave master left, the slaves were at odds with each other, and because that's the way they were taught.

We fought constantly.

I'm not talking with your hands. Try sticks, bricks, knives or any weapon that would do justice. We were a violent family.

Where do you think we got the violence?

Men have been violent towards moms; she has been violent towards us.

She has drawn her gun on us, on more than one occasion. Telling your children you hate them, then act violent against them, will have kids looking to the streets as a way out. Beating you upside the head with shoes, brooms, or whatever she had her hands on.

I mean will hit you up side the head then will have the nerve to tell you to tap a nap.

Hell, we could have gone into shock, or she could have hit us in the wrong spot. She didn't care. She was a violent woman, and that caused us to be violent kids.

She didn't care about the consequences.

She shot our dad in the head when I was two. Still don't know why she did it, and no one will really tell me either.

Waited later in life before asking dad, why moms did what she did.

He tells me to ask her. She tells me to ask him.

Rochelle was either there or knows what happened. She was never really asked about that day.

Either moms or dad will eventually tell me. I won't count on it.

That is messed up, when your mom or dad can't share information with their family. A lot of the stuff mom and dad went through is none of our business, but inquiring minds want to know. So whatever Rochelle knows that will be helpful to us, then we need to know.

Rochelle would tell us how moms would tie dad up with ropes or ties while he was drunk then she would leave. Everyone says my dad was a good man, but moms has painted a picture like he is a nobody.

Don't believe he was there, but Rochelle would get mad, and say moms kept him from being there.

That's where hostility set in, because we would disagree on that issue.

When he would drive down the street and see us walking, he wouldn't even offer us a ride.

He was probably scared of moms.

There are a lot of unanswered questions. Like, what did he do to moms that made her want to kill him?

She meant to kill him, because he was shot in the head. You don't shoot anyone in the head and expect them to live through it.

The only reason he gives for her shooting him is, they were arguing.

If you are going to shoot someone in the head for just an argument, then it would be a lot more dead people on our hands.

I know it's more to it than that. Rumor has it that moms was at a club, and either dad had to go to work, or he just wanted her home. Moms didn't want to leave at the time, and that's when the argument started. Then bang and the rest is history.

I know there are hidden truths that need to be told.

One thing that bothers me is that he hints around about Tara not being his child. Paternity wise.

He'll say things like "I was in California at the time," or "I know who all my kids are."

There's a lot of speculation that Tara may not be dad's child.

Everyone knows he's her father, but it's still a lot of unanswered questions.

Look at the evidence, Tara doesn't really look like us.

Why is she the only one out of dad six kids by moms that has sickle cell?

He claims he was in California at the time. Could this be a case of momma's baby daddy's maybe? I would wonder why Jim would come by every other day and pick up Tara only. He would buy her things or give moms money for her. And as sad as it may sound, Tara and Jim favor. I wish there was a blood test taken, to end all the speculation.

Even if Tara is not his child, there shouldn't be a loss on his behalf.

He has never done anything for her or the rest of us. I'll take that back, he use to and still does take care of Rochelle and her children. He gives Rochelle kids birthday gifts and money all through the year. Little Joe can be around and he wouldn't give him a damn thing.

Then had the nerve to tell him he would buy him a bike when his birthday came around. And when it did come around and Little Joe asked him about it, he changed his mind and gave him five dollars. What in the hell is he going to do with five dollars? Buy a happy meal and say my granddaddy fed me.

My son is not hard up for a lie and certainly not hard up for five sorry ass dollars.

I'll tell you what you keep the damn five dollars and buy yourself some liquor. My treat. That's the only thing I see we had in common.

In March nineteen ninety-one, I came down to Jackson to visit. My father offered me a drink.

He saw that I had my own when it was removed from the bag. He asked "What are you drinking?" I told him E&J Brandy.

What a coincidence, he had the same liquor.

Several years later, I visited Jackson once again, but this time he was offered a drink. He had his on and what do you know, he was also drinking Paul Masson.

Now when Jackson became my home, in May nineteen ninety-seven, who would think lightning strikes in the same place three times.

This time no one offered each other a drink. The crazy part about it was someone he was drinking with was on their way to the store to buy his liquor. When they came back, I'll be damned if he didn't send them to get some Seagram's Gin.

How do you explain something like that?

Three different times, years apart and we have the same thing to drink. Is this all we have in common?

If so, you can keep the memories. I don't want to go through the rest of my life thinking the only thing we had in common was we liked the same poison.

I guess since he gave me no money, he could at least give me something that he liked.

Well let me take that back, he did give me some money.

Looking back one day he gave Lonny and Rochelle I think two hundred or so dollars a piece. Then he gave Mike and I like fifty dollars a piece.

Yes we were mad about it because he would always give them money. A few minutes later he must have found out Mike and I was mad.

He called around to my grandmothers house and told us to come back it was a mistake in the money. When we got around there he took the money back from us and gave us two dollars a piece. That was the last time I had any respect for the dude. I think that was like nineteen eighty.

Never asked him for anything and don't expect to either. He would throw up in my face, how his social security checks were to take care of us.

Oh well.

There's no hate for my father, but it's a need to understand what happened to him and moms.

Right to this day, no decent conversation can be had with my father, or better choice of words would be the sperm donor. He hasn't been a father or a daddy to me.

I try to hold a father and son conversation with him, but hell he stays to drunk to concentrate. And when I try to talk, it's nothing but cussing and derogatory language. I try to give him the benefit of the doubt. I want to talk to him sober so it can at least be legitimate. Maybe he stays drunk to escape what he's been through. That's the way drinking had me to think.

I can't help but to feel this way. My mother won't tell me anything.

Her sisters and brothers are very limited with what they say. All they would say is your mother needs to tell you the truth. What truth are they referring to? But, they are quick to put her down.

They would say your mother was a pill freak, or a Nyquil freak. That was another reason why we were so in love with Nyquil. Moms would drink a bottle or more everyday.

They would tell how she would leave us days at a time, with different members of the family. Some of the things said are true.

Every time moms was asked, about some of the things that are being said, she would say they were lying. A lot of times, it was just left alone.

The reason for me knowing the truth is it will better help me understand why we hate each other as a family.

The way we are to this day reflects a lot of the things we seen coming up.

It was so much violence, with the men my mother chose, we thought that's the way it was supposed to be.

I'm not just talking curse words, try blood drawn fights.

We would be sleep, and then awaken by glass breaking.

All you could hear was cursing and fighting.

She was still with Satan's daddy around nineteen seventy-seven or seventy-eight. Then, at the time, he was the most violent man she has ever known; at least from what we seen over the years.

On one of their club nights, they came home arguing as usual. Then, that escalated into a fight.

He must have locked the door, because she was screaming trying to get out. We felt helpless.

Some how moms made it out of the room and locked her self in another room.

Bro, as we called him, kicked the door in and hit her across the head with a two-by-four.

That was probably the most blood we had ever seen. Blood was everywhere.

Another time when they were fighting, he hit her in the head with an iron. All of this abuse, and she still stayed with him.

She was riding with him one day, and they had a car accident.

Don't believe that one either. How can she fall out the car and break her jaw, without her face being scraped up? If I seen this man hit a dog and a horse unconscious, and with his bare hands, what do you think he's capable of doing to a human. Her mouth had to be wired back together. Believe me, he hit her, and then pushed her out the car. Her wrist was also broken, after he pushed her out of the car. You know something, she still stayed with him.

His mother would always tell her, don't have a baby by Dirt, his other street alias.

With a name like Dirt, she should have known he was up to no good.

She was hard headed.

He said he would give her something that would haunt us forever.

He dealt with voo doo or witchcraft and was going to put a spell on her.

That would have been too easy. What he did was worse. He got her pregnant.

Then come along Satan.

Listen to those two names. Dirt and Satan.

When Satan had his first birthday, his eyes were red on the picture he took. And no it was not the camera nor the angle.

Satan is not your ordinary character.

People consider 666 as being the mark of the beast.

A beast so desecrated and evil that goes around wreaking havoc on human nature.

Evil though Peanut is the 6th boy born in the 6th month on the 6th day does not mean he is evil.

Now if Satan would have bore the 666 on his name you may have convinced me.

Look at him.

He has several personalities.

He would talk to different people at night when we were trying to sleep. He was not yet seven years old at the time.

He was even smoking weed at seven. Where he got weed from at seven still puzzles me today.

We had not been in Michigan a year and Satan had broken into two houses, in one day at seven. The police came to the house to arrest him, and no one could believe it.

Moms was like, "you have to be talking about Mike or Joe". Yes it was Satan.

Moms had to pay for the windows Satan broke.

Little did she know that was the beginning of living hell for the whole family.

He was driving teachers at school crazy, and it was his first year.

By the time he was in the second grade, teachers couldn't handle him. He had already been expelled from three or four schools in Battle Creek. Because of his behavior, he was not allowed to enroll into any public schools.

He would always assault the kids, and even the teachers. Kids were being transferred to different schools, because they were scared of him.

He pushed a handicapped boy down some stairs, and laughed about it. They were done with his behavior, after that incident.

He was being treated at Child Guidance Center, for mental retardation.

They couldn't do anything with him. They told moms, either she signed him into a mental institution, or the state would take control of him.

What's the difference?

So she admitted him into Pheasant Ridge in Kalamazoo Michigan. The same place Malcolm X mother was placed.

He would be there for a while, before they decided their treatment could not help him. Then they sent him to Coldwater, Michigan, where his stay was short.

He got on the staff nerves so bad, that they probably didn't want to treat him. He had assaulted every staff member that came across him.

He caught hell, when they sent him to Detroit, because they weren't going for the assaulting.

He had plenty of chances to get out of the mental institutions, but refused to change his behavior.

When they let him come home for visits, he would act worse than ever.

So the majority of the time, his visit home was never complete.

One night, while on visitation, he wanted to watch Halloween on TV, and moms said no.

Later that night, he walked up the steps with a knife to mom's room.

He told her what he was going to do for not letting him watch TV.

He wouldn't be home for a visit one day, before going back to the institution.

No one could handle him at all the institutions he had been admitted to.

At seventeen, Detroit didn't tell moms they were bringing him. They just put his clothes on the curb and drove off.

Who blame them for doing that?

Now, after ten years of being in three or four different mental institutions, the animal was back at home. Let's see if you can see why Satan would act the way he did.

Look back at his father's life. Bro was crazy, and violent, and to add injury to insult, a voo-doo worshipper.

Guess that's probably why moms tried to kill him? One day, he was going to jump on her as usual. She probably said to herself, no more ass whippings. He was probably about to hit her, when she pulled the gun out.

So she shot him, and then took him to the hospital. She already knew the police was going to be called. She told him, if he told the police who done it, she'll finish him off.

She really didn't care about whom she shot, or shot at, or even pulled her gun on.

It was even that way in Michigan. She shot at people that didn't bother us, as well as the people that did.

She has either shot at one of her kids, or has pulled out the gun.

Me personally, she has pulled her gun on me several times, but was never in her face long enough for her to pull the trigger. Was never worried, but I mean why be stupid, or her next victim.

When she did go get her gun, if we were arguing, by the time she came back, she didn't see me.

I would just leave for a couple of hours then come back. Why? Who knows?

I was living better, hustling on the streets, than at home being put through hell. And that is the GOD honest truth.

Why would you want to pull your gun out on your kids? We were never violent towards her; she was always violent towards us.

That's a hell of a predicament to put your kids through. And then wonder why we hate each other, and ourselves. Wonder why we can't get a grip on reality to raise our kids.

Its bad feelings about how my sisters would be beat up. They would say things about me that wasn't liked, but the violence displayed behind it was painful.

It was almost like a violent relationship that is in denial.

What I'm saying is, when my sisters would get beat up, an hour later, we acted as if nothing happened.

And there were no bad feelings at the time. They knew how my temper was so why anger me?

They knew violence was a way for me to express manhood. And my mother helped me to perceive life that way.

Coming up watching all the violence, and being involved with a lot of it; she didn't say you shouldn't fight your sisters and brothers. And if she did, it would have been contradictory.

How can she tell me not to be violent toward the family, when that's the entire family saw? She was an example to me that violence should be a way of life. She didn't tell the men in her life not to beat her up, so why tell me not to beat my sisters and brothers up.

The girls were not the only ones to get beat up. The boys caught hell with me as well. They would get me as a child at nine or ten.

But as the years went by, fighting became a challenge with my brothers.

If they won, they knew not to go to sleep. When I won the battle, more was to follow.

A defeat could never be swallowed as easy as that. If they got the best of me without a weapon, I would use one.

Don't say that was dirty fighting. They were just treated like were enemy.

And to me, they were. Since we had no family love, and didn't act like a family, you're an enemy and will get taken out.

It was a case of street fighting. When you're fighting, you don't stop to think they're family, you do what you can to win.

The anger we displayed to each other, as sisters and brothers, was almost the same as moms showed us.

The beatings we received, not whippings, were not meant for even criminals to receive.

Whatever we did, moms punished us severely.

We would have to hold an encyclopedia, in each hand, and stand up for hours. Sometimes we had to hold the books standing on one foot. If the encyclopedias fell, then another one was added. And every time another encyclopedia was added, we got hit, with whatever she had.

Some times, when she was really tripping on us, we had to hold three encyclopedias in each hand, and stand on one foot.

You couldn't hold three encyclopedias in your hand standing on two feet, how in the hell were we suppose to balance them on one foot?

If we really pissed her off, she would go and 'load the boot.'

She had these black leather boots that was so pointed, you could kill roaches in a corner, from three feet away.

And when we did something, or she felt like practicing, she would put on one boot, and then kick the point on the floor so her foot could be all the way to the tip of the boot. Have you to bend over, and then kick the hell out of you.

Ah Lord please don't move and let her miss. Then you really had hell to pay.

Man kicking you in the crack of your butt, with that boot was no laughing matter.

If she got a good kick in, you'll see us walking stiff on our tips toes. Butt cheeks would be so tight from the pain, if air got through the crack, it would hurt more.

That wasn't close to the other treatment we received.

Tara and Fran would get beat with extension cords, or thick branches, not switches. The few times she did beat me with an extension cord that was enough.

So, every time she went to get the extension cord, she had to try and catch me.

On her good days, she would break brooms and sticks on us.

That's how we treated each other. And we paid for it dearly.

One thing that wasn't liked is when; she would hit us across the head with something, and then tell us to go to sleep.

Why should suicide be committed, when she damn near killed us herself?

Hitting you in the head and telling you to go to sleep, was enough to make you fall into a coma.

We must have been really bad, or moms was always on a trip.

One day, she beat Tara or Fran, or both, with a garden hose. They were good to stay around and take that.

She didn't have to pull a stick or broom on me, before tracks were made. You would run to, instead of getting beat down. Every time she went to hit me with something, I took off running, and wouldn't come back, until she was gone.

She only got me good a few times, before my lesson was learned not to hang around. And was a child, when she got me really good.

We were outside burning leaves, and Fran was picking with me. She was told over and over to leave me alone. Devious thoughts were always being displayed, and it was time to put some into practice.

She didn't leave me alone, so the broom was taken, and the straw part was laid in the fire.

I waited until the straw part was good and red.

Fran hair was let down and was moving freely with the wind. Soon as she came by me, the flaming broom was put to her hair.

It flamed up quick, especially when she started running. They told her not to run, but she panicked.

It burned all of her hair, and I paid for that dearly.

When moms came home, she saw what had happened to Fran's hair. She took a long black leather belt and

tried to go to work.

I wasn't buying a beating that day. I hauled ass through the house, while she was trying to catch me.

Then she asked the others to join in.

What we didn't like was, when you run, she always tell some one to help catch you.

That's how moms was. Tell someone to catch you, and then you're now mad at your sisters and brothers. Then it's pay back time, when moms hit the streets.

Moms is like that, even to this day.

She always played us against each other and then act as if nothing happened.

So when she told them to catch me, the bed was the only place for me to crawl under. I thought it was safe, but that thought was wrong.

The bed started lifting up, and it was time to run again. The rest of the family was on stand by, like they were the National Guard.

Just sitting there waiting on her next move she twirled the belt around. Then she turned the belt into a lasso, and throws it around my neck, then drags me from under the bed. Wished that day I had some hair to give to Fran, because no beating was worth that. Fran please forgives me for burning out your hair. And what a coincidence, she grew up to be a beautician.

Often ask myself, how did moms take the time to beat the hell out of us, when she was rarely there.

Then I thought, it doesn't take long to beat you, then leave, and then come back home, to do it all over again.

Moms didn't care what she used to half kill us.

Whatever weapon of mass destruction she put her hands on, look out.

She beat Tara real bad for something that was done by me, one day.

The refrigerator was unplugged, and something spoiled, probably her beer.

Anyway she asked who unplugged the refrigerator, and the blame was put on Tara. I didn't want to get in trouble, so Tara was the first person to come to mind.

I don't know what was worse, the broom getting shredded, or Tara getting beat down for no reason. Tara I apologize for you getting a beat down for something you did not do. Mom made toothpicks out of the broomstick on

Tara. She still has some of the marks from that, and other beatings.

We hated it, when everyone were sleeping, she would be pissed off for whatever reason, then come and beat us with a stick, broom, or whatever weapon off mass destruction she had, in her arsenal.

Forget Iraq, the weapons of mass destruction were in my home.

We all have two or more, of Moms wounds to display. She didn't care about what she would use.

The men that beat up my mother, and used weapons, they didn't care about that.

She was a little woman and they still used weapons. And she didn't care, because she thought more of her men, from my point of view, than she thought of her kids. And I must be right, because what loving mother will put violent men over her kids and keep them there. They didn't care about her. And that's how I felt about my sisters and brothers.

Moms, we really needed you.

Watching your mother get beat up on, bleeding from everywhere, you feel so helpless.

Then see her with them again, the next day, as if nothing happened.

That's why violence was ok, to me. It was seen in the household constantly, and we felt as though that's the way a family was supposed to act.

My mother would have stitches in her head and still be laughing and joking with the fools.

And knowing how crazy these fools were, moms would still have three or more boyfriends. Guess Momma was a rolling stone. Then when she decided to have just one, he was even crazier.

Greg was really the only father we knew. I met him before moms, and the rest of the family did. He would come up to store so his gas could be pumped, and water put in the radiator.

He was a cool dude, until he got with moms. He was the only man that ever gave us allowance, and spent time with us. Guess that was to get closer to moms.

He fished a lot, and gave them to moms, and she would cook some for him. Then he took us fishing a lot. That was the only times I could remember doing things as a family. Moms would take us to this fishing spot, called the pump house. She would take grease, and meal with seasonings, to the pump house. As the fish were caught and cleaned, moms would throw them in the hot and waiting grease.

Greg had a nice job at the time, and he showed a lot of interest in her, and us.

After the interest wore off, the problems started. They used to call him two-dollar Greg, because of his blue top Vodka he always drank. It only cost two dollars for a half pint. Bootleg prices.

He would work everyday drunk or sober. And on payday, he would give us an allowance. Sometimes it was cool when he got drunk. He would send us to Church's chicken for a ten piece, with a ten or twenty dollar bill, and say keep the change. He would eat the whole ten pieces then send for another one.

That lifestyle didn't last to long. They started to argue a lot. Then the violence followed shortly after.

Well it may have been started, but we didn't see any.

One day Greg was drunk and arguing with moms. Then he slapped her in the face hard. Moms don't stand but five-three, Greg, about six-two.

I was a little older, and wasn't going for men beating up on moms anymore. All of us tore into him. We beat him down that night. He chilled for a while on the fighting. One night, don't know why I was with him and moms, but I'm glad. They were arguing as usually.

Moms got out the car and started walking. All could be seen was Greg picking her up, and she hitting the concrete. Then the low life had the nerve to stomp her in the chest.

She had a collapsed lung, and was taken to the hospital. The doctors were unable to save the lung, so now she has to spend the rest of her life with one.

We found him, and tore that ass up as usual. Like the other men in previous times, she went back to him.

It wasn't long after that beat down he received from us he moved to Michigan.

Guess he got tired of us beating him down, since we were tired of him beating moms down.

Chapter 3

We were still enrolled in school, when Greg moved to Michigan in ninety eighty-two. One day, moms said we were going to Battle Creek, Michigan. This was the Easter holiday, for Spring break.

I had never in my life heard of a Battle Creek Michigan.

All that happened was moms bought me, Satan, Peanut, and herself, a one way Greyhound bus ticket to Battle Creek.

Come to find out, Kellogg's, Post, and Archway Cookies, all were started in Battle Creek. Even the great Sojourner Truth is buried there.

It was more to that, for moms to just leave Mississippi with no notice. To add insult to injury, going to a place you never heard of.

Didn't move or give notice, just said we were going on vacation for Easter.

That was the longest vacation any one could go on.

Being only thirteen at the time she still could have told me what was up. To me she had inclinations to move up there, without the idea of returning.

We went to Michigan with no money, or she said we didn't have any.

Aaron, my oldest brother, gave momma, Claudia Smitten number.

She was the pastor of Bethlehem Church in Battle Creek. How Aaron knew her still puzzles me.

Pastor Smitten looked out for us, when we first moved there. My first day in Battle Creek, was April 14th, 1982.

After that day, life would never be the same for me. And believe me, Battle Creek would never be the same.

It was so much snow on the ground, you couldn't see the street.

If money was at my disposal, I and Greyhound would have had another date.

We stayed in a hotel for a week, before moms found a house. Or better yet, an igloo. We were cold in Mississippi, but we froze in Michigan. The first house we moved into, we were always cold and hungry.

Moms never really believed in gas, so you can imagine living in Michigan, in the wintertime, with no heat.

Yes we froze. Thought living in Mississippi with no heat was terrible, but icebox Michigan. Nobody deserved to live like that.

Tara, Fran, and Mike finally came up in July. They liked it, until they got a taste of the cold weather.

Can't remember whom they lived with, while they were still in Mississippi, but my guess would be her sisters and brothers. Millie always kept Tara and Fran so it's safe to say they lived with her.

Moms family always had us when we toddlers and she had to go away.

Was glad they had come, because there was no one to talk to, or kick it with.

And of course, by then, moms and Greg was back together. That seemed like a set up plan to me. What do you think?

When we made it to Battle Creek, she contacted Greg to let him know we were there.

Begin to wonder if that move was premeditated.

Why would Greg up and leave his job, and leave Jackson with no prior plans.

I didn't put it jumping up and leaving pass her, because she moved to Dallas with Bro, Satan's daddy. If she moved to Dallas and didn't ask if we wanted to go, why ask if we want to move to Michigan.

Why did moms want to leave Jackson?

We truly believe that she sent Greg there first, with the intentions of leaving immediately after.

She didn't give any one notice, just up and left, with no where to live.

I don't recall any real stability in Mississippi either. By age thirteen, there were at least 10 different places we lived. Streets: Brown, Minerva, Gallatin, Dudley Alley(twice), Winona, Topp, Bell, etc. Also lived in Dallas, TX, and Brandon, MS, as well as aunts and my grandmother.

So moving to Michigan didn't surprise me any. We only lived in four places the first three or four years after moving there.

The first house we moved in was a disaster. We still had no heat, and it was still cold in April.

It was better for us to live on the outside, because it was warmer than the inside.

The house had three levels. It had first and second floors as well as the basement.

We only lived in the first house about seven months, before moving into a different dump.

Nick Wilson, the landlord didn't really own the house, so we had to move. He was just collecting free rent. How she met him and thought he owned the house is beyond me.

It was November, cold and we had to move.

Even though it was on the same street four blocks down, we had to move everything in a grocery cart.

Can you imagine, pushing a couch down the street in a grocery cart?

We had to move everything with that grocery cart.

Glad it was nighttime, and no one was out.

The second house was no better than the first. It was colder and bigger, and that doesn't mix.

By then, we had met the two of the 'fellas', Marshall and Rodney.

They would go to the house next door to us and steal grapes.

They were walking by one day, laughing at the way we were talking.

You know how it is when you're coming from the South with a southern country accent.

Marshall lived a few houses down, and Rodney lived around the corner.

After we met them, they had started coming over to visit.

We would be mixing records, or trying to rap in a cold house.

They had come over a few times, and then they stopped.

We found out later why they quit coming over. It was because we had no heat.

I wouldn't have gone to their house either, if they didn't have heat.

They would laugh, because it would be ice all on the wall paneling.

Ice would be inside the windowsill.

It would be so cold you would have to go outside and get warm, then come back in the freezer.

You literally had to put meat in the freezer to thaw it out.

We left milk or whatever out all night, and it wouldn't spoil. Even that would freeze.

Sometimes we put food in the snow to keep it cold.

Never had roaches in the wintertime, because they couldn't even take the cold.

But the roaches caught hell in the summertime. Moms wouldn't let us kill the big black ants, because she said they killed and ate the roaches. And we wondered why the ants around the house were bigger than the roaches.

Anyway, you know when it's cold outside; it's colder on the inside.

Felt sorry for the rest of them one day. It must have been below zero outside, and don't forget, no heat.

Moms had Greg to put some wood in an empty metal garbage can, and made a fireplace out of it. Duh, where's the ventilation?

Then it started to get really smoky in the house, with no ventilation anywhere.

To make a long story short, they almost died from carbon monoxide poisoning.

Ambulance and fire trucks were everywhere.

I am surprised social services did not come and rescue us.

You would think after the same thing that happened in Mississippi, would happen anywhere else, and that moms would have gotten some heat. Think again.

Why moms didn't like having heat is beyond my thoughts.

We use to sleep two or three to a bed, so to her I guess that was enough heat.

When morning came, you would hate to get up, because it would be so cold.

Even though we went to bed with the clothes we were going to wear the next day, that didn't help. You had to go first and lie in a cold bed to go to sleep.

We, all eight of us, would sit in moms room to keep warm. She had the TV and heater in her room. When it was time to leave the room, it would be so cold outside her door, you would almost cry to get back in. Because of so many house fires with space heaters, we could not burn one all night.

The house was too big, to try and heat it, with the little heaters. We complained about it, but she would tell us to iron the bed, before we laid in it.

That worked, but we still had to get up, and faced the cold weather, in the morning.

And can you imagine taking little baths out the sink. That stuff is ok when you need to get a quick wash up. And you only do stuff like that every once in a while. What about everyday?

Having to boil your own water for a quick bath is cool every once in a while. Having to do it on a regular basis can become a discomfort.

Instead of being cold every night, we just didn't take a bath.

So what it were eight of us, we still should have had some heat.

Moms was getting social security for at least four of us. So that was at least several hundred plus dollars a month.

Greg worked, giving up over half his paycheck each week. That's another two plus hundred plus dollars a week. That equated to about eight hundred plus dollars a month.

We had summer jobs giving moms half. That was another one hundred twenty five dollars apiece, every two weeks the four of us gave her.

Then we would still have to pay her if we borrowed lunch money through out the week. That was cold. Giving up half your check first, then pay back what you borrowed. Oh Well. Life goes on.

With the money moms was receiving from social security, Greg, and us working, we should have at least ate good, and had heat.

When we first moved to Michigan, the thought of my days hitting up garbage dumpsters was over.

Think again.

The times when Church's chicken, or KFC's garbage dumpsters were hit up, were still fresh in my mind.

The French fries and burgers, from Mickey D's, or Burger King, weren't all that bad. It may have had a few coffee grinds on them, but were still good.

A lot of the food was still wrapped in paper, because workers may have dropped it, or they made the wrong order, and could not sell it. So they had to throw the food away, and we would be there to receive the goods.

The garbage dumpsters were a lifesaver many of times.

When we moved to Michigan, we had to start back hitting garbage dumpsters up for goods.

Sometimes you couldn't resist going into a trashcan to see what's in them. I can't lie about that.

It would be some good stuff. Slightly bent canned goods, chips, and cookies were always found. Whatever you wanted, the dumpster had it.

We even knew what were in the canned goods that didn't have labels on them. We could guess if it was ravioli, or fruit cocktail, or vegetables.

Each one us probably had our own can opener, so we wouldn't have to share.

Sometimes, workers would put things in the dumpster for themselves.

Kind of like it used to be in Mississippi at the service station.

There would be whole cases food, milk, or meat, waiting for someone to come along and claim it.

God must have been with us, because what if we would have gotten food poisoning?

It was cool, when Mike and I hit the dumpster, because we did it discrete.

Moms and Greg did it all in the open. People would be passing by looking, and she would say "they do it to, we just got here first".

Greg didn't care about what he did, or when he did it, he just did it.

When we would go to the duck pond, to feed the goldfish and ducks, Greg would always talk about the ducks.

It was fun to catch the goldfish, only later to find out that we were not suppose to eat them.

After we found that out, we didn't feed them anymore. We would just feed the ducks. Why feed the fish, if you couldn't eat them?

It was two ducks we would always feed. We named them whitey and swany. We watched them grow from little ducklings to whatever grown ducks are called.

Moms had a taste for duck one day. She sent Greg and me to the duck pond to get her one. Greg was looking at the wrong two ducks.

He was told him not to get those, but to choose some different ones. None of the other ducks were falling for Greg's scheme. He was trying to get them to come up the hill.

The only reason whitey and swany came to Greg is because they knew me. So they came to Greg when he called them.

He was throwing little pieces of bread up the hill. Then he sat down so they could eat out of his lap. Then he grabbed both ducks by their necks. I'm sure you know what happened next.

On the way back, we passed a turtle laying eggs in a hole.

Greg found a brick and hit the turtle in the back. The turtle must have gone five or six feet in the air. We bagged the turtle up to, and even took the eggs. Guess you can say we hit the jackpot that night.

The next day, we had duck, and later that week we had turtle and eggs.

Guess eating some kind of meat was better than eating bologna sandwiches everyday.

That's probably why bologna and I don't get along today.

We ate so many bologna sandwiches, that we would take empty coffee jars, and use the rim to make little circle sandwiches. Anything to make the same food looks somewhat different.

Eating ketchup, mayonnaise, syrup, and sugar sandwiches wasn't all that great either. But you ate it, because you knew that's all you had.

And half the time we would get the ketchup from restaurants around town.

You know how it is when you don't have the basic commodities around the house you go to places like Churches Chicken for your napkins because you didn't have toilet paper at home. Don't get me wrong, the newspapers, fig leaves, or dried up corn on the cob came in handy when there was no toilet paper. So when we made it in to town we would make stops at different restaurants and stock up on napkins, little packets of ketchup, mayonnaise, mustard, sugar, or whatever was handed out free. Well free to customers that bought something. We would act as though we bought something so they could give out more.

That lasted us a while.

Now when we have rice, or grits, or even mush we can have sugar with it.

We would eat so much mush (boiled corn meal, water and salt or sugar), that I thought were grits.

And not to mention oatmeal, we would have to add saltine crackers to have enough for everyone.

We had to do whatever it took to make it.

Guess you can say the mush and oatmeal came in handy since it wasn't hard on your teeth.

And moms never took us to the dentist until we were damn near grown.

I was like seventeen when my first trip to the dentist happened.

After my first trip they drilled nineteen fillings of silver crap in my mouth.

Boy oh boy did that drill hurt.

That was in the winter of eighty-five. My mouth was sore and I couldn't eat.

Can look back at the times when it would be cold and no food would be in sight. Moms would send us to the store, and we couldn't wait to go to the dumpster.

Can remember going into the basement at the first house we moved into.

It was cases of Ralston cereal spread about the basement. Some was molded from sitting in water, but a lot of the top boxes were good. We ate cereal for months.

Moms would buy milk and sugar, if we didn't find any in the dumpster.

Speaking of cereal, when moms would get WIC for Satan, Peanut, or all, which was another lifesaver. We would fight over the buckwheat cereal. That was the only cereal they gave away, that was already sweetened.

When we didn't have regular milk, we had to use Similac, Enfamil or the nasty tasting PET milk.

We didn't care. We ate cereal out pots, pans, and skillets. When you're hungry, you'll eat cereal from a glass to get full.

One day milk supply was short, and we had to share. We took turns using the milk, because it wasn't enough for everyone.

When one was done, they had to pass the milk to the other. You had to eat the cereal with a fork, so the milk would drip through the crevices, and could be saved.

It was Mike's turn when Rochelle had it. She was letting the milk drip from the crack of her mouth into the bowl. She must have thought he didn't want it after that.

Mike was mad but, he still used the milk. As you can see, we really know what it's like to have it hard.

"Couldn't wait till tha gubment cheese was in town." This was the best cheese ever made. I mean people were buying and selling the cheese like it was shares of stock.

We would eat grilled cheese sandwiches with the other commodities the government handed out. And you would be happy to receive the commodities, because you were already eating stuff you were tired of.

By that time, we were really sick and tired of living the way we did.

Nothing to eat, can't take a bath like you want to, and tired of washing clothes with your hands. You would think it was the sixties instead of the mid eighties. I can't lie sometimes we did come across a wringer washer.

Those were the days before we had a washing machine.

Washing clothes out on your hands every night, and by morning, they still wouldn't be dry. We were use to it, from never having any heat. We had to walk to school, with cold and wet clothes stuck to our bodies.

The days of having to boil water in a pot, to take a bath out of the sink was still a headache.

What was the purpose?

You would still be cold, even though it was a space heater in the bathroom. As soon as you left the bathroom, you would freeze instantly.

Then you would have to get in an ice-cold bed and try to go sleep. Even though we complained, moms would still tell us to iron the bed before getting into it, because it would be to cold to lie on the mattress.

Then we would have to sleep in what we were going to wear to school. That way when we got up, instead of dressing in the cold, we would already be dressed.

And still, right to this day, my mother has no heat, and still boil water to take baths.

People that knew us said we should have been use to the cold, after a few years.

We're still not thawed out.

That's one reason Mike dropped out of school in the tenth grade. After going through the ninth grade with a rough winter, who can really blame him? It was our second winter in Michigan.

We would have to walk through slush and ice to get to school.

This didn't happen in Mississippi.

In Michigan, we were cold when we left the house, and would be cold when we made it to school. Then it would be cold when we left school, and it would be cold, when we made it home.

At least we were consistent.

So I dropped out of school with Mike.

Since moms didn't say anything about him staying home everyday, she wouldn't care about me. And she didn't.

For a while, she didn't know we had dropped out of school.

She had the TV, coffee pot, her pee pot, and heater in her room, so she rarely came out. We couldn't roam around the house, because it would be too cold. So we would lie in the bed until we hit the streets.

We would have come out better staying in school, because at least we ate and was warm.

They had even put me in the right grade, because of dropping out of school in Mississippi.

Fran, Mike, and I were all in the same grade, when we moved to Michigan from Mississippi.

They thought it was best to put us all in the same grade, so that we could finish at the same time.

So we were all in the ninth grade except Tara. She was in the eighth but wanted to go back to the seventh grade.

Never understood why she wanted to go back a grade, instead of staying in her right grade.

Even after they were going to put her in the ninth grade with us, she still wanted to go back to the seventh.

I really didn't want to go to high school, because of all the fights in the ninth grade.

It was too many enemies going to the same school.

The first day in a Michigan school, got into a fight.

Think they suspended me five or ten days.

The first day back from suspension, got into a fight.

They suspended me again.

By the time the ninth grade was up, the counselor and the principal said, more fights were by me alone, than the whole school put together.

You know how it is when you move from a different state. Especially coming from a southern state, where people want to try you. And there was no going for it anymore.

The first week in Michigan, a lot of people tried me.

A boy and his sister were trying to jump me one day, coming home. They were not at all a match, but a weapon was still needed.

A bottle that was close by was broken, and the girl's hand was slit with it. They tried to jump on me, but they called the police. That was the first trouble that came across me.

After only one week in Michigan, was already in trouble, and received probation for what had happened.

After that, a lot of enemies were made, and that was the beginning of a continuous hard life in Michigan for me.

They didn't like me and the feelings were mutual. One of the reasons was because of different gang affiliations.

By me being a Vice-Lord and they were Disciples, we fought all the time. It was a lot of them, but there was no backing down.

Rodney taught me about the Vice-Lords.

All his cousins were Disciples, and they never bothered him, but it was always about me.

They would chase me through the hood everyday. They wouldn't fight you one on one, it was always a five on one situation.

Since my desire was to fight all the time, meeting up with those fools didn't phase me any.

Learned a lot about the Vice-Lords and went to Jackson Mississippi to share the knowledge. There were no Vice-Lords around Jackson, and none to be found. Not to say there weren't any. Recruiting was started locally in Battle Creek, to see if we could expand the organization. It went well, but more status was needed.

Even went to Jackson in nineteen eighty-five recruiting soldiers. Telling them all about the knowledge that had been obtained, nearly all of them were interested. The fellas in Jackson were like me, when they first learned about the Vice-Lords. They were ready to put in work, and spread the knowledge.

Wouldn't say Vice Lords were taken to Jackson by me, but after returning a year later, the foot soldiers that were recruited be me, were ruling.

Never have I had so many people wanting to learn something so different.

Jackson never was a gang-affiliated city, so anything from the North was good to us.

As kids in Jackson, we would go around calling ourselves names that was often compared to gangs, but were never involved in criminal gang banging activity.

The new recruits were popping up all over Jackson, and the prestige was being enjoyed. We were having kids to believe we were the best thing that happened since sliced bread.

They were skipping school just to learn some new knowledge.

They would hang around me from sun up to sundown, listening and learning. Doing what ever it took just to join.

They didn't mind getting beat down by other members just to prove their loyalty. They would disown their parents because we would have them believing we were their true family. Having them to believe if they got into trouble we would get them out of jail. All lies just to get them to do the dirty work.

If kids would put the same effort into school, as they do gang membership, it would be a lot of graduates.

The Vice-Lords in Jackson were graduating more kids than Murrah, Peeples, Lanier, Provine, and Rowan.

Even the elementary kids wanted in on the knowledge.

Kids were actually remembering everything that was taught to them. I would even test them, just to see if they were serious about learning. Going back from remembrance, they all would score a hundred. And they even got the extra credit questions correct.

Kind of feel bad about the situation now. Jackson was recording record murders, assaults, and other crime stats. Gangs, crime and crack were the order of the day in Jackson. It seems as though this hit the city all at one time.

Went back to Jackson in nineteen eighty-six to visit and train more soldiers. This alone assured me the notoriety that was yet to come. After making my self a self appointed leader, this allowed me to serve as a four star general with my own Army. Four positions were created and of course the top spots were held by yours truly.

Secretary of Treasurer, Secretary of Defense, Minister of Information, and Chief of Security. I would have my own security to move with me.

After appointing lieutenants on down to foot soldiers, this created one of the largest gangs Jackson would see.

I controlled the Wood Street area, the Lanier School area, the Rowan School area, as well as the Jackson Mall area. I went to areas by Jackson State, Blackburn Junior High, and the Farish Street District to start up sets.

We would even move out on rival crews that were causing problems.

The police was harassing me with every move that was made. They knew who the leader was, but couldn't prove my involvement, in anything. I think this guy name Vincent Martin, a police or gang enforcement agent, was trying to move in on me. I was not called Mr. Untouchable for nothing. He never got the chance. I don't know if the guy is in law enforcement any more or not.

One day we had a gang fight, and people started shooting. A guy on Silas Brown got shot in the back of the head, by his partner. Five-o just knew my people and I were involved.

They took my ID and noticed the Michigan address. They held me downtown, asking me dumb ass questions about my affiliation with the Vice-Lords.

Told them I'm from Michigan and don't know what you're talking about. Some of the foot soldiers that were recruited punked out and started telling.

The police weren't lying, because some of the names being called were recognized.

Well so much for having true foot soldiers.

I stayed in Mississippi a short time, before an emergency came up. So my return to Michigan had to be quick.

We were at a school called Poindexter Elementary break dancing, when the principal tried to put us out.

I had a smart mouth couldn't resist. A PTA meeting, was going on at the time, we were break dancing.

He was trying to get us to turn the music down, and we wouldn't.

The crowd was into it, and thought it was part of the meeting.

When it was over, the fool (probably the principal) pushed me in this room and hit me in the temple. He must have had a ring on, because blood was trickling down my temple.

All hell broke loose.

We tore that ass up, but he wasn't done. He was chasing me all around the school.

I got tired of running and saw a stick with nails in it. Soon as he came around the corner, wham.

The nail got stuck in the bone part under his eye. Snatched the stick back, and blood was sprouting every where.

We told him to call the police, but he said everything was all right. He knew he was in the wrong for what happened. And knowing he hit me in the head first, he knew he would have gotten in more trouble. Guess his scared ass called the police anyway. That was smart though. Tell us everything is ok, then after we leave call the police to make it look like we were guilty.

Since they wanted me anyway, I was not about to be given the pleasure of catching me.

They were looking for me as though murder was committed.

They wished a murder was committed. The police came by my grandmother's house thinking they would find me there. Sike, I was at school still trying to recruit more gang members.

It was Wingfield High, and I don't know how the school found out the police was looking for me.

Can't remember if it was a teacher, or a principal trying to hold me until the police came. Whoever it was, got hit in the process of trying to retain me.

That evening, I was on a Greyhound bus back to Battle Creek.

I was going back to change my life around, since I was getting into so much trouble. I tried to enroll back into Battle Creek High School. They said no, because Jackson

Police had a warrant for me. The school told me the police may come to transport me back to Jackson.

For some reason there was no worry, because jail never scared me.

Getting caught is what scared me, because real men move in silence.

When you're a smooth talker and persuasiveness is your meal ticket, you fear nothing but getting caught.

If you don't get caught, you become more and more invincible.

If you get caught, no one respects you, because now you look weak.

No one was able to touch me, and I really believed that.

Even called my boys, and myself 'The Untouchables.'

And we were untouchable.

The South was a little slow as compared to Northern City life, and I took advantage of that.

That's one reason I appeared untouchable.

When my security moved with me, they did everything to protect me.

Knowledge is powerful.

The more knowledge that was learned in Michigan and Illinois, people in Jackson respected me.

A lot of the neighborhoods we would recruit in, the turn out were spectacular.

Meetings would be held, as to where fifty or sixty people in one neighborhood would show up just to hear what I had to say.

It was cool, because the Vice-Lords became all the family they really had.

And they were joining at a rapid pace. The ones that were joining came up under the same general conditions as me.

They felt good about having something to belong to, since they had no fathers, or mothers.

No one was around to show them that home family life is better than gang family life.

I would rather for them to have had a good home life, than to have a gang to look up to.

The kids looked up to me, and respected everything that was handed down to them.

Being familiar with the street life, and showing them the street life, and the way, was like me giving something back. But they had a pipedream full of lies.

A lot of the youngsters died during the cause, and there are feelings of sorrow.

Look at some of these kids today, and the talents they possess.

Kids standing shorter than me were dunking a basketball with not one, but two hands.

Now look at the condition they're in. Either they have dropped out of school, or they sell or use dope.

I try and tell them, if they would only stay in school, let the colleges pay for the education. And if they don't make it to the pros, at least they will have an education to fall back on.

Where are all the foot soldiers that were under my command?

Did they consume what was handed down to them, and survive? Or did they get caught up in the rapture?

I'm not saying the foot soldiers I trained got taken out. Maybe they have, or are in prison somewhere.

It's just the fact of another brother with nothing to live for is gone.

I was teaching kids before the gang recruitment started.

They learned from me about how to survive. We never carried any weapons.

At least when they were under my command they didn't.

People criticized me for a lot of the things that were shown to kids.

They learned how to hustle legally, when they could have been shown how to sell drugs, or rob, or do b&e's. (Breaking&Entering)

They received true leadership, under my command.

They were taught how to wash cars, pump gas, and put people grocery in their cars.

A lot of the things I learned legally were shown to them.

Some of them were older than me and was still looking up to me.

There's no regret showing the brothers the knowledge that was obtained. The regret is the trouble that was surrounding me.

I wish this mentality would have stayed this way before the gang banging teaching started.

People were getting stabbed, shot, killed, and robbed in great numbers.

We were soldiers for the devil, satan, shatain, Lucifer, Iblis, or whatever else name evil was called.

Yes we will take your kid and turn them against you parents.

Kids, come into our world and let us show you how to completely ruin your life.

Because they won't let you do what you want to do, they are the enemy

You say your parents make you sick. Then let us heal you the gang banging way.

You say they are hard on you and don't care. We will let you think we care as long as you are doing the dirty work for us. Oh yeah and go to jail. You'll find out quick how much we care.

You'll have another family that will look out for you in prison. Some joker with a life sentence is waiting to make you his girlfriend.

Oh and don't try and tell.

You remember the first code of conduct on the street is you don't snitch no matter what.

That same code applies to prison, but its worse.

See on the streets you can snitch and hide out or run for a little while until you get caught.

In prison, you snitch you have no where to run. If any of this seem fun and admirable to you, then come see us. Or let your parents guide you into something they would like to achieve.

That is for you to be equal or better yet greater than them.

The school principal incident mentioned earlier caused me to move back to Michigan in nineteen eighty -six. Life was getting a little out of hand.

I was supposed to be graduating that summer, and dropping out of school was beginning to make me realize something.

Some education was better than none, and even though my diploma was received on the streets, there was nothing tangible to show for it.

Now realizing that you couldn't graduate from the hood, me getting a diploma could have been something special. The thought was there for a while, about giving up the streets and going back to school.

I went back to Battle Creek High to see if they would let me back in school.

I had to lie about the Jackson Police not coming to Michigan to pick me up.

They told me that was fine, but still couldn't enroll because of the credits needed to graduate by June.

Michigan schools, wasn't like Mississippi schools.

In Michigan, you can flunk the tenth and eleventh grade.

If you don't have enough credits at the end of the 12th grade, you don't graduate. And you can't come back the next year.

Then in Mississippi, if you don't have all your credits, you can keep going until you finished.

When it came time for me to graduate, only two and a half credits were accumulated, and those were from the ninth grade.

There goes me trying to turn my life around.

Seen Mrs. LaCrosse, a Battle Creek High teacher, at the store. She was telling me about going to night school where she also taught. She was the real life saver in changing my life around.

They had a program that was like getting your GED, but a little different.

If you go to adult education in the daytime and night school in the evening, you could accumulate all your credits to graduate.

It was only one catch, it would take two years.

Or just get my GED.

I didn't want to go to day school.

When the chance was there, I didn't go, so I definitely didn't want to go to night school.

I ended up enrolling into both day and night classes, for some reason.

Well, it was really to get off the streets, since there was no gang affiliation anymore.

It was still in my heart "thug till I die" but the gang banging stopped.

But the enemies still hated me, and now it was all about survival.

I was even doing well in adult education.

The teachers were telling me to take the tests without coming to class.

Because of my enrollment in night school, I told them there was no need to get a GED.

They said it didn't matter, I could still take the tests, and the credits would go towards my high school diploma.

So there was no need for me to study.

All five tests were taken and passed in one week.

After that, it was only one full year of night school to go.

I walked to school every night, except on Fridays, because it was only four nights a week.

Through rain, sleet, or snow, they always saw me going, or coming from school.

Walking never bothered me, but this lady that also went to night school would sometimes offer me a ride. It must have been two or three degrees outside one night, with wind chills below zero. When she offered me the ride, I was about to say no thank you.

My bones said take the ride, because my mouth didn't speak.

Got into the back seat and saw this white girl that didn't like me, and I didn't like her either. We were in the same class and had always argued.

Again we started to argue. And we argued all the way to the front of my house.

The lady dropped me off, and while getting out of the car, the girl kicked me in the stomach.

Without even thinking, she was hit in the nose and it split open instantly.

Went to class the next day, and the school officials said I couldn't come back to night school.

Was almost done, and there was no turning back. Went back the next day, and talked to the night school administrator.

The girl lied and said that we were arguing and she was hit first.

They called in the lady that gave us the ride, and she told them the truth. They allowed me to come back, under the condition my class with her changed.

That was cool as long as I finished. And through all the trials and tribulations, it happened.

January 15th 1988, they awarded me my diploma. A year and a half after I originally supposed to have received it.

That was the greatest feeling in the world.

Greater than anything you can imagine.

If you ever finished high school you know what I'm talking about.

If you haven't, then you could never miss what you never had.

If you are planning on going back, whether young or old, do so.

I had to congratulate myself for completing high school. Now the only thing that bothered me was, now what do you do?

Chapter 4

This army recruiter was hounding me to enlist. He was telling about how all I could never be in the military.

The military was never for me, or any other brother.

He would always be told no there's no interest.

We would talk about the many wars that were going, on for me to join.

Why fight for a country that has never really cared about me?

Every time America went to war with someone, it never benefited me. And why America has never went to war with anyone other than people of color since the world wars.

Look at the Korean War, the Vietnam War, Panama, Grenada, Libya and Iraq.

All people were of color.

I'm impressed.

So joining the military was never an interest to me.

You can talk about freedom all you want to.

America has done some foul things to other nations, and we think its right.

Look at the war with Iraq.

People say America did a good thing because Iraq took Kuwait from the Kuwaitis.

America took Oregon, California, New Mexico and other states from the Mexicans.

What's the difference?

Now they're bombing Iraq again, to get rid of their weapons of mass destruction. Then why don't we get rid of our weapons of mass destruction?

They sold the country all the weapons, made it the fourth largest military in the world, gave Sadaam Hussein the key to the city of Detroit in nineteen eighty, then a decade later try to remove him from power.

You had the Axis Powers consisting of Germany, Italy, and Japan calling them hostile nations.

Now you have an 'Axis of Evil' consisting of Iraq, Iran, and North Korea. And you want to rough speak form democracy for them.

Please spare me the agony.

It may sound unpatriotic, but think honestly, who's really unpatriotic. There's a war going on in my neighborhood, and I'm trying to win that one first.

These fools shooting at me and chasing me every chance they get. And you want me to fight who?

Hell at least I'm familiar with the gang banger, the drug dealers, and the thugs that are trying to take me out. Most of them anyways.

At least I know how to sometimes maneuver through the hood and escape harm's way.

What chance do I have on the streets of Baghdad when a citizen is trying to protect their country roll up on me?

Should I shoot an innocent man for coming into his home when I will kill someone for coming in to mine?

And you want me to go to war with whom?

It's a war going on with my family I'm trying to win.

I can remember when the living room, bedroom and or dining room was a modern day war zone in the house.

Hiding in closets you call trenches to take out the next enemy family member.

Standing behind doors so when your enemy family member walked through, you tried to take his or her damn head off.

So what they are family and I consider them my enemy and you want me to go fight someone I never seen in my life. And I don't know why.

I'm suppose to believe because you said they are the enemy it's true. What did they do to me, and what are the real reasons for being a stranger in a strange land?

They never tell you what the war is about anyway. What I look like fighting someone, and don't know why.

Those people haven't done anything to me.

Look at the battle in my household?

It's a war with my family and I'm trying to call a truce. Moms is always bugging and the only person she cares about is Fran.

Fran and Tara were always at each other's throat. Moms would be mad at Tara and protect Fran. So Tara received protection from me.

Not to say she was always right, I just wanted to make sure moms gave her fair treatment.

One night, when Tara was pregnant, she was arguing with Fran.

Fran kicked Tara in the stomach for no reason. Well even if it was a reason, she still shouldn't have kicked her.

I was really tripping on that, and was all over Fran's case, when moms stepped in. She didn't say anything about Fran kicking Tara, just why you are always taking up for Tara. Yall must be sleeping together or something.

Moms and I got into it bad that night.

Then she's always accusing me of being on drugs.

I'm not being funny but how can you do drugs, or have done them then accuse someone when you have never seen or heard of them doing them.

Yes my temper is bad, but she doesn't have to accuse me of things that are untrue.

I really started tripping when she said leave those drugs alone. She accused me again, so the VCR and the TV were picked up, and then thrown out the picture window.

Guess my violent temper would reflect on me coming up. She hated me for that, but it was all good.

But she hated us from day one, so nothing ever changed.

Moms used to always say to us, "I hate yall", and "I wish I wouldn't have had any of yall."

She would say this like we really asked to be here. Like we enjoyed some of the pleasure she was having at the time we shouldn't have been conceived.

Sometimes there were thoughts if things like that led me to be suicidal, or have suicidal tendencies.

And the times when moms was around, she beat the hell out of us every chance she got. I'm talking about breaking brooms across our backs.

Extension cords were a favorite of hers. How can you beat you child with an extension cord?

If my memory serves me correctly, she would dip the extension cord in alcohol, or grease to make it worse. Or she would beat you with an extension cord then make you take a bath in alcohol. Guess so the scars wouldn't get infected.

Let me reminisce for a moment, if you don't mind.

I can remember when she was beating me for going trick-or-treating.

She was hitting me with a belt, and there was not a care in the world at the time.

Was just hoping she would hurry up, and get her thrills on, so my candy could be eaten.

Since there was no response to the beating as she wanted, she turned the belt around and hit me in the mouth with the buckle.

Blood splattered all over the door, and she didn't even stop to see if I was ok.

She just walked away, and never said anything about it.

It's ok, because that night, my candy was still eaten, swollen lip and all.

Yeah there was plenty of hate from just that one incident.

That was one of the many marks moms left on my body.

The one dimple on the right side of my face is homemade. Or should I say, momma made. She came home one day tripping and she was mad because we didn't clean up.

As we were walking up the stairs, I don't know what was said or done to make her hit my jaw into the corner of the windowsill.

Blood was running down my face, and she did nothing to help stop the bleeding.

After some form of visible scars were shown, she didn't react to it as though something was wrong.

It was almost like if she saw evidence of the so called chastisement that meant justice was served.

Then we really caught hell when she would come home from the bar drunk waking everyone up in the neighborhood.

Then to top that off, we would have to be up in an hour or so for school.

Often think of those times every time I look at the scars on my face and lip.

Ahhhhh. Enough of that.

Any ways.

The same night the VCR and TV went through the window. Guess she really thought I did drugs after that episode.

I was also mad because she put Tara out the house while being pregnant.

When Fran was pregnant nothing was said, but it had to be a stint about Tara.

After that incident, the recruiter was called the next day, and we talked about me joining the military.

Being all I could never be in the military was better than being tortured at Momma's Concentration Camp.

The army was something that was vowed, never to take place. What other choice did I have?

It was April nineteen-eighty-eight, and July was the month for me to go. With nowhere really to go, that month had to come quick.

Was deeply in love with Mindy, and she was pregnant, so there was no other way out. Mindy was the only person there at the time, and a way out was needed.

Told her about me joining the army, and when things got situated, will send for her and the baby.

It seemed like the closer July came, the more moms would trip.

Moms was bugging at an all time high, and things at home were just getting worse.

Called Sgt. Willis, my recruiter, and told him the date needed to be pushed up earlier than July.

He set a date for May twenty third nineteen eighty-eight.

Just knew that was a messed up thing to do, when we were at the processing station.

The enlistment people were saying you had one more chance to change your mind before you sign.

Was about to raise my hand, but changed my mind, when I thought of momma's concentration camp. I stayed the night at a hotel in Detroit, before they sent me to Ft. Dix NJ, my basic training site.

That was going to be the last time to party for a while. So I thought.

The first few days in basic training were not bad at all.

I wasn't in the army two weeks before Mindy left me. She told me about loosing the baby. There's still some disbelief about that.

Before joining the army, Mindy would go to the doctors almost every day. They told me everything was fine, so how did she loose the baby. She claims a miscarriage happened, and it was hard to adjust to that. I would just cry through the night, saying why.

I was ready to leave basic training, but the adjustment set in, along with being heartless again.

Basic training wasn't all that bad.

I got into about seven fights while being there. That's what the military is for right, fighting.

The drill sergeants would tell me to fight the enemy, not my fellow man. That's who was being fought, the enemy.

One night got into a terrible fight with one of my fellow comrades. Yeah right.

They had the nerve to call the MP's (military police) on me. Couldn't believe they put me under arrest in basic training for fighting an enemy.

It didn't matter who was fought, because everyone was an enemy to me.

They tried to get the streets out of me but hey 'thug till I die.'

Did everything that wasn't supposed to be done in basic training.

I would leave the barracks at nighttime to get beer. It was always a hustle in basic training. Cigarettes, beer, candy bars, and whatever else that made a dollar were being sold for three times the value.

The others were scared to leave, so they would be charged triple for whatever they wanted.

A few of the envious, jealous, playa haters started telling on me.

No one could buy that snitching shit.

Fools were starting to get broke down every chance that came my way.

People in the barracks hated me, until the day we graduated.

Some of the loyal ones to me filled me in on a little secret.

The night before graduation, the enemies were going to give me a blanket party.

That's when people hold you down with a blanket, so you can't move, while the others beat you down.

So that night, slept with one eye open, and the other one was on the look out.

When late night came, someone came to make sure I was sleeping. It was Krueger.

I opened up both eyes, and told him to go for it.

There was no sleeping the rest of the night. Told Krueger if we ever met again, you're mine.

Graduated and went to Ft. Lee, VA for my AIT (advanced individual training).

Got into trouble the first weekend in Virginia.

Policy was that if soldiers made it to the base on weekends, they have to stay in the barracks until the drill sergeants returned on Monday. Like hell. I wasn't there an hour before being out and about. Heard about this club called the Sword and Key is jumping on Fridays, and 24 South on Union Street, be jumping on Saturdays. They saw me at both that weekend kicking it.

On Monday, drill sergeant Vanderwise called me into his office. I knew then, someone snitched on me. Now this man had never seen me a day in his life, had the nerve to tell me I couldn't go a way from the barracks for a month. He had a lot of nerves.

I was back at the Sword and Key that weekend to be with Jackie Wicks, a nice female that was met the week before.

On Monday, was back in the drill sergeant's office again.

This time he didn't say don't go anywhere, he just took my civilian clothes. Now all that was left was the BDU's (battle dress uniform).

Spent the week wondering what would be worn to the club the upcoming weekend.

I didn't care about no training or anything else. I was straight up party time everyday.

Man, that weekend I was back at the Sword and Key club with the monkey suit on, like it was a three piece suit.

Of course I was back in the drill sergeant's office again.

This was really ticking me off right about now.

You guys are not going to change me and that is that.

They didn't change me in basic training and they are supposed to be hard, they are not going to change me here.

Tried to sneak away one night and go to the store. Was running down this hill and tried to jump a ditch. From going downhill I didn't realize it was wide until I leaped. I'm sure it was twenty feet wide. Anyways, I cleared it but came up short a few inches. As soon as I landed, it was a loud crack. Now I see what paraplegics go through. A feeling of paralysis had set in for like an hour. No movement of feeling in my lower body. I just laid there and prayed. Somehow someone came and rescued me. I think that was the first time riding in an ambulance. That messed my back up permanently and I'm paying for it right to this day.

Broke up and still trying to have fun my last few days in Virginia.

So much fun was had at Ft. Lee.

Went back to Battle Creek October nineteen eight-eight to visit before going to Texas where they stationed me.

It was so much fun in the Creek that it seemed as thought I was there forever.

Eventually went to my permanent duty station, in Ft. Bliss TX, outside of El Paso. El Paso is a city in Texas with a population of 600,000 people with ninety six percent Mexicans, surrounding it. You rarely seen a tree in El Paso, and there were nothing but mountains.

Only stayed in El Paso nine months but a permanent stain was put on the city, and the army base. It was just that bad.

When I first got there me and some more soldiers (suckers) ended up going to HHT Maintenance Group.

Some of us were supposed to go to HHT Support Group. Even after finding out about being in the wrong area, we still didn't go to the right one. Support group was where the boring suckers, I mean soldiers stayed.

Maintenance Group was the rowdy ones. I couldn't wait to rename Maintenance Group, Mafia Troop. Everywhere we went, we wreaked havoc. Thomas Jenkins, we called him Teddy Ruxx, was the center of Mafia Troop. He was a Disciple from Chicago, and even though I was a Vice-Lord, we were really close.

Teddy Ruxx did everything you weren't supposed to do in the military. I'm not going into detail on the things he done, but can tell you about some of the things, that were done by me.

Before leaving Ft. Bliss, I went to jail for beating this Mexican down. The hoe-lice, I mean police, arrested me, and it was the Mexicans fault. You're probably saying to yourself, how anything can not be your fault, when you have displayed nothing but violence for minimum reasons.

It was his fault.

We (the Mafia Troop), were all drinking when this fool started tripping. He already knew my reputation as a fighter so why step to me and have your head caved in like a cavity.

He stood around six two, two hundred fifty pounds. If guns never frightened me, don't stop to think one minute somebody's size worried me.

All that was wanted that day, was a good time, and no fool was about to destroy it.

This fool was all up in my face for no reason. Who was he trying to impress?

Don't really know, because he didn't impress me.

I was drinking on a forty ounce, not saying one word to him. He was told he had one more time to get in my face talking shit.

I'm left handed, and was drinking the forty with my right hand. When danger in sensed, my left hand is prepared for action.

He said, "What are you going to do hit me with the forty?" At the same time he was saying that, he knocked the forty out of my hand, and all hell broke loose.

He was hit one time in the temple, and he was out cold. He was being stomped and kicked and I didn't want to stop.

He was out cold, and another forty was opened, and the party resumed. Someone decided to call the ambulance for him.

They thought he was dead, because it took paramedics like fifteen minutes to revive him.

Yeah it was a gruesome site, but hey, I can 'kill a brick' and 'drown a drop of water.'

The police were asking everyone what happened. Knowing what they were going to do, the Mafia Troop said they didn't see anything.

Some other witnesses told them what happened and said it wasn't my fault, but they arrested me anyway.

You can expect that to happen. City of six hundred thousand people, with ninety six percent Mexicans, think of what percentage the police force was.

They gave me a five thousand-dollar bond, but since I was in the military, only needed ten percent of that.

Then I found out that's for anybody.

Mafia Troop brought the money, but the prejudice ass holes told them a bail bondsman was needed.

Got out of jail about six hours later, and was back doing what was done best, getting into trouble.

Almost everyday at Ft. Bliss, on or off the base, you would hear about a fight. One guess to you, who is the star?

Roll the red carpet chief royalty arrives. All rise. Thank you. Thank you. You may now be seated.

Drunk or sober, it didn't really matter. I was on a suicide mission, with no return.

On Fridays we would show up at the All Graders Club, nick named the All Brothers Club. Now this club was actually on the military base. It didn't take long before the Mafia Troop would be in action. We were bound to run into an enemy from a different platoon, or even outside the base.

When it was all done, people would be chilling in the parking lot. You can hear people say, it was them damn Mafia Troop fools. People would speak up on me and would have never laid eyes on me.

You can hear them say, It was Shorty and Teddy Ruxx in there fighting, they're always fighting. I would be right in their face agreeing with them.

And be saying to myself, people can just hear about you always being into something, and put it all the blame on you.

They were never wrong.

There was no secret, as to which direction my life was headed.

I just refused to let the army, or anyone else change me.

This was me. No sugar coating it. No additives or preservatives. Just a straight up out the ghetto thug that believed in one thing.

You don't stare at me and I won't cuss you out. You don't swing at me and I won't fly your damn head off. You don't shoot at me and your whole family won't receive early obituaries.

Mafia Troop was not the only people doing dirt in the platoons. More dirt came from the so called leaders in charge, than from the subordinates. Insubordinate is the more proper term.

Captains and lieutenants were smoking crack in the barracks. Can you imagine the same men that are calling you into formation every morning, is buying crack from the Mafia Troop in the evening.

These are the same officials that are supposed to be training you for combat, but they are at each others throat over rocks of crack cocaine.

That's another reason there was no respect for the military.

They are supposed to be teaching you about how to survive, and they were the biggest drug dealers and users around. I'm not saying dope was sold from me, during my time in the military; it was just other Mafia Troop members that did the selling. They were actually selling dope out their rooms on base.

Would often wonder how they were passing drug tests. They were using golden seal and some other purification, to rid their bodies of drugs. Well not rid their body but make it look like there's nothing in the system. And the sergeants would manipulate some of the test results, to make everything look ok. I can remember them telling us when the next so called surprise drug testing would be. Besides selling the dope, the fellas were also using it themselves. That's one thing that baffled me at the time was how can you be your own best customer. And what if you didn't have money, you give yourself credit.

Good thing I was never into drugs, because it was easy for me to say no.

Chapter 5

I had flirted with a few kinds of drugs, but never was an abuser. Drugs like opium, speed, acid, and weed were drugs that I played around with, at one point in time. Guess I was trying to fit in or something. After they made me do even crazier things, I knew then, drugs weren't for me.

Only wished the other family members felt the same way about drugs. Drugs have torn my family apart. Crack really hit the males in a horrendous way.

Mike, my brother and one time business partner is heavy into drugs. Rumors were Marshall got him into smoking crack. They tried to get Big Rod to smoke some, but he was like hell no.

I was never really into drugs, so it was kind of hard for me to understand how Mike got started.

After we moved to Michigan, we kind of went our separate ways. We still hustled together for a while, until he just wanted to do his own thing.

He was never a leader anyway. He has always followed. This white girl name Angie Vincent got him to smoking cigarettes. She wasn't even a teenager yet, and I think he was like sixteen no more than seventeen.

We were heading our separate ways after he started smoking.

Any kind of smoke was a turn off to me. I don't even eat barbecue if it was cooked with charcoal and lighter fluid.

Also I have never had a relationship with a woman that smoked. If they did smoke, it was like a drunken one nighter going on. Well except for Deb. She smoked the skinny Virginia Slims. I told her when we were first talking it was either me or the cigarettes. So she chose Virginia. I'm just kidding. She left the cigarettes alone.

Moms, Greg, four brothers, and two sisters smoke. Only three out of moms nine kids don't smoke.

My mother is a heavy smoker. God I wish she would quit. She claims that will never happen. Trust me, keep smoking them and you will quit one way or the other.

She smokes about three and a half packs a day. She would send me to the store every three days for a carton of cigarettes. She's would say, Greg, Lonny, or Satan were helping her smoke the cigarettes. Now they're all gone, and she still has excuses.

Now she says they burn in the ashtray. As much as cigarettes cost, you're going to let them burn in the ashtray. Yeah right. Moms you're fooling no one but yourself.

The doctors are always telling her to stop smoking. She's already taking medicine for her heart, nerves, asthma, and high blood pressure. Anyone knows Valium and heart pills don't mix.

Now, there's understanding why doctors had me on Valium, all those many years.

Plus with the asthma being really bad, moms smoking is not healthy for the one good working lung. That means all the tar and carcinogens are going in to one lung instead of two.

Never could understand how someone could inhale smoke, swallow it, then blow the recycled smoke back out. Then to top it off cigarettes are the biggest killer year after year.

Coming up, my share of cigarettes in the past taught me a valuable lesson.

Mike should have had known from the last time we tried to smoke cigarettes not to try them again.

Don't know if we found or stole a pack of Marlboro short cigarettes. Knowing us we stole them.

We were walking down the railroad tracks in Jackson, splitting the pack. He had ten, and the other ten went to me.

It must have been a hundred degrees outside. We smoked all twenty cigarettes. Then the sun started to beam on our foreheads. The only remembrance was waking up to smelling salt from the paramedics. They said some train attendants reported two males unconscious.

Right to this day, never have I had a headache, as painful as that one. Every time a cigarette is looked at, that terrible headache re-appears, especially if it's a pack Marlboro's.

Then tried to chew tobacco, but that was even worse. It was at Baker Elementary in Jackson when Tom Parkson, a classmate, brought some Levi Garret chewing tobacco to school. Thought you were supposed to chew the tobacco and swallow the leaves. That's what I did. The bad part about it was, we had lunch, then went to recess. It was hot, and vomit with chewed up tobacco leaves, was coming out of my mouth and nostrils.

I was sick for days, before that feeling was gone.

After those incidents, you didn't have to worry about me trying anything like that again. Well, until marijuana was tried, and that was only a few times.

The fellas would smoke marijuana on a constant basis. They tried to get me to try it, but there was no need for it.

One night, they finally got me to be down for it. Mitchell McMahan, one of the other fellas now living in Sad Diego, said "hit it", and let me hold you around the waist for ten seconds.

Hit the weed, then held my breath for ten seconds while he was squeezing me. Then he let me go, and I passed out instantly. It scared me so bad, that weed was only tried a few times after, and that was years later, years ago.

Crack, now it took a toll on Mike and Marshall. As for Mike, he has been to prison twice for crack, and he still won't leave it alone.

The first time he went to prison, he could have avoided. Crack was being sold from his house, when he came to me with something that sounded too good to be true. He told me this white dude he never seen before wanted to buy three hundred dollars worth of crack.

Sounded good but I couldn't touch it.

Told Mike something was up with that guy. He insisted he was straight, but I couldn't do it, so he went and bought the crack from somewhere else.

Then he came back to me again, and I still wouldn't sell to him. Then on the third time, I was like Mike, this man is spending almost nine hundred dollars for some dope. What bothered me is when he said the man hadn't smoked any of the crack. This man spent all this money and didn't smoke one rock. Something was up. Mike said he was looking for a prostitute. You can get a prostitute for two or three dollars or even on credit now days. So you want me to believe that.

That took place in May, and in November he got arrested. Guess the grand jury was in town, and they had a warrant for his arrest. Then he tells me, the guy that set him up, was an under cover agent.

I'm glad my instincts told me not to touch it, because we would have went to prison together.

I have shared a bed, clothes, and even food with him, but Lords knows I didn't want to share a cell with him.

If he didn't start slipping, he wouldn't have got caught.

Before he went to prison, he was stealing from everyone he could.

Here's a prime example.

Moms sent him to pay the rent one day and he spent the money.

When the next time rent was due, the landlord wanted two months, and moms didn't know why. She told moms, no rent was paid for the last month.

When she asked him about paying the rent, Mike said he forgot to tell her he lost the money.

He did Tara the same way. He was suppose to get a money order for her rent, and never did. And the people told Tara that she was two months behind on rent. No record of a money order, or rent being paid was found.

He would steal his girlfriend money and food stamps. Then turn around and buy crack with the money. Kids hungry and you want to steal the money that kept them fed. That's the lowest thing any one could do to their family. That hurt me more than him stealing from me.

He stole a seven hundred-dollar diamond ring from me, and sold it for a twenty -dollar rock. Eventually got the ring back, but he swore to GOD, he didn't take it.

Fran and Tara saw this girl working at a gas station in Battle Creek. They saw the ring and told her it was mine, and wanted it back. Of course she didn't give it to them.

They told me where the girl worked, and I went to the store to confiscate it.

The manager said the girl quit, about two days earlier.

She told me where the girl lived, and I marched over to her house. Sure enough it was my ring.

They gave Mike twenty dollars for it. Then found out it was Steve's girlfriend. He was Mike's neighbor.

We knew Mike had stolen the ring the first time it came up missing.

When he was asked about the ring, he swore to GOD that he didn't steal it. He literally had me crying with him, because it was just that much belief there. So much for using GOD for a lie.

That's what dope will do to you. Make you say and do things, and use the Creator to prove you are innocent, when you know damn well you are guilty.

I was still in the military, when they told me about Mike smoking crack. Then found out Lonny and Greg were also smoking crack.

Greg was no better than Mike with the stealing. He had a damn good job, and started stealing from the company. He stole thousands of dollars worth of electronic equipment, from his job. I was mad, because he didn't sell any of the stuff to me.

Think he got caught for selling his boss wife one of the TV's he stole. That's dumb, stealing something, and not knowing the people, you are selling the merchandise to.

Away to prison he went.

And like Mike, prison didn't stop him from smoking crack.

Prison only let addicts rehabilitate for a while, then once released back to the streets, they start smoking crack all over again. People have also mentioned to me that in some prisons, you can get more dope in there than on the streets. Guess the warden on down to the corrections officers have to get their share.

Have you ever seen a rehabilitated crack head? Me either. I'm sure there are some out there, but never met any.

For one thing, they never get over the craving. Then how can they be rehabilitated going around the same people that used to smoke crack with them. They still smoke it, but you are a recovering addict. Then when something goes wrong, they use crack as justification for the problems they incur.

Don't feel sorry for crack heads, addicts, users, or what ever name you want to call them.

The same is felt for my family members.

They were grown when they started smoking crack, and seen what it had done to others before them.

Oh you thought it couldn't happen to you?

I don't think they were forced into doing something they didn't want to. They were not retarded, so they knew what the outcome would be like, once they got started.

How can you work all week, then get a check, and smoke it up on drugs in a few hours. Then you would have to wait another week or two to get paid again. Or if you got a social security check wait a whole month before another check.

Addicts are waiting a whole month on a check to let it go up in smoke in a few hours.

That's a hell of a condition to be in.

Mike was a good customer of mine. Yeah my brother always bought from me. Guess you can say my contribution to his habit was appreciated. He was keeping the money in the family. If he didn't buy from me he would have bought it from some where or someone else.

He would also bring a lot of business to me. His crack smoking clientele was so powerful that there was no reason to street sell anymore. They all became personal customers of mine.

This business partnership seemed more legitimate than the undercover one, and it profited well.

They would give him the money to buy the crack from me, and then he would break the cocaine rocks in half.

If they sent him to buy five rocks of cocaine, he would use a razor to cut them in half to produce ten.

Whatever amount they bought, Mike would still split the rocks in half. The people never knew what he was doing because my crack rocks were big enough to do it.

So he ended up getting dope both ways.

After hiding what he cut, he would then ask for some of their dope.

They had to give or smoke some with him because he had the connection through me.

Never knew why, when he split the dope in half, he didn't sell it to the next customer and get paid.

To him, it was all about getting high.

After the high started, he was really slipping.

Dope would only be sold at his house, in the afternoon, and no where else.

Then he started coming to my apartment. Even after he was told not to, he didn't listen. He figured, since dope was sold from his house, he could come to mine and buy. But the difference is he was paid twice for his services.

Then what would make me mad was, the people that he would bring to buy dope, would start coming on their own.

That kept them from having to give him some.

And the people he brought remembered where I lived then came back on their own.

The majority of them were never seen before. Then they really tripped when they knew he was cutting the rocks in half. I didn't cut them like he did. So when they saw what they were getting they informed more and more users.

When the crack heads started coming to my place of residence in drones operations had to be ceased.

Battle Creek had adopted the zero tolerance drug policy and I was already on probation from a previous drug charge.

So when the crack heads came by, they were told business was shut down permanently.

That was the only way for they would go look elsewhere.

A crack head is not going to keep coming to the same place if there is no dope available.

So once again Mike and I were not business partners anymore.

I would often wonder what it would have been like if we were still business partners. The way we used to be in Mississippi, we would have had Michigan sewed up.

I would have handled the business part as usual, and he could have handled the distribution. But that would be senseless to let a crack head handle the distribution of dope.

Letting others influence you to do things, other than business, or money making tactics will find you always broke.

I'm always talking about how hitting up garbage cans would be the order of the day, but there were never any broke days for any long periods of time.

When crack hit the scene, it paved the way for a lot of hustlers like me.

That wasn't long after the days of selling cans and bottles in Michigan. In Mississippi, selling coke bottles for two cents apiece didn't make you much money, but it helped.

That was around nineteen eighty-one. In nineteen eighty-two, when we moved to Michigan, cans and bottles were ten cents each.

That's when Mike and I started to branch off. I wanted to do what it took to keep us hustling together. We maintained hustling only after the bottle hustle started to die off.

When my bottles and cans hustling days first started, it seemed as though no one else were doing it.

I would go all around Battle Creek with my cart, looking for returns all day.

Mike had quit hustling with me by then, so there was no love lost, only money to be made.

The profits were all mines and that was cool. He had his own thing going on and I had mine.

Bottle hustling brought about ten dollars a day, easy. On Friday through Sunday thirty dollars a day was not a problem.

People would be at Claude Evans (Nigga) park, chilling, kicking it and drinking. As they would be finishing forty ounces I would be there picking up the bottles.

I was waiting around like a hungry vulture swooping down on bottles.

Every time my grocery cart would fill up, it would be taken to the supermarket to cash in the returns.

Once returning to the 'nigga park' from cashing in one load of bottles, it would some times be enough to fill the cart again.

People saw how good hustle bottle collecting was. Everybody and their momma started doing it.

People were looking out for me though.

Instead of throwing them on the ground, for some one else to pick up, they would keep them in their trunk until my rounds were made.

Fe Fe, a good friend of mine, would have ten to fifteen dollars worth of bottles in her house at one time. A lot of people would hang around her house, drinking all the time. I would go by her house everyday and collect, before my other rounds were made around town.

Some times when she didn't have but a few bottles, she would put some dollars in my pocket. Then she would apologize for not having a lot of bottles. Still don't know why she would apologize. Then she would flirt with me constantly.

I was into girls and women at fourteen, but Fe Fe was just a little older. She would always say "hey hustler come here, you want a date?"

She gave me the nickname hustler, and I lived up to that name everyday.

Since every one was hustling bottles now, it started to phase out. A different kind of hustle was needed now.

One day, Mike and I were passing through the back of a hospital when we saw big plastic bags of cans. It was more cans than we had ever seen at one time.

We didn't take them that day, because we had to case the area out first. Plans were drawn up immediately to launch an assault on the cans.

We went through the front door, sneaked through the kitchen, then out the back door. Man what a gold mine. It must have been ten five feet tall garbage bags full of cans.

We knew they must have left the cans out for the truck to pick them up, on the next delivery.

We each took one bag. When we took the cans to the store, they were fifty-five and sixty dollars a bag. Later that night, we took about four more bags. That brought us another hundred plus dollars each.

Begin to wonder if that's the only time Mike would hustle with me, is when paydays like that came.

That lasted a good while, because the hospital thought the drink delivery people were probably taking the cans.

Then Mike told Timmy Lee, a friend of ours, about the cans. I could not understand why Mike would invite people in on our hustle.

At least we were taking the cans at night, so it wouldn't look obvious. Timmy would go in the middle of the day, even when people were at lunch. He started taking the cans every day, even half bags.

Either Timmy got caught or the hospital found out the drink truck wasn't getting the cans.

After that, the hospital started locking the cans in a cage on the inside.

Soon as that hustle was over, Mike went on with his life again.

We still hung and kicked it. Just not as much.

We had started to hang more at the Hart Hotel, a place where you can just about find anything illegal going on. The Hart later turned out to be a gold mine also.

The fellas would either meet up there, or we would all go together.

When we hustled on the streets, we would spend the money on video games, and food at the Hart.

One day, David Hudson, the owner of the Hart, left one of the video games door open. He was emptying the money out and didn't shut the door to the game all the way.

All we wanted to do was put some credits on the game.

Our surprise was even better, a spare set of keys were in the door panel. We took the keys and locked the video game. When we wanted to play the game, we would open it up and put credits on it. And when other people played, we took the money.

For some reason, we tried to see if the keys worked on any other video games, and they did. They worked on almost every game. And the games they didn't work on we found keys in the others that did.

Now we had keys to all the video games. David would see us playing games all week, and knew he had a gold mine. On the weekend, we would be there when he emptied out the machines. David didn't see any quarters in the video. Stanley, David's son, would sometimes take the money out also. So when one or the other checked the machines, they assumed the other emptied them out.

Then one weekend, both Stanley and David were there to empty out the machines. When they saw that all the money was gone, they then realized, we were hitting them up.

After that, David hired Keith, one of the fellas, to watch the game room. Keith was with us hitting the machines, before David hired him so we were still in the house. We were still hitting the games up even harder.

We never had to worry about a meal all the times while being at the Hart.

We were even stealing the food they served in the dining room. Pizza, ice cream, fish, chicken, and what ever the restaurant sold, we took it.

Keith, the new watchman, was taking more than we were, and was getting paid to make sure we didn't take anything.

David found out that hiring Keith was costing him even more and there was still no money in the video game room machines.

David eventually closed the game room down. Another business closed down with the help of our service.

Closing the game room didn't stop us from hitting up other ones, because we had the keys that fit other games. We would go around town finding games the keys would fit. It didn't take long for businesses to catch on to what was going on, before they started putting pad locks on the games.

We didn't have the keys to the pad locks so another operation had to be ceased.

After that was over, my hustling days came to a halt.

Sitting around all day, I had to wonder what would be my next hustle.

I would either walk around to gather my thoughts or think of ways to modify or enhance old hustles.

I was walking through downtown Battle Creek one day passing by a bookstore.

It was called 'Read Mor' and I went in to steal some candy. That's when these colorful pencils were noticed, and about fifty of them were stolen.

Didn't take me long to figure what to do with them. Was at K Mart five minutes later, selling them for a dollar or a donation.

People were told my school was raising money for either music equipment or a trip. Would tell them the pencils cost a dollar or a donation. That word donation would help me out in the long run also.

Some would give a dollar, or sometimes five. Made about one hundred dollars off the pencils, because people that gave a donation would say keep the pencil.

I got caught up one day.

This lady was asked if she wanted to buy a pencil or give a donation. She asked me what purpose the money was going to be used. She was told Battle Creek High was raising money for music equipment. We started talking, about how active she was in her son's music class.

She said he went to the same school and didn't mention anything about new equipment being needed.

She knew lies were being told, because a little while after she went into the store, the manager came outside to talk to me. He asked what school was raising the money, and I said Battle Creek High. He wanted the music teachers name so he could call and assure it.

He was told a fake teachers name because there was no doubt he was not going to call. I had dropped out of school at the time and didn't know any music teachers.

So when he turned his back and walked away, he didn't see me again. I made it to another business doing the same thing, until that hustle got old.

Well, the hustle didn't get old, a better opportunity was implemented.

I was hearing about how you could make and sell products in Junior Achievement.

After immediately signing up the things we were making, and selling wasn't going on to well. My first item was a ceramic penholder. Who didn't have one of those? And, who needed one?

That didn't bother me. Because of my previous hustling days schemes were about to be set into motion. Someone was bound to buy one, and a lot of them were going to be sold.

About thirty penholders were made the first and only time. I went everywhere trying to sell pencil holders, and people were like "we already have one." Then when you tell them, you can give it to some one as a gift; they would say "no I don't know any one that needs one."

I was out there two or three days selling penholders, in the cold. They were five dollars, and only one was sold.

Thought to my self this legal hustling is not making any money.

Even went to the wealthy side to try and get the other twenty-nine penholders off. People were turning me down left and right.

Good ghetto selling tactics were being used but no one wanted a penholder.

Thought something different would be tried at the next house. Rang the doorbell, and a lady answered. That made me happy, because women were easily persuaded.

Men are no problems, women were just easier to convince, especially if they see young kids trying to do something positive.

After she answered the door, I said "hi I'm from Junior Achievement and we make and sell products to keep the youth off the streets. We're selling penholders, and would you like to purchase one, or make a donation?"

There's that word donation again.

She didn't want a penholder, but said she would like to make a donation. I can remember her giving me five dollars and she still wouldn't take a penholder.

I couldn't understand why the penholders were five dollars and she didn't want one, but will give a five-dollar donation. People wouldn't take the penholder from me, even though they only gave, a one or two dollar donation.

That word donation was used after every selling line. Hardly ever sold a pencil holder but nearly every one gave a donation.

Junior Achievement found out about me asking people for donations. They told me my participation in the program had to end.

They were mad because it was nothing coming back to them.

Who really cared?

It was time for March of Dimes anyway.

I had participated in March of Dimes the year before and that was a gold mine.

People would sponsor me for the number of miles that would be walked.

After the walk they would multiply every mile walked times the amount they sponsored.

After the first walk only a little money was made.

It was a thirty-mile walk and a lot of people sponsored me from fifty cents to a dollar a mile. That was fifteen to thirty dollars a person. The problem was every person that sponsored me for the big dollars paid me with a check. Madness was there but they would be paid back the next year and years after that.

When it was time for March of Dimes again my second year, after the Junior Achievement hustle, it was going to be a good year.

This time people were told up front that March of Dimes didn't take checks this year.

Last year it was so many checks written until I felt like a damn bank.

Some of them were saying never mind until my famous donation line was used.

Money was pouring in from all over. That's what you would call a good ghetto technique. If no one is buying anything, or pay you with something that can't benefit you, like checks, you always have to find ways of getting over.

Checks were still being given after the walk. They were turned in, and all the cash was kept.

Mike was turned on, to my newest hustle.

Every time a new business venture was implemented, Mike was turned on to it.

Then the rest of the fellas were in on it, because they saw all the money that was involved. We would argue and fight over which territory we would go to and get our hustle on.

That go to show you money will destroy even a friendship.

None of the territory or money was ours; we were just hustling and arguing.

The good part about it was we walked. Well some of us did, the others just profited and never walked.

Mike eventually told Timmy Lee about the March of Dimes hustle. And like always, the hustle ended when he joined in.

It didn't matter that he told Timmy, it was just that Timmy went about hustling the wrong way. The people that would sponsor him he stole from them.

He walked but when it was time to go collect the money something always came up missing from the people's house.

Then he would tell people to put the checks in his name. At least from me they were told, March of Dimes didn't accept checks.

The people knew something after Timmy told them not to make the checks payable to the March of Dimes.

One year it's to March of Dimes, then the next it's to the individual.

The only good Timmy was is when he would steal for us on our next hustle.

He would steal these three-dollar chains, and we put ten or fourteen carat gold clips on the ends of them.

We sold the fake chains for about ten dollars each. People thought they were getting over, because they would buy three to four necklaces, at a time.

You can see by now, I have just about done everything that represented hustling And I wasn't even out of high school yet.

Chapter 6

Having finished high school, and been to the army, the little years ago sidekick hustling days were over.

After being discharged from the army, just knew 'I could be all I could be.' I'm talking about in the job world. Even though my stay, in the army was only for a year, I thought veterans got treated well. I thought wrong. Every time an application was filled out, the military was used as job experience.

Employers don't care about any army experience, all they want to know if you are able to do the job they have for you.

Tried to find employment all over Battle Creek and nothing was happening but temporary services.

The fellas were making big dollars on the Ave. selling crack, and a piece of the action belonged to me.

Being broke ain't a joke, and it wasn't simple to get in on the action.

It was hard for me at first, to compete with fellas like Marquese, Jesse, or Patrick.

They had all the clientele, and I was just 'a new kid on the rocks'.

It didn't take long for me to be in competition with the top. They didn't want to merge, so there had to be some kind of hostile take over.

Like Nino said in New Jack City "you don't want to roll with me, I'll roll right over you."

When people came to buy, they would be offered more from me than anyone else.

If their customers wanted three, twenty-dollar rocks for fifty dollars, they received four from me. If they wanted six, for a hundred, they would be given eight.

They would think the dope was fake for the reason so much was offered, for so little price. They didn't know my plan was to take over, and eventually be number one.

For the people that thought fake dope was being sold to them, they would smoke the first one in front of me. This showed them how real and how good my dope was. Then, they would go to crack alley and finish smoking, or they would go elsewhere.

After about two weeks in business, several thousands of dollars were in my pocket, and another thousand in dope.

Business was booming, and before long, number one was mine. One of the reasons for being on top was, because the rest of the fellas were selling for other people. I and I alone started my business. The dope was bought in large quantities, and deals were given to crack heads the others dealers only dreamed of giving.

A lot of specials were offered, to my customers and the fellas customers. Some times they were offered, five twenty dollar rocks for sixty dollars.

People on the Ave. envied me. What they fail to realize is that, they were selling long before me, and now the top spot belonged to me.

The HSP(Hanover Street Posse) were a money generating group. We didn't know what to do with all of the money that was generated.

Clothes were bought and worn once, then thrown away. Shoes were bought, worn once, and then thrown on the street wires.

We would give crack heads money and dope, to wrestle and beat up each other. Or, make them walk down the street naked.

We made money, and didn't know what to do with it. We could have made money, and then opened a legitimate business.

A lot of the street sellers don't think that way.

It was all about who made the most, and who spent the most.

No one bothered me either. I already had a reputation for fighting. So who ever tested me, knew they had hell on their hands.

Like Tyson in the beginning, refused to loose to anyone.

Jesse Carson called me 'CAJ.' (pronounced cage). The acronym means Crazy Ass Joe.

Everything would be done in a crazy way. Dope was sold in a crazy way. I would fight in a crazy way. So my life was lived in a crazy way.

Never have I had so much money at one time. I never worried about spending it all at one time, because on the Ave., more would be made.

It didn't take long for me to make another thousand if all my other money was spent.

If it was a weekend, two grand could be made easily. If it was a weekday, five hundred dollars could still be made. And that wasn't bad for the size of Battle Creek, and the number of dealers around town.

Like any other baller, I couldn't wait until the first, the third, and the fifteenth came around.

And food stamp day was lovely. I would really make a killing, with the food stamp hustle. Customers would get ganked for real. Sixty five-dollar books of food stamps could be bought for a twenty-dollar rock. It would have cost me only five dollars cash.

Ten-dollar rocks would be bought for five dollars, and then sold for ten in cash. Then if they would have food stamps, they would be told they are twenty-dollar rocks. Then they would get two rocks, to make it look good for a sixty five-dollar book of food stamps. And to think they were getting over on me.

Then, more and more people would come to me saying they heard about the two twenty dollar rocks, for a sixty-five dollar book of food stamps.. I'll hook them up.

Food stamps would be sold for half the value. A sixty-five dollar book has a street value of thirty-two dollars and fifty cents. And if they were given two rocks, street value forty dollars, they couldn't wait to jump on the deal. But they were given two ten dollar rocks from me only cost me five dollars a piece, for a sixty-five dollar book.

Not a bad profit, for one quick exchange.

I gave a lot of the food stamps to moms because shoeboxes of them had accumulated. More food stamps than anyone would know what to do with.

As my empire started to grow it was like a pawnshop being operated out of moms house. TV's,

VCR's, microwaves, and camcorders were beginning to line the basement walls. Anything of value was bought with the crack that was being sold.

Moms didn't know about me putting those items in the basement.

It was cool being in that kind of situation.

Had the respect, the money, the women, and the guns. I was sitting on top of the world, but fate caught up with me one day.

We were on the Ave., trying to make that last dollar, before Big Rod went to get something to eat. Something told me not to go. Every time the Ave. was left, my dope would be hid. There's no reason why the dope was with me at that time. Because no one expected one time (police) to be out at that moment, we assumed it was safe to leave.

As soon as we bent the corner, five-o flashed the lights. Didn't want to play Big Rod, and hide the dope in his car. It was balled up, and thrown out the window.

Just knew the police would not find it.

Told Big Rod, and Marshall, to tell the police 'Snake' threw the dope out the window, if they found it.

Snake was a fictional character that was made up that night. They laughed at me, for coming up with that idea.

Big Rod still laughs at me to this day.

Thought I was going to get away, because they couldn't see the dope.

Then, this punk ass cop named Track Star, pulled up. He would be the one to find the dope. By them finding it didn't scare me at all.

It was my money and all the dope that would be probably lost.

Over five hundred dollars in cash, don't remember how many food stamps, some weed, and seventeen rocks(three hundred and forty dollars street value), were about to be gone down the drain.

They took me to the county jail.

They had me in the county jail fourteen days before a court date even came. The fourteen days, seemed like fourteen months.

Half the jail cell was stinking, the other half smelled decent.

Some of the brothers that were in the same cell came from the same hood.

The only thing for them to do was play cards and shower all day.

They took showers like three and four time a day. I had a hard time wondering why these brothers would rarely keep their hygiene up on the streets, but get in a jail cell with all men and stay clean. It made no sense.

The ones that did probably keep their hygiene regularly on the streets took three and four showers for other reasons.

The funny sounds they would make, in the shower were disturbing. I can understand they were incarcerated and all, but to play with your self that many times a day was ridiculous.

Brothers were going through jars of grease like it was food.

They would always tell me that eventually they'd hear me in the shower doing the same.

When my court date came, that would be my release, and playing with my self was only a thought.

Being in a hellhole like that was not a pretty sight.

Before you can go to a main cell, you have to be in a holding cell. Sometimes it takes a day or two, or you could be waiting weeks. The holding cell they placed me in was only big enough for eight people. Twenty people tried to share the holding cell.

There was no other area in the holding cell to place my mattress but by the toilet. Since that was the only spot available, I had to make do.

Woke up one morning, thinking the ceiling was leaking, but some fool was pissing, and it was splashing on me. It was time for me to go, after that incident.

Brothers being held in cells packed like sardines. We don't want to stop doing the things we do, to keep from going to jail, so that's what happens to us.

As long as dope was made available to the hustlers, it was no stopping. I didn't care about going to jail, because of over crowding.

We knew more jails were being built. Then we'll sit around a jail cell waiting, as though we are getting a dream home built.

So what they have a three strike law.

You have brothers right now that are waiting to cash in the two other felonies, in exchange for the twenty-five to life sentence.

After a few days of being in a holding cell, they put me in a regular cell. That didn't do any good, because the floor was the only place to sleep.

It was three of us waiting for a bunk, and me being number two, seemed like it was a long way off.

One was released the next morning and the other posted a bond that afternoon.

I was taking my mattress to the empty bunk, and this white boy tried to check it in. He knew who was next on the list, but still tried to take the bunk.

Because he only hung with brothers on the streets he felt as though he had clout.

Skip the small talk he had to be broke down quick. His back was damn near broken, when he was slammed on the iron bed rail.

He was getting stomped and kicked and then he started to scream like a little girl.

The guards came up to the cell to check things out and he told them who jumped on him. The guards asked the people in the cell what happened.

Everyone said they didn't see anything. Not saying they were scared of me, they knew one rule in jail was not to be a snitch.

Nothing happened to mc, but they took the other dude to another cell.

They knew if he was left in a cell with all blacks, and he just snitched, dental records would not have recognized him.

It was getting pretty bored in the little cell. Playing cards and checkers all day were a headache.

Church was on Sundays, and we went just to get out of the cell.

The pastor man would be reading from the Bible, and everyone would be conversing with people they hadn't seen in a while.

The food sucked. I didn't eat pork, and they wouldn't give you anything else. They had this sandwich we called a MOP sandwich. The acronyms stand for 'mayonnaise, onions, and pickles.' That's all the sandwich consisted of between two pieces of bread.

And that water down Kool-Aid didn't help. They probably used one pack of Kool-Aid, to five gallons of water, with one cup of sugar.

The wine we made was better than the Kool-Aid but everyone couldn't drink.

You had to donate your juice everyday in order to get some of the wine. They had a bookkeeper keeping records of who donated, which days, and how many juices they donated. Never knew how the wine was made but everyone in the cell that donated was drunk. People would get high and drink the wine like they were back on the block.

The way they got high would amaze you. When they served breakfast we sometimes got bananas. The inmates took the banana peelings and let them dry.

Then they took paper and rolled up the dry banana peelings.

You're probably wondering how they lit the what ever you want to call it.

They took a paper clip and stuck it in the socket until it sparked enough flames to light.

It amazed me how people used substitutes to maintain their habits.

I couldn't join in on any of those habits.

The only thing you mainly could do was to try and sleep during your time there.

Don't sleep too late, or your food will be eaten by the time you did wake up.

It was on more than one occasion that I woke up to an empty tray. You can only ask one time about someone eaten your food and people will look at me you as if to say "you knew it was going to happen."

Yeah that's true, so there was no more sleeping, when it was time to eat.

People had ways of doing anything they wanted to in jail.

There was so much hope of being bonded out that I couldn't take it anymore.

My bond was one hundred thousand or ten percent.

No money saved up for bail and I knew that much was in goods stashed in moms basement.

They were trying to charge me with delivery and manufacture of a controlled substance.

How in the hell would they know?

The dope was already rocked up when it was bought, so how could they call it

manufacturing?

Moms was going to get me out, as soon as the court date was set. So I thought. They set my preliminary hearing for November 14th, 1989.

Moms left me in there because she would always say if we went to jail, the only way she would help us out if we were defending ourselves. So when they let me make my call, she was told they are trying to put a dope charge on me. That didn't work because after the jailer told her what my charges were she just said oh well.

During my preliminary hearing the judge dropped the delivery and manufacture charge.

Officer Helmet Head, as we called him was the arresting police officer. He was out of his jurisdiction at the time of the arrest. He was also spying on me with binoculars that weren't police issued.

The judge asked him how he could see anyone that far away at night with binoculars selling dope.

The judge said if anything he could have seen me passing out phone numbers.

So the judge had me to stand trial on possession of cocaine and marijuana.

The judge set a ten thousand dollar personal recognizance bond since they had no record of me being in any serious trouble. They just never caught me doing anything illegally in a while.

After fourteen days of being in that hellhole the system sent me back to the streets.

Money was needed and no there was no thought of me giving up selling dope.

I just needed to be more careful.

Helmet Head didn't like it, when the delivery and manufacture charges were dropped. He was always harassing me thinking there was dope in my possession.

Dope would be hid under the rings on my fingers, or some where close, so a sale could be made.

They knew dope was still being sold but needed to catch me red handed.

Especially with the possession trial coming up soon catching me again would solidify their claim.

I made enough money to stop and lay low for a while.

Called myself chilling on selling dope for a moment until Big Rod told me they where going to Chi-Town that weekend.

I wanted to go, but was really low on funds, at the time. Borrowed ninety dollars and bought me a ready rocked sixteenth. (crack that's ready to sell, instead of cooking it yourself). Made about three hundred off that, and it could have been more, if there wouldn't have been any deals made.

Paid that ninety dollars back and bought me two more ready rocked sixteenths.

My boy knew about me being a marked man so he didn't deal with me directly any more.

He would put the dope in a Jell-O box and throw it out the window as he passed. The dope was hid, as he circled the block to pick me up, so he can be paid.

Smart move.

Five-O hadn't been around all day so money was consistently being made. Just as the thought of the police not being around all day, Track Star drives right up behind me.

It was bad timing because the grand in my pocket and about two hundred more dollars left in dope was feeling good.

Just tried to keep walking, saying to myself, "Joe if you get caught, your ass is grass."

I heard Track Star say "Joe". I started to run, but turned around anyway. I was trying to play it off like we were cool. I was like "What up track star?" We called him that because he ran track in high school and would run all the brothers down. Most of them anyway.

That's another reason why there was no need to run. And plus it had just snowed. Track Star would let you get a good head start then chase you down and will catch you.

He spoke back and asked me what I had been up to, since he had not seen me on the Ave. in a while.

I told him just chilling and trying to stay out of trouble. Then he asked me that fatal question, "Joe do you have any guns or dope on you?" Like I was going to confess and say yes.

I told him about me not messing around with dope any more. He asked if he could search me, and I told him yes.

As we were approaching each other I took off running though some empty houses. He may have been a track star that day but he wasn't about to catch me.

I ran all the way to the Eastside in a matter of minutes.

The fellas threw snowballs in Track Star's police car, while he was trying to catch the real track star.

He told them to tell me not come back to the Ave.

My Ave. My block. My livelihood. Track Star you can go straight to hell, with a one way ticket.

We left for Chicago that evening. It was over a thousand dollars in cash and the two hundred dollars in dope in my pockets.

The dope was given to another member of the Hanover Street Posse and we split for Chi-Town.

We only stayed in Chicago two days and came back broke as a joke.

It was probably from the way this waitress was being tipped at this club called the Elks.

Everyone was being treated as usual, and the waitress would receive a twenty dollar tip.

She lived at my table that night. I didn't mind sharing the wealth especially when there was more where that came from.

When we made it back to Battle Creek I had to be extra careful after the incident before we left.

It was also February, and my possession charge trial started in April.

Dope was still continued to be sold on the Ave., despite what the police said about me staying away.

A new tactic was being used for selling dope that was fool proof. A lot of these plastic roses were bought and a ten or twenty dollar rock was placed in each. When the customers came to buy they were handed a ten or twenty dollar rose. The role had to be played like that now, because Five-O was either on foot patrol, or riding beach cruiser bicycles.

Now-a-days, it takes a lot to make a dollar and we had to survive some how.

Dope was continued to be sold all the way up to my trial.

On the first day of my trial it went quick, because my lawyer postponed it.

We found out the seventeen rocks the police confiscated for evidence wasn't there. Only three rocks showed up in court. Didn't remember how much weed was taken but it was more than the five dollars worth that showed up in court.

The prosecutor offered me a guilty plea with four months to twenty years in prison.

Why in the hell would I accept a felony plea with three rocks of crack and five dollars worth of weed?

Why plea to a felony that will haunt me the rest of my life?

Not being able to vote or leave the country or even buy a firearm to protect my self.

Prosecutor, go straight to hell. Now plea on that.

The prosecutor knew he would never be able to win a felony conviction so we had to go back to court at a subsequent time.

I'm glad the police did something with the rest of the dope and weed, because it helped me out in court.

On the next court date, my lawyer thought it would be best if I pleaded guilty to use. That was cool, because using was not a felony. Didn't think the judge would by a story like that. Thought he would ask for a urine sample or something like that, if we did enter a guilty plea.

On Friday, April 5th 1990, the judge accepted my guilty plea to use of cocaine and the he gave me two years probation.

Of course that didn't stop me from dealing, it made me more invincible.

Woke up that Saturday morning, the 6th of April, the day after being sentenced to probation I was on my way out the door, to make another dollar.

Moms told me she had a dream of me getting shot. I never really paid any attention to it because there was a dollar to be made.

Business was booming that Saturday, and it showed no signs of letting up. The Ave. was really pumping hard that day.

For the first time after winter the barbecue grill was lit. Crack customers were flocking everywhere, and everyone was making money.

We went to Casey's Store and bought numerous cases of beer and bought hundreds of dollars worth of meat.

All compliments of the crack heads being loyal customers.

Kids were outside enjoying themselves playing and running around.

After leaving a crack head making a sale Leshawn Swanson(a crack user) was walking out of Milby's house at the corner of the Ave.

He was asking me something, about why we're always beating up on his family. He was referring to the Hanover Street Posse, better known as the Ave.

We were trying to explain to him that it was not me, and had no idea about what he was talking about. Guess he didn't believe me, because he put his hand in his pocket, and we started to argue. I had no idea what was about to happen next.

I kept trying to tell him that it wasn't me. All he would say is I'm tired of HSP jumping on my family.

After he said that again there was a click. Then he hit me in the left side of my temple with the gun.

It went off, and there was a loud bang.

I tried to run and that's when he shot me in the back of my knee. Fell to the ground and for some reason, I couldn't get up.

Then he put the gun to my temple and said "I should kill you". My eyes were closed, for about a half of minute, before opening them.

I was sure he was going to pull the trigger again, after the first hit. He probably figured, since he has already shot me once, it wouldn't be any worse to finish me off.

By the time the half minute was up, my eyes were opened, and he was driving off.

I'm still in a daze, wondering, what in the hell just happened.

People were sometimes shooting at me, whether it was in Mississippi or Michigan.

You never really think of getting shot.

You never worry, because you feel so untouchable.

When a bullet grazed my head and missed, the first time getting shot at, there were thoughts that nothing could happen to me.

That moment after getting shot, my whole life was flashed before hitting the ground.

Sure the thought of all the bad things that were done came back to me.

Even the bad things that were done to other people, never made me feel bad. You live on the streets, you hustle, you survive, and you die.

That simple.

You don't think about kids, family, or anything. You don't even care about waking up another day. You live the day like you're going to die that night.

Everyone on the Ave. was in a daze also. They couldn't believe what happened either.

The police caught Leshawn within minutes.

But some of his family members were already at my mother doorstep, saying what they were going to do if charges were filed.

My mother was telling me to press charges, because he tried to kill me. That was a no-no, because if his family couldn't get to me, they would get to some one close to me. It wasn't worth the risk. The police said they couldn't offer us protection before and after the trial, so why press charges. And you learn not to be a snitch, because it makes it worse.

The police still had Leshawn in custody, so we told them to let him go. If you lived on the streets, you died on the streets. That is still a belief. And if you snitched regardless of who was the cause, you really don't live long.

Snitches are found in ditches is like a household name on the street.

Nine days were spent, in the hospital because of the damage from the bullet.

It was cool after the first day, because the fellas would bring forty ounces to my room. By the time evening came, we would be buzzing like my first cousin.

I must have been inebriated everyday while being in the hospital.

All kinds of women would come and see me. Some of them that didn't like one another still stayed to see me. No argument ensued. Guess they were just happy to be in my presence.

Susan and Marcelle got in to it, and I think Marcelle was put out the room.

The bullet shattered my bone, and the doctors had to put in three plates and eight screws, to put my leg back together.

Guess I was one of the unlucky ones. Some people get shot in the flesh part of their body, and then go home. As for me, my stay was nine days. Because they had to reconstruct the bones, is why my stay was that long.

People would always tell me how lucky I am to be alive.

It really didn't matter to me, because there were no reasons to care about living or dying anyway.

When the fellas would leave and the alcohol was gone, it was often I would think about the best times of my life.

It would have to be the old school hip hop era.

When break dancing was popular it settled me done for a minute.

I mean we would write music and lyrics. Have dance and rap contests.

This gave us something to do day in and day out.

When traveling back and forth from Michigan to Mississippi entertainment was a big part of knowing there was something else to do besides gang banging.

I was really good at it.

Even in nineteen eighty-five or eighty-six I was talking to my aunt Dorothy Moore about signing with Malaco Records.

Since she had already put out hits like Misty Blue and was nominated for a Grammy with the song, I figured she could help me out.

But low and behold the streets and gang life ended the best times of my life.

These were the actual thoughts while lying up in the hospital bed.

When they discharged me from the hospital, Dr. Comai told me to get twenty weeks bed rest. How can a street runner such as myself, stay in a house let alone a bed, for twenty weeks?

I was back on the Ave. the next day selling dope. Walking up and down the street, on crutches, with staples and stitches in my leg.

They inserted a tube inside the wound to drain of the tainted blood. I would just hop, sell dope, and let the blood drip.

I never wanted let up on dealing, even if it cost me my life

Dope would be sold for a few hours then my leg would rest for a while.

That's the life of a real hustler.

It seemed as though bad luck was following me everywhere.

I was resting my leg at Marty's house one day, when one of the fells ganked this bass head(took a crack user money).

The guy kept asking for his money, but no one would give it back.

We didn't think he would come back either. We didn't think of him bringing a gun, because if he had one, he would have sold it by now.

The door was open, when this orange Honda Civic pulled up. The guy didn't say anything. He didn't even get out of the car. He just pulled out a pump shotgun and started unloading. All could be said was "it's a hit".

Every one ran and left me. Guess that's the real meaning, when they say every man for himself and God for us all.

I was trying to hop out the back door, and the guy was still shooting. After all the shells were dispensed, the he pulled off.

One of the fellas got hit in the back of the head and legs with some pellets. No real damage was done, but a life was almost taken.

This guy we knew was driving by at the time the shooting was going on.

Guess he thought some one was blazing at him, because he ran into a tree in Keith's yard. All of that could have been resolved, if they would have given the guy his twenty dollars back.

That's what the fellas would do when it was a cocaine drought, gank people. When you're so use to making money, you would sell fake dope to get paid.

We would sell anything that resembled crack, when it was a drought. (no dope to be bought then resold)

Frozen French fries, sheet rock, chalk, and even soap, are just a few things to name.

One of the fellas was selling this white dude some soap. The guy told him if it was some good dope, he would buy a lot of it.

My boy was trying to get away, but the guy insisted he waited until he got a blast of the dope. My boy was like all right man. Dude took a big hit, and was holding his breath.

Then his eyes got real big. His girlfriend thought it was some good dope. As she was waiting for her turn to hit it, the dude let out his breath and said "this is some damn soap".

My boy was like "yep ivory soap, it's the next best thing to get your lungs clean."

We did also have fun selling dope as you can tell.

Selling fake dope was becoming more and more popular, the summer of nineteen ninety.

Don't know if the police 'zero tolerance' drug policy was working, or cocaine was just hard to come by now.

Thinking in nineteen ninety about the future was an everyday thing. I would say to myself, "you have did so many bad things, dropped out of school, joined a gang, went back to school, went to the military, got out, went back to Michigan, started selling dope, got caught, on probation, got shot, still selling dope, and every thing else that fell in between".

What do all this add up to? Nothing. The nothing they would call me, and the nothing they always told me my life was going to be.

I didn't have any harsh feelings, about the situation that was plaguing me. No one ever told me "Joe you are going to mount to something one day."

Think about the slavery days, when black people would work for hundreds of years for no money.

I mean working from sun up to sun down, for no money.

Now we can get a job, and get paid, and we still rather not work. These are the thoughts that were never carried into practice.

A lot of that reflected on my mother telling me that my life would be nothing. She kept telling me I was never going to live to see sixteen, and how she hated, and wished she never had me.

If you have your mother telling you these things, and no one to argue that, that's the way you live. As a child thinks, so is he.

My thoughts were like a nobody, acted like a nobody, and lived like a nobody. So that was me a nobody.

I was somebody to the people that dope was sold to. I was somebody to the people that money was given to. I was even somebody to the women that received the best times of their lives from me.

How can my life be somebody unconditionally? I always wanted to be someone that people loved, and respected. The love and respect people had for me was from street fame.

The people that called me crazy respected me also. They knew what would happen when they crossed my path the wrong way. Yeah it was an image that had to be protected. If they knew me as a violent type of person, why not live up to that image?

I'm not trying to portray myself as a person that is supposed to be bad. I have been hanging on the streets far to long, to try to be that, other than what was real about me. And yes I did a lot of horrendous things in my life. Yes I still wonder if God will forgive me.

But I don't need people to keep telling me I'm going to hell. If all bad things are done in life and no change ever came about, then of course I know what the ultimate outcome will be. But don't tell me day in and day out about going to hell, because if I asked you about your life, then where would you go. So when people told me about going to hell, I would just reply and say "ok, I'll see you there." I just wish I had money like them, because while they are flying first class to hell, I'll be taking coach.

See I have never considered myself a role model to kids either. Everywhere kids see me; they would speak and ask for money.

Some of them knew me without ever having contact with me.

Money was given to kids from me every day. So much that they got accustomed to me giving them money. That's why the kids gave me the nickname 'Daddy Joe.'

The nickname Daddy Joe was cool, because it made me feel as though kids were looking up to me once again.

The kids even had feelings for me. When the shooting went down on the Ave., the kids were more concerned than the grownups.

Guess it was because some of the grown ups wished it would have been murder, instead of attempted murder.

That's another reason why there was no love for anyone in reality. Especially for the men that envied me. It is some women that get no love or respect from me either.

I never had a conscious about the crimes that were done. The crimes that were being committed at the time, never made me think twice.

Not even with the violence that was associated with it. Now that the bad things could be looked back on, there is somewhat sorrow and compassion for it. The only reason there's a feeling of compassion, is because some innocent people got hurt.

Hell was always a place that was in my future. Some of the things that have been done, GOD will not forgive me for them.

And I know that.

Chapter 7

Spiritual concepts never played a part in my life.

GOD knew my doom, the first day my existence started.

HE is that intelligent. HE knew some of the things would be inhumane, and a displeasure to HIS eyesight. HE knew this, but where was my knowledge? Who should take the blame, for not telling me about GOD at an early age?

If knowledge about HIM had been shown to me, there would have been a different perception of HIM.

I think.

Moms didn't really go into detail about GOD. She would only mention HIM by name, with no description. She didn't pray with us, nor did she tell us what a prayer was. I can only remember going to church as a kid, and that was a few times then.

Cars would have bumper stickers that read, 'a family that prays together, stays together.' That's probably why we hated each other as a family. No kind of family prayer, or unity or love was ever displayed.

Never can remember going to church as a family. Not even once, can that be recalled.

That's not a lie it's the truth in clear form.

There was no love for one another, and there are hate feelings right to this day.

How can sisters, that live a few blocks from each other, don't even speak?

No legitimate reasons behind it. Only no love was shown.

They can't be around moms, and have peace.

If one comes to visit moms, and the other one shows up, they don't speak to one another.

Everyone is sitting around looking at each other, with hateful thoughts.

Moms is scared to say something.

Whoever was over first to visit, feel moms owe them the attention.

If moms talk to one, the other will get mad and leave.

Then, no matter which one leave first, moms will talk negative about them.

That is what kept us divided, as a family.

Moms should have intervened and brought them together, instead of playing us against each other.

And this is why a lot of hell was caught from moms.

It's more than her disliking me.

It's because I'm not afraid to stand up and tell the truth. Yes our family is screwed up, and moms, you are the main one that is keeping the hell going.

My oldest brother is supposed to be a preacher, living only a hundred miles away. He doesn't even come to visit her a lot.

It may be holidays before he will come, or bring his family to visit.

Fran live in Michigan, and she visits moms, more than he does.

I'm not saying he's wrong for not visiting; he doesn't want to get caught up in the madness, with the rest of us.

He knows how moms use to treat him, when he was coming up. He remembers the times when she would pull her gun out on him.

Rochelle remembers the same.

As a matter of fact, she has pulled her gun out on seven of her nine kids that I know of.

Those of you in the family, who may dislike me for the truth, prove me wrong. The family doesn't care too much for each other.

Who can not attest to that?

And it's not just my immediate family.

I'm also talking about the extended family also. They never liked me, and it was the same from me.

Noella, you and most of your family, they were not liked. Those days of talking, and dogging us out, will never be forgotten. You, and your family, they know who they are, are so two-faced. That's why you don't see me grinning in your face, and at your house. No need for that. You know how my mother has treated us, but you laugh in her face, as though you never spoke ill things of her.

And the rest of you, in the extended family, the same is for you. Time and being bored, will not allow me to name all of you. But the guilty ones, you know who you are.

And even though I forgive you now, and there are no hate feelings, I can now move on.

No one in our extended family got along with each other.

I'm thirty-one years old, and can't remember one family reunion. The only family reunion we had was after a funeral.

Then, a lot of them didn't show up, because it would be someone there that had animosity with another. Or an argument would ensue, and that would be the end of that get together.

One family thought their family was better than the other.

All the families thought their family was better than ours. It was true, but never put anyone down because of them being without.

My mother had nothing to praise us about; so she praised her nieces and nephews.

She would always say, "my people kids got dam good jobs, and dam good homes, and a dam good education."

Their mother's and father's were there to make sure they were given those things. Their mother's and father have provided good homes and meals for their families.

They may have struggled during this, but they made it out ok. Like most of us made it out ok. But our struggle was different than theirs.

Did they have heat? Of course they did. We lived in several places to attest to that. Did they have decent holidays? Of course they did. We saw what there families were doing during those times.

It would sadden us, as a family, to hear moms speak so highly of other's.

She could have given us what her sister's and brothers gave their kids.

At least we could have gotten something new, from moms, every once in a while.

There's nothing wrong with the Salvation Army, or the goodwill.

Moms call it the good house.

It wasn't until I was older, before realizing that the Salvation Army and the Goodwill were not department stores.

The way my mother shopped there, you would think they were household names like Sears or J.C. Penney.

Our school clothes were from the Goodwill, and our household things were from the Goodwill.

If the Goodwill sold used food, we probably would have been there shopping there also.

Moms would take us into the Goodwill, and load us down with goods.

She would tell us to go to the car and unload, then come back to reload. It was enough to make you embarrassed.

But you did it to get clothes, and shoes.

If our shoes were ragged, we went in, put some more on and left the other ones, to be sold.

Now you can see where my hustling comes from.

And don't go to a restaurant with Moms or Fran. They will spend six or seven dollars on the buffet, then leave with a hundred dollars worth of food.

I'm talking about silverware and all.

Fran probably have different sets of utensils, from every restaurant she has been to.

With moms with you, it brings back the harsh days of the Goodwill and the Salvation Army.

I'm not making mockery of the Goodwill, or Salvation Army. That is what a lot of people depend on, that really are unfortunate.

When the word unfortunate is used, it's in reference to the people who are really in need.

Not the one's whose parents spend the money on crack and alcohol, and then buys cheap things for their kids. Not the one's that buys brand new outfits for themselves, then buy their kids second hand things.

When Christmas came around, we didn't get anything. Then moms started going to this place, where families would adopt you at Thanksgiving or Christmas. That was cool, because we received a lot of good things from the strangers that cared.

We could have at least been giving something decent by moms, at Christmas.

I'm not saying my mother didn't ever get us anything, but new things some times, would have been nice.

Moms would tell people that our clothes came from J.C. Penney or Sears.

I'm not saying our clothes didn't come from either one of those places; we just didn't wear them first.

This is not a put down to my mother, but the truth needs to be told. While she is telling people we had the finer things in life, that's not true. I'm sorry my mother never really had much so to her it may have been the finer things to her.

There is much love for my mother, and will be to the end of this earth. I would die for my mother, without even thinking about it. We just know she could have done better, and should have done better to bring us up as a family.

And the same one's that she praised, and spoke so highly of, look at most of them now.

Look at your so call people now. And look at most of us.

They're either crack heads, alcoholics, in prison, dead or have gone crazy.

That is why you have to be careful about who you praise. Charity starts at home moms.

Once again, this is not a put down to my mother, but she didn't influence any of the good decisions, we would later choose.

There's no remembrance of coming up in a church. I knew there was a GOD, but would always curse HIM for the things that were going on in my life.

I don't know why. There are others I'm sure have gone through similar situations. You can go through life, for a short period of time, and not learn anything about GOD, and the things HE has given the world.

I wished moms would have taught us about GOD, and we could have probably been better acting kids. There was belief about GOD, so why we were not taught. There were no family prayers going on in the house. No grace saying before dinner, only at holiday dinner. And that ceased, as we got a little older, and it was rare for us to eat as a family.

But then it hit me one day. How can she teach us if she doesn't know?

Maybe no one taught her and she didn't know how to relay it over to us.

Now that there is some knowledge about GOD but is it enough to be forgiven?

Coming up as a child, with no spiritual teachings around the house, children will fall off the path of righteousness.

I was just living every day, and doing bad things, not knowing there was a GOD watching every move that was made.

Very seldom would this GOD, that was supposed to have created the Heavens, and the Earth, be talked about.

The only time my body was ever in a church, is when it was broken into.

I didn't think there was a GOD for black people, because everyone was painting HIM white. So I figured the figurines they were calling Jesus, was for the white people along with the churches.

I'm saying, the statues were white, the followers of Jesus were white, and the prophets were white. Every thing that dealt with religion was white.

So the thought of GOD only caring for white people, made me think, that's why black people were, in the condition they were in.

The thought of we, as black people, didn't have a GOD, or GOD didn't care for us, was always on my mind.

Would say to myself, "if there is a GOD, why do we live the way we do?" Wondered why we would have to eat out of the garbage, or why every house we moved in, were cold and a dump.

Why we didn't get along as a family? All of these thoughts plagued me for a long time.

We were never exposed to any white ghettos, or seen little white kids eating out of the garbage cans.

I'm sure there were little white kids, in the same predicament we were in, but just didn't see any.

Yes hating GOD was in my vocabulary, because there was no knowledge of HIM.

It's sad a person has to wait until they're grown, before even trying to learn anything about GOD.

Life could have been different, if moms would have been a little more spiritual and less barbiturate. She loved the bars and clubs, probably more than she loved us.

Learning more about GOD, at an early age, would go a long way, and kids would probably turn out different.

We should have been introduced to HIM in a more spiritual way. Every one looks at GOD in a different kind of way.

Blacks want HIM black, whites want Him white. Didn't know whom to serve, so I served myself, and was god to myself.

Bowed down to myself, and others bowed down to me. So there was no need to serve GOD, when it was so much havoc over HIM.

It was a commandment that said 'thou shalt not use God's name in vain. But we would always say "I swear to GOD, on a stack of Bibles" just to get a point across. Even when we were lying, we still used that scenario, because it was supposed to be used to display the truth.

The example was used to say, that my mother is still right to this day, saying that. Instead of telling us that it was wrong, she influenced it. Instead of telling us not to steal, she was showing us how.

If she didn't serve GOD, then why should she teach us to? She didn't show us that man was supposed to serve GOD.

Why serve something that has never served me? There's no need to lie. These were the actual thoughts being displayed as a kid.

GOD knew about the lack of understanding, from me, about HIM.

That's why I feel HE didn't do to me what HE could have done.

Have said I'm sorry to GOD over and over again. Wanting to learn more about GOD became clear, when HE was understood, and that HE was true.

The only thing that bothered me was the need for something that was different.

And that's when Islam was found, or should say, that's when Islam found me.

It was a different kind of understanding. Islam was plain and to the point.

There was no color in Islam. No statues or images to bow down to, but to bow down to one GOD and to one GOD, alone.

That's why I embraced Islam, with little or no disagreement about it.

It's one verse in the Quran that made me really want to know about GOD.

It says "In the name of ALLAH the Beneficent, the Merciful. When ALLAH'S help and victory comes, when thou seest men entering into the religion of ALLAH in companies, celebrate the praise of thy LORD and ask HIS protection, surely HE is ever returning to Mercy".

Think about that statement. "Surely HE is ever returning to Mercy."

That means, no matter what a person has done in life, if they ask for GOD'S forgiveness, He will forgive them. Of course they have to live right the rest of the way.

My first encounter with Islam was when I was station at Ft. Bliss, TX. Guess the guy's name was Terrence Mitchell, and he was from Detroit.

He was telling me about this guy name Louis Farrakhan. Had never heard of the name before, so there was really no reason to be bothered.

I was eating bacon and sausage one morning, and Terrence was putting pork down. I told him we have been eating this stuff for years and it never bothered us. I didn't know about high blood pressure and stroke associated with eating pork either.

That was my ignorance about pork. Now there was understanding why my head hurt, when pork was eaten.

Anyway, he taught me a lot about pork. Enough to make me quit instantly. He was showing me these scriptures, in the Bible, and the Quran where GOD had dispelled swine as an unclean food to eat. That bothers me today, as to why so many followers of Jesus eat pork, when it was made an abomination.

But hey to each his own, and I'm not perfect either.

Chapter 8

Started reading the Quran and listening to a tape every now and then, because what it said was every bit of what I didn't need to be doing.

I couldn't stop doing the things the Quran and Bible opposed.

Like drinking.

I never liked drinking, but it was a way out for me. It really did alleviate some of the problems that plagued my mind. Well, the thought of alcohol did.

Began drinking at six and never turned back. Hustling on the streets, eating and drinking through the day was the only lifestyle that was known to me.

I didn't need anyone to buy it for me. I would go into the neighborhood store and buy any kind of beer that was cheap. Couldn't have been, more than ten years old at the time, when beer was first bought. Hustling for food and beer as a child was not anything strange to me. Hustling was just a way of life, and every thing was done to keep the habit flowing.

If the hustle were good, then it would be Church's chicken and beer. If the hustle was not good, it would only be chicken.

That's because the beer was easy to steal, and Church's chicken wasn't.

When we moved to Michigan, the drinking didn't come to a halt. Actually it got worse.

People would often ask me about my drinking at such an early age. I didn't have a legitimate reason, because there wasn't one.

After that first sip of beer at six got me hooked, there was no turning back.

After feeling comfortable with drinking beer, the liquor started. The world has never been the same. I was about fourteen when liquor became a favorite of mine. The way it intensified the beer high made me feel extra good. Just didn't like the violence that was associated with drinking liquor. Now it seemed as though the liquor was a dependency.

If we didn't have money, crazy things were done to get beer or liquor.

We would go to the store, find a receipt on the floor, and go get two cases of beer. We would have the receipt hanging out of our mouth like we paid for the beer.

Then we would walk through the check out line, like the receipt was legitimate.

No one ever said anything, because they thought no one would probably have the nerve to do something like that.

Some of the people that hung around me have done crazy things for money, just to get something to drink. Richard and I was walking pass the hospital, when he saw this old man. It happened so quickly, when he hit this man in the back of the head, with a table leg, for his wallet.

It wasn't but two dollars in the wallet, and he went and bought a forty ounce of 'olde english 800' malt liquor.

I didn't know whether to feel bad, or help him drink the forty-ounce.

The forty was cold and good.

One time we needed some money, and don't know if it was the right place at the wrong time, or the wrong place at the right time.

Anyway, these guys that rarely hung around with me were always doing dirt for anything.

They saw this old man coming from the ATM machine, and walked up from behind him.

Don't know where the tire iron came from, but seen where it went.

They hit the man, in the back of the head and took his money. The man didn't have but a hundred dollars, and that didn't matter to them.

We walked away, and the man was left there shaking, and kicking.

For some reason, that didn't cause me to feel bad about it.

Since there was no conscious, there was no reason to get emotional. People would actually hurt other people for money for no reason.

I have gotten drunk and did stupid things, but have never assaulted anyone for money.

We would get smashed with other friends then go throw bricks through people windows.

Looking back at that, and would think to myself, how could such things be done to innocent people. Innocent people were used, because it has been done also to people that deserved it.

If someone pissed me off, some of the homeboys would go to brick the houses with me. It wasn't like I was scared to do it alone, I just wanted to make sure a lot of damage was done in a few seconds.

We would all be at a window with two bricks each. When the signal was given from me, it would sound like cannons for two or three seconds, then we would run.

The next day, we would walk by to survey the damage. A lot of the houses we hit, would be boarded up, and never to be repaired again.

People would pay me to bust car windows, or flatten someone's tires. After the money was received, they were told something better would happen.

By them knowing about the violence, they would tell me not to hurt anyone. They would be assured that no one would put a finger on the victim.

The next day, the person that paid me, would hear about the damage that was done. They would be asked, if the services were worth it. They would give me extra money, for a job well done.

The people houses that got hit and they didn't know me, feelings of sorrow are there. You can't blame alcohol, but when you get drunk with the fellas then you do crazy things like that.

Never knew why, the innocent people got hit. Probably just to keep up practice.

Not really.

There was no respect for anyone, or their property. I owned none of it, so it was easy for me to destroy someone else's property.

Houses weren't the only destruction we did. We would hit cars also, and mainly police cars.

We would be in the bushes drinking for hours, waiting on a police car to pass by.

And when one did, you could hear the boom blocks away.

Some police would loose control, and drive off the road, and others would drive fast to get away.

That's the pay back to the police, for the anger we had built inside.

The anger that was built inside from me, was from growing up down in the South. People were still living like it's still the sixties.

Some still live that way, even as we approach the new millennium. People in the South still say colored folk, or Negro.

They stop for a funeral, but will hold up traffic for an ambulance, or fire truck, going to save someone's life.

I mean all kinds of wrecks and accidents dealing with the public safety officials, because citizens refuse to stop or pull over to let them by. How backwards is that? And the bad part about it is there's no law stating you have to stop your car in the middle of the road when a funeral is passing by. If anything people, you are breaking the law.

That's a hell of a mentality to still have.

Anyway, there was never a thought about being the kind of person that nature intended me to be.

The nature that was there is that the world must revolve around me. It was either my way or no way. It was no room for compromising, and no room for negotiations.

With me, you couldn't even voice your opinion, without being drowned out.

Just thought being right about everything, was the way it was, even knowing that you was wrong. And I was never wrong.

The things that were unsure, in my eyesight, became reality anyway.

That's because of this motto. "I would be sure always."

A lot of things that were learned from growing up on the streets, there are no regrets. The street mentality is still being used to this day. With the exception of the bad things that were done.

The street knowledge is a lesson, of not to do some of the things that would put you in places no one likes. Jail or hell.

There's no gang banging anymore. There's no hanging around negative people, or disrespecting people anymore.

If it had been positive people in the beginning, there would be no need to say a lot of these things.

I'm not saying the fellas were negative people, because we were all victims of the ghetto.

When the change came, some of them were opposed to it, when they were always on me about changing.

They were there, when the fights ensued, and had my back. With all the enemies that hated me, they knew it would be needed.

When I got into a fight, they would say, "Here we go again." It was nice to know that you had that kind of protection.

All of the fellas were not there for me. Marshall, he would always run or hide, when it was time to battle.

I wouldn't fight a blind man, if Marshall were with me.

Sorry Marshall, but that's the truth.

Drunk or sober, I would still be trying to fight, and take whoever out.

Sometimes the thoughts of how I would defend myself staggering, still amazes me.

I almost got caught up one day.

It was February nineteen ninety-three, when we were at this club called the Speakeasy.

My homeboy, Kenny Kut, and I were dee jaying at the club. We teamed up with this guy named Dr. J to split dee jaying.

The deal was, we split the door money, and the bar keeps the liquor money.

It was Saturday, and you know it was the day after payday.

The club was packed Thursday, Friday, and Saturday, and we knew it was jamming those three nights, and it was time to get paid.

This fool tried to give us somewhere around a hundred dollars.

Who he thought was going to buy the line, that only two hundred dollars were collected those three days. Then he said he used the money to get out of jail, for shooting someone in Lansing.

First of all, you're not about to shoot no one and get a two or three hundred dollars bond. Then, on a weekend, you're not about to get out of jail on a weekend for a felony like that.

He was a crack smoker, but I didn't think he would spend our money, and not pay us.

Kenny Kut was scared to ask for the money, so a real man had to ask for it.

Told Dr. J we need the rest of our money, but from the look in his eyes, it was gone.

He was saying it didn't concern me, when it was some of my equipment being used.

It wasn't the fact of the money; I was just looking out for Kenny Kut. My pockets were always on full, so there was no need for me to bitch about a few hundred dollars.

We started arguing about him giving Kenny the rest of his money.

Yeah my drunk was on, but there was no backing down. The two Long Island ice teas', that were drank earlier, had me feeling too good.

Dr. J stood about six one or two. At the time two hundred twenty plus pounds. You know what crack will do to you after you become an addict.

Anyway, there was no need to be scared to rumble. Let's get it on, because his size didn't faze me.

I don't know who swung first, but when he was hit, he didn't budge. Guess crack will do that to you also.

After connecting a few times, and no response, my thoughts were to give up.

Then he swung at me. Luckily I ducked, and he missed. The wind alone from the swing was strong enough to knock a child down.

Don't know if the liquor had my equilibrium off, but found myself stumbling after every swing. If he would have connected a punch, LORD knows.

I was dancing and joking with him, about the way he was missing punches, then he tripped me. I messed around and tumbled about two or three times.

On the last roll, he jumped on top of me, and put his knees on top of my arms. He was too heavy for me to try and lift him off. Then he started hitting me.

Keith grabbed Dr. J and said "that's enough man he gives up."

Then the fool slapped me. As his hand was going across my mouth, one of his fingers got caught in my teeth. Bit down on his finger and it instantly snapped off. When he stood up, blood was squirting out of his finger.

I spit out the finger, and it rolled around in the parking lot.

It scared me more when he said "I'm going to knock your ass out now."

He didn't know his finger was bit off, until Keith told him. Keith was trying to tell him to go to the hospital, but he wouldn't listen.

He was being teased by me saying, "I bit your finger off, I bit your finger off."

He left, with me thinking he was on his way to the hospital.

After that, the finger was picked up, put in my pocket, and we went home.

You can remember the incidents after they happen, but when you're drunk, you don't think about the consequences. You just do whatever, and wait until you are confronted with the situation at a later time.

The next day I realized what happened, but it was too late.

The finger stayed in my pocket for two days, before it was thrown away.

Guess the police talked to him about the incident, and he didn't want to press charges.

Then, about a week later, the police came to the apartment to arrest me, for some kind of assault charge.

The police told me he changed his mind about pressing charges.

I was thinking to myself, if he really wanted to press charges, or was he being coerced into doing it.

The story they gave me was as if he was beat up by me.

Like I beat him up for no reason, and he was unsure at first about pressing charges.

Maybe I'm wrong, but it was more to it, than him being unsure if he wanted to press charges.

When Leshawn shot me, there were no thoughts of pressing charges. It wasn't because he frightened me. Not hardly.

My family was completely innocent, and they were being thought of in the long run. You don't want anything to happen to them, because of your street life. You live on the streets, things happen whether bad or good, and you pay for it.

When people did things to me, forget about pressing charges, despite continuous pressure from the police.

All that can be said is, Dr.J I'm truly sorry, for biting your finger off. The liquor was doing all the talking, but you were taking advantage of us.

Never meant to bite you either, but that was the only way to get you off of me.

There's no legal way to fight on the streets, and you're not the only person that has been assaulted that way by me.

And to my niece daddy, I'm sorry for biting a hole in your neck.

I'm sorry for that, but if you really look at it, even you can attest, that it was your fault. We use to be boys, but you took advantage of the situation.

Don't know if we were mixing records, or playing video games, but you were getting to irate, about it being your turn. Every one was drunk and was having a good time, until the arguing started.

Then, like every other time I'm drunk and arguing with some one, a fight ensued. That ended the friendship we had.

James Spade, I'm sorry for the time, when the skin was bit off your finger. That was your fault also. We were boys and the argument was not called for. Why you stuck your finger in my face still ponders me today.

But hey, look back at the fight we had, can only say I'm sorry for what happened man.

It's a lot of people that apologies can be given to, for the things that happened, but it's not necessary.

It's necessary, but those that know me, have already forgiven me. And those that don't know me, apologies are made to whoever pleases.

And the drinking excuse can be used, but that won't do any good, because the damage is already done.

Being drunk is no excuse for the way a person should act, but there are.

Those excuses have to deal with what a person is really going through.

Drinking was used to take my mind off what was going on with me. Beer was cool, but the liquor will make the buzz feel better.

I never really had a preference of what to drink. If you can sit and drink the stuff they make, in the county jail, you could drink just about anything.

Gin and juice was a favorite of everybody's. The slogan "gin make you sin" couldn't have been put a better way.

Besides the fights gin would make me get into; was also a wild person.

Like doing wild things to women. Would get drunk, and do things to women, you wouldn't do to a farm animal.

Here's only one example.

While being stationed in El Paso, I met this lady at a club called the Dirty Floor. Drinking was going on as usual, when she approached the table.

Can remember she voluntarily put my hand under her skirt. She wasn't wearing any panties at the time. We conversed for a little while then she asked me to take her home.

Of course there was no refusing.

We made it to her house, went in and kicked it. Guess it was good, because she started to stalk me.

Well, she didn't stalk me at first. She would just drive around town looking for me.

It was at least ten women on my list, so there was no time to be dedicated to one.

She was getting too attached, and had to be scratched off the list. The bad thing about it, she was married. Her husband was in the military also. Of course that didn't matter, because my discharge date was coming soon.

My mind was already made up, to stop seeing her, a few weeks before learning about my discharge date.

I didn't tell her about the plans that were made, because of the deep feelings she had for me.

One night, on my way to her house, stopped and got a fifth of Seagram's gin. She had her own, and I had my own.

She asked me to do something that night that was unbelievable.

I was into rough things, but what she wanted was a little outside my league.

She asked me to beat her. I was about to ball my fist up and go to work.

She brought this long black belt to me and said "use this."

I told her that wasn't my kind of party. But the more that was drank, the more she asked me to do it.

After half the Seagram's was gone, I finally agreed to do it.

This was going to be the wildest moment ever witnessed, or performed in.

The gin was almost done, when she called me into the room.

Went in and she was bent over the bed. The only thing that was visible was her booty shining in the moonlight.

The moon wasn't the only thing that was full that night.

The belt was in one hand, the gin was bottle was in the other, and work was ready to be performed.

She was saying "beat me Shorty". That was a name Teddy Ruxx gave me.

Anyway, I tapped her on the butt lightly with the belt, then hit the gin.

She said "beat me harder Shorty", then she was hit a little harder. Once again she said "beat me harder Shorty."

After hitting her a few more times, and hitting the gin even harder, control was lost.

She wanted me to just hit her on the butt, but she was starting to get lashed all over. Guess when she said "beat me harder" it turned me on.

I went from being shy of doing it, to breaking her down like a stuck horse.

I continued to hit the gin, and then she would get hit. I would take a step back, run, and then hit her again. After doing that a few times, I was coming down on her, like it was a WWF match.

She was getting hit everywhere. On her back, her legs, I'm talking everywhere.

Then she started to run. Now she was being chased all over, getting hit with the belt. She made it to the door, and out the house. She was running down the street screaming and yelling.

There was no need for me to hang around, so my disappearance came quick.

When she saw me again, we never talked about that night.

I went over to her house the night before my discharge, with intentions of saying good-bye to her.

While telling her it was my last night in El Paso, she asked me to take her. Of course the answer was no, with the reason's her having a husband and kids.

It blew my mind, when she said they wouldn't have to know where she was. I'm glad; she only knew it was Michigan, and not which city I was going to.

As we were saying our good-byes arguing, she had a knife in her hand.

I was twisting the doorknob to leave, when she stabbed me in the wrist. I couldn't believe that just happened. Then she stabbed me in the arm.

For some silly reason, I was standing there asking her, why she do it.

We were getting no where with the answers she was giving so it was time for me to step.

I tried to leave again, when she was going into her purse. She always carried a gun, but didn't think it is what she was getting.

She aimed the gun at me, and something told me to duck, as she pulled the trigger. It was a loud blast. Then, she aimed the gun at me again while I was on the floor.

This time, she wasn't given the chance to pull the trigger again. She got hit in the face and fell to the floor.

We were wrestling for the gun, and then I got on top of her.

She was hit in the mouth, and she started choking on her bottom tooth, that got knocked out.

She was still relentless.

Carpet burns were on the side of my face, from wrestling with her. The gun was kicked under the couch, and I tried to leave.

On my way to the door, heard police say open up.

I'm assuming, some one heard the fighting and a gun shot, and then called the police.

The door was opened, and the police bum rushed me. Guess it's a natural response to come to the rescue of women. But this time, a man was the victim.

They had me contained, while asking her the questions. She was pointing at her mouth, and the carpet burns, she also had received while we were fighting.

Everything was going through my mind. I'm thinking, what the hell is she telling them? Then thought to myself, all hell I'm hit.

The police came to the car and asked for my identification.

If they called my name in, it was a one way ticket to jail.

They had a warrant for the assault charge on that Mexican, because it was no court appearance from me.

Why should I appear in a court ran by Mexicans, being charged with assaulting a Mexican? Hell no I didn't show up in court.

Luckily, my id wasn't with me. Of course they searched my pockets for it, and I'm glad she didn't know my full name. All she knew me as being called Shorty.

The police claimed she was jumped on, and was the one that was shot at. I gave my side of the story, and explained to them, what really happened.

Even showed them the gunshot, in the wall, where she tried to shoot me. Showed them the stab wounds

in my arms, and the knife she used.

The story from me made sense to them.

They asked me if charges were going to be filed, and the reply was no.

Because tomorrow was my last day in El Paso, getting back to the army base was my only concern.

Made it back to the army base, thinking that was the last time she'll ever see me again. So I thought.

The next day my final exit rounds were being made, when someone said "Shorty, wait a minute."

Charlotte was driving towards me, calling my name. I started walking towards the military police barracks to tell on her.

She got escorted off the post, and that was the last time we seen each other.

Sometimes, you hate it when things have to end that way, but that's life.

Like people tell me, you shouldn't have gotten involved with her in the first place.

That's true, because the love at the time was for this girl name Jo Ann Sims. Met her walking down Dyer St., with her sister, and offered them a ride.

I really loved Jo Ann, even after only knowing her for a short time.

The kind of fun that we had was different from any other of relationship with a woman.

The talks and walks, we would have on Scenic Drive, meant something special to me. It was an instant attachment, and wanting to marry her, only came a short time later.

A call was made to my mother, and she was told about the thought of asking Jo Ann to marry me.

Moms started crying and told me that wasn't a good idea. The plan was to marry Jo Ann and stay in El Paso, and not go back to Michigan.

Moms wanted me back in Michigan, instead of getting married. The relationship with Jo Ann ended quick, and once again, all alone. Jo Ann left on July 1st nineteen eighty-nine and my last day in El Paso was on July 6th. To this day, don't know why she left El Paso, but that was even painful to me, than Mindy leaving me, and loosing the baby.

Like the other women in El Paso, Jo Ann left me, never to be seen again.

That was the same way with Jackie Knox. Fell in love with her, and she also left me. Met her in Juarez Mexico, and she was also a decent woman. Jackie had much flavor, and we got along well. She was having problems with her mother, and needed somewhere to go. She moved to Brooklyn or somewhere in the five boroughs in New York, and was never heard from again.

I would often wonder what happened to the special women that were in my life, in El Paso.

Duchess Kelly, how are you doing, you are not forgotten.

In several different states you meet people, can fall in love with some, then you leave the state and the special people.

I met Janie Ricks at Ft. Lee VA. She was from Chicago, and was going to Germany soon. After we met, things went well for us. We spent a lot of time together, like any other couple, when they first meet.

And, it was like any other good relationship couples have.

You spend time with each other, enjoy each other's company, and you wonder if you should fall in love or not. Those thoughts went through my mind, a little after we met.

Even though Jechiel, JoAnn, and Duchess were mentioned, but JoAnn was the first woman that captured my heart, in the military.

Only Janie gave me her address, with the hope of us keeping in contact with each other.

Needless to say, she left, and no contact was ever made with her.

The situation was being treated like all the rest of the relationships.

You meet people, can fall in love, when it's over, it's over.

You leave, or they leave, it was just another relationship.

I was faced with things like that all my life. Had a crush with this girl name Fronza in the seventh grade, and knew we were going to share lives with each other.

It was a deep crush, and had to fight my best friend over her. She lived on Bon Air Street in Jackson, and I lived by Enoch's, the Junior High school we went to.

She lived quite a ways away, and I would still walk to her house almost everyday, just to see her. She had a nice family.

Her mother and father were the kind of parents a child would dream of having. They probably had some disagreements, as a family, but they were a happy family. They would sit at the table to eat together, like a family should. Instead of a family scattered all over the house eating. Even though we were young, I still believe there was love in one another.

Then, just like that, with no notice, Fronza was taken from me. Moms left Mississippi, to move to Michigan, and my life with Fronza ended that simple.

Chapter 9

That is why people never want to fall in love, especially when you are young. You get hurt, and then others have to suffer for it. Tracy being the first to hurt me, then later Mindy.

Women I later dated have suffered, through other women leaving me.

It was hard to commit myself, after the first time a woman hurt me. It's even worse, when the relationship has to end, because someone has to move out of state.

Girls at a young age, and women at an older age, have always looked out for me. Even at seven, girls enjoyed giving me money, candy, or whatever. They may have been doing that, because they were kind. It was taken differently from me. It was the young pimp in me.

I can remember around six, being under the house with girl name Doris. You know how the houses are in Mississippi. A lot of them sit on bricks, so it's easy to play under them. Only there was never any playing with me.

I didn't know what we were doing, but we were trying.

And to be honest with you, don't ask where the ideas came from, or know if I it was ok or not.

Don't remember if my pants were down, but do remember my head hitting the wood under the house.

Moms came outside and asked what was going on. She didn't see Doris, so she thought it was just me playing with myself, I mean by myself. Calm down that was just a little humor.

Anyways, that wasn't tried again. Not for a while to be exact.

Moms did catch me one time. Well, she almost caught me. I was around eight then, still trying to creep under houses.

That's what every curious young male go through at that age. Well at least I went through it.

When she asked me what we were doing under the house, I was just being quiet. Didn't have any under wear on, at the time, she was talking to me.

It was funny, because she asked me why my thing was hard. Could only tell her I had to use the bathroom, was the reason, for being under the house.

When I did go to the bathroom, the scariest thing happened to me.

Something gray was coming out of the tip of my thing. I was scared to tell moms what was happening, and I didn't know what to do either. There was no one I could ask about it.

Diseases were foreign to me then, so the thought of the girl giving me a STD was far from my mind.

It scared me so bad that nothing was tried with another girl, until my teenage years started.

Then, the world was never the same, after those years started.

I became sexually active at an early age. I was popular with girls no matter what age. From my adolescent years to my teens then on to early adulthood, I have always had a woman by my side.

Must have known what was taking place, because women were being satisfied. Even older women were attracted to me, at an early age.

I was dealing with twenty-five year old women, even in high school.

Thirty-year old women were nothing to get at age eighteen.

Why the older women were so attracted to me even kept me wondering.

I knew how to talk to women on a much mature level than most men at my age. Relating to women for so long was already a thing of the past to me. No matter what age they were, I could hold my own in any given situation.

And I never really wanted to deal with one woman. One woman alone could not give me one hundred percent satisfaction.

One woman could satisfy a man physically, while another woman could satisfy them emotionally.

Another may satisfy mentally, one economically, and another one socially.

What I'm trying to say is there are no complete women. That's why so many women were in my life. There was no physical relationship with every woman that came into my life. It was several women, for several different reasons.

Every woman couldn't satisfy me physically, even though they could be satisfied.

That is not a modest statement, it is just plain truth.

I had potentials to converse with women that were much older, but found out even sooner, the potentials to satisfy them physically.

The women that knew me would often flirt, even if that wasn't on my mind.

A lot of the drinking would be done alone, or with the fellas, before it started with women.

Being in clubs, at an early age, kicking it with women, was not a problem. My first real encounter with a club was in Michigan, called The Parkview. I was about fourteen, and would be in the Parkview kicking it with the grown folks. Even in Detroit at places called the Purple Passion, or Chuck's, I was able to get in before I was eighteen. And these were no hole in the wall clubs like in Mississippi, where a ten year old can get in and do whatever. These were high profile clubs.

Laughing, drinking, and getting to know all the women around. Prostitutes were the first, because they will look out for you. They teach you and show you things you never seen or heard before.

The point that's trying to be made is prostitutes were my first encounter with women.

We would hustle in the same areas and bumped heads a lot.

They would talk trash to me, and it would always be talked back to them.

I would listen to the way they talked, and absorbed it all.

Men that wouldn't have any money would try to talk the prostitutes into getting a freebie.

The old school game the men were running on the prostitutes or even other women wasn't working.

The old school game was taken, and some new school flavor was put to it.

When the older men tried to talk their old school game, it still wouldn't work. Told them that the women were not going for that old school trash anymore, they need some of this new school flavor.

The women would say "what you know about the new school."

I was scared to run the new school flavor to them, at first. So it took me being drunk, before it could be laid down.

They heard things from me that you couldn't hear in a triple X movie.

I was never taken up on an offer, but it got their attention.

They would say "you're too young," or your little ass couldn't squirt a gun.

Never knew what that meant at the time, but when I did find out, it made me think of being eight again.

The time when moms caught me under the house and the stuff was leaking from my thing.

So when we moved to Battle Creek Michigan, The Parkview was the first place my new school game was initiated.

I was only thirteen, maybe fourteen, buying drinks at this club. I would talk to the prostitutes, as well as getting my drink on.

I wouldn't talk dirty to them at first, only conversations that made me appear to be older. It worked out well with them, because they were falling for every line.

What tripped women out the most was, when they found out my age, they didn't believe me. It wasn't that my facial features made me look older; it was the way my conversation was presented to them.

The game was talked to the older women, but the younger girls would get the dates.

See, it was easy to get the young girls with the new school game, but the older women would just listen.

Until that changed one day.

I was dating this girl, but me and her mom would always converse, or hang out.

We would always talk about her daughter, until she told me, how attracted she was to me.

I never thought anything of it.

The more we talked, the closer we got. And the closer her mom and I became, interest for the girl was immediately lost.

Her mom helped with getting me farther away from her daughter.

She would tell me how her daughter was no good for me, and how she could be better.

I listened to what her mom had to say, and eventually fell for it.

Before kicking it with her mom, we agreed to keep it a secret. I didn't want her daughter to be calling me baby one day, then the next day calling me step daddy.

I was only fifteen and the girl mom was around thirty. You don't think anything of it at first, and having any thoughts about caring was out of the question.

So the girl was with me in the day, then her mom at night.

How it was done was, the daughter would let me out the front door to go home, then her mom would let me in through the back door. Then I would leave before daybreak, so her daughter wouldn't see me.

That was the start of me being with older women at a young age.

The older I got, the older the women got.

Women started coming in dozens. Being only eighteen, at the time, women were ranging in age twenty to thirty. They were on my jock constantly.

Eventually, the thirty-year-old woman was kicked to the curb, because her daughter was better.

Guess women play the same games men play.

Tell a man how good they are just to get some, and then a man find out it was just all talk. "Just to get some, now you feel dumb."

That's how I fell for my girlfriend mom. She told me how good she was, and my silly butt fell for it.

She couldn't back it up to save her life.

A valuable lesson was learned from that situation. Never say what you could do, without being able to back it up.

That lesson made me even bolder with women.

The game that was being ran down on women, left them curious. The new school flavor, that they had learned, was never introduced to them by anyone else.

The more game that was ran down, the more curious women would get.

And alcohol helped intensify the curiosity. I'm not saying women would get drunk, and they would be taken advantaged of, it just helped when they were about to go home.

I would talk to them sober to get their attention, and then run game when their buzz was on.

My game was so tight I guess you could call it the verbal date rape drug.

And before you knew it, my name was ringing all over Battle Creek.

Every where my face was seen, women would respond instantly.

Every where my feet were planted, I was always the center of attention.

The prestige was there, and a new identity was needed. The wardrobe was the first thing that was changed.

Suits were started to be worn out to the clubs. That was to attract the women that weren't down for the gang banging.

The suit scene fit well indeed.

Frosted jeans and tennis shoes, were still being worn, but the suits were to impress the image.

Guess you can say I was the junior J Anthony Brown. That brother knows he can dress.

Some women bought into that, but the market of ladies, needed to be widened. I'm not talking about weight either. But all in all no matter where you go in life, hey big women need loving to.

I couldn't wait to get dressed up and step out, so the women could be all over me.

It would be two to three feet of snow outside, and I would still step into a club with a suit on.

The good thing about it was I didn't have a shirt on. No socks, and sometimes, on good occasions, the under wear stayed at home also.

Women loved that kind of dress style. Some of them anyway.

Men playa hated on me a lot. Don't ask me why because, there was nothing I had that they didn't have, or couldn't get.

I would be dressed up, out and about clubbing; you can hear those making little innuendos about me.

I paid no attention to it, because they were the jealous ones.

Money, cars, clothes and, women, I had it all.

Was it enough to make the playa haters jealous? Maybe.

Did I have anything they didn't have or couldn't get? Maybe.

So why put me down for having, or wanting to have the finer things in life, and getting what I wanted.

That's motivation. If they had put half the motivation into getting what they wanted, instead of putting me down, they would have succeeded.

Even the ones that had never laid eyes on me would tell me I wasn't anything. That's not the words they would use, but you get the point.

I'll say, "Man you don't even know me." The reply would be "Yeah, but I heard about you."

That's the worst condition for anyone to be in, is for someone to hear something about them. Especially when they know it's not the truth.

Some of the things they were saying were true, but none of my actions affected them, or their family.

They condemned me on the fact of what others thought of me, not what they witnessed for themselves.

There were bad things about me, but it was also good things.

It may not sound like that statement makes any sense, but it does.

It was bad in a sense, that being a drug dealer, and a gang banging, was not anything to be proud of.

That got me the prestige that was needed to make it with the women, and my own life style.

It was good, because all that was known and had, it was shared with someone's wife or girlfriend.

Because of the love that was shown to women, I hated to see them sad or misused. That's one reason it was never a long relationship with a woman. It was too many sad and lonely women out there to be dedicated to just one

Having one woman I just couldn't take it. Women and I were in the same predicament.

They needed something that was missing in the relationship they were in.

Whether it was physical, mental, or social, they were missing out on that.

They may have had a boyfriend or husband, but they were still being mistreated in some kind of way. That's when it would be time for me to step in.

There were never intentions of building a relationship with the women, whether it was physical or not.

Women just needed to know they were more than what their mates perceived them to be.

Women needed to be treated like the queens they are. Men would tell women lies, filling their heads with empty promises that will never be fulfilled.

Never make promises to women, or women to men, that would cause you to go back on your word.

The promises that were made from me were only a good time. And that's what they received, a good time.

The only problem that plagued me was the women would fall in love. I couldn't deal with that, so the relationship had to be ended.

It wasn't the fact of them having a mate; they would just receive neglect from me in some kind of way.

You're probably thinking, why put women through that?

You put women through that, because the best times of their lives have just been fulfilled.

So now they know it's a better life out there, than the one they're stuck in.

Women would tell me how much they loved me. It flattered me, but there was a job that had to be done. Trying to satisfy every woman wasn't a hassle it was the fact of dividing up the time.

Sad or lonely women had that look on their face like it was saying "Joe come rescue me."

They would be told up front about the kind of person they would be dealing with.

I would let them also know that it was strictly a conversation that they could choose whatever else they wanted.

After socializing with them for about a week or two, they would be interesting in things going a little deeper.

That's where it had to come to a halt. They would be told, about me not being the ordinary person they perceived me to be. They already knew that from the conversation.

But the thought of that being your friends, girlfriends only came across your mind once or twice.

That's because you wonder if you really have a conscious or not.

And besides, since real men move in silence, how would they know anyway?

Who's to blame when you are backed up in a situation like that? No one made their girl come on to me.

And if it were the other way around, they would have told on me. So when they came on to me, it was played off like they would only be playing.

So their girl starts calling or telling you to come by, when you know your friend is either at work, or not around.

It's almost like you accept the challenge, with the thought of you being set up also in mind.

If you get caught talking to them, or he come home while you are there, then you kind of know something is up.

And that happened a few times.

I mean we were straight up chilling when my friend had come home. He was like "What up man?", and I couldn't look him in the eye from trying to wipe the lipstick off my clothes and me.

He asked, "What are you doing over here?"

Being the cool, calm and collected liar that could look GOD in the eyes and lie to HIM came up with something smooth like "man my car is down the street stalled and need a jump."

Now that wouldn't be a lie, because my car would be down the street. It wasn't down the street from being stalled, it was just so nobody would say they seen my car over to his house.

He just said, "Come let me help you out, so I can go to bed."

Now you are left wondering for a day or two, just to see if his girlfriend will hold up to the lie you just told.

And it wasn't a day that went by before she tried something else. So I just did like any other male would do, rolled with the punches.

Yeah you converse with them behind closed doors, and then a peck on the lips may takes place.

Then the next several days you are chewing on their tongue like a piece of super bubble.

After a while, you can sense something else is destined to happen.

Then something physically may happen, but they would hold back after a few kisses.

That was enough to make them feel weak in the knees. They would be kissed slowly and softly, while lightly breathing into their nostrils.

It causes them to wonder, just how great the encounter may be.

I would let them go home and think about it for a while. It didn't take them long, before they were ready to see what the talk about me was really about.

They would be treated like it will be the last time in their lifetime, they would be satisfied.

Welcome to the greatest show on earth.

After you seduce their mind, you already know in your heart, you can take them to a place no man has ever taken them.

So it's Friday night, and I'm the hound dog that's looking for the bird. I'm the hunter, not knowing I'm the hunted.

Of course the cell phone rings, and it's not the call that was being waited for, but for some strange reason, I'll take it.

The number on the caller id is recognized, and I think it's my homey. Damn is he home at this time? Nah he should be at work at this time so the call is answered anyway.

A soft hello is replied. All that could be heard in the receiver was "oh Joe that sexy voice turns me on, every time I hear it.

It's been close to a year, and his girlfriend has been trying to get with me. The gin was talking, and Tupac got me hyped, so let's get ready to rumble.

She said it was something she had to discuss with me.

I was like "I'm listening."

Said she'd rather tell me in person, and asked if I would come over.

I'm like ah hell something has gone down because her voice was shallow.

Agreeing to the idea, my car was left at home, and I took a cab to their house.

She went into detail about the affection and attraction she had for me, but none of that was new to me.

I said "Is that what you really wanted to tell me?"

Noticing the gin bottle with the pink grapefruit juice on the side, she lit the strawberry candles to set the scene.

Even the aroma in the air, was putting me in the mood. I was already in third gear, and the tank was on full.

I have had a lot of experience with knowing how to make a woman feel, so there was no need for me to try and come up with something. I never made love, always created it.

The body movement. The talk. The touching. The kissing. The gyration. Oh it's so intensifying.

On you march, get ready, get set, go.

Remembering how his kisses always increased her heart rate, the supreme grind master took her by the hand, and led her around the room like a seeing eye dog.

The reason for this is because after a few hits of the gin, the staring into her eyes had her mesmerized.

Leading her to the bedroom, the supreme grind master sees his boy picture on the headboard. Ignoring the pictures, because he knows none of this that is happening is his fault.

It's just a case of another woman wanting him to 'justify his love.'

The moisture from his tongue lightly wets her cleavage. Her eyes rolling around like a merry go round.

Treating her like a sick patient coming to the emergency room, dr. supreme grind master wasted no time giving her an I V.

He penetrates his needle, but a little resistance causes him to hold back from fully injecting it.

As being the master of healing, and the king of seduction, he now changes his game plan.

He gives her a deep passionate kiss. He sticks his tongue so far down her throat he can taste the filet of fish she ate at McDonalds earlier in the day.

Now she feels as though she's under anesthesia. Her body is numb, and before the I V needle is inserted again, he stands like superman atop the bed, with his flagpole at attention.

The I V is inserted, and little does she knows, the slow dripping liquid will have her more sedated.

Her words are slurred, as she try to say "oh supreme, what are you doing to me?

Hearing that, he knows that after tonight, her life will never be the same. Mine either if my friend finds out that he's another victim of the supreme grind master strikes again.

But that thought never bothered me.

Think about it, and look at it from a street point of view.

If one of my friends slept with my girlfriend, there would be no animosity towards him.

She's the one that may have initiated the contact, and it would have obviously taken place more than one time. Even if he was the one that initiated the contact, she didn't reject the offer.

She took the time to set something up, go meet him, take her clothes off, have fun, and then it would come out in the open at a later time

Well the next day, or when we would see each other again, she told me that was the best time she ever had.

Once again, that was nothing new to me.

I'm not saying every woman that slept with me, said it was the best, because you never give your all too every woman.

Chapter 10

A lot of women were slept with, just to be doing them a favor. They wanted to see if what other women were saying about me was true.

You're probably thinking I'm conceded. That's not being conceded that is as truthful as it gets.

Can be in a club chilling alone, then a woman would come and sit with me. She'll be offered a drink, and the order would be placed. Sometimes they'll say "no, but I'll buy you one."

Found that to be comical at times. The way women try to use reverse psychology on men.

Take the drink and think to myself "oh boy, here's another one."

A lot of times couldn't even tell them my name, because they would already know it.

I'll say "my name is," then they'll say "you're Joe Henderson." and "I heard a lot about you".

That's probably how my name started ringing in the first place. Of course they'll be asked about knowing my name.

It would usually be "you kicked it with a friend of mine."

They never told me the names of their friends. Their friends can tell them my name, but they won't tell me the name of the person that supposedly kicked it with me.

Already knew what the women would want, so there was no need for me to beat around the bush.

We would talk until one thirty or one forty five. The club closed at two, and it would be time to close the conversation.

Plus the stores stop selling liquor at two a.m.

I'll make a move for the door and the woman would ask, "What are you about to do?"

Tell them about going to the store and getting something else to drink, and then get something to eat, and then go home.

They would say something like "we could go to my house, and finish talking". Yeah Right.

No need to explain what happened next, because scenarios like that happened to me all the time.

Years ago it went from trying hours to get a woman to take me home with them, to women damn near begging me to take them.

Men hated that also. They would tell women how much of nothing they thought of me to be, but the women friends spoke differently.

That's what you would call free advertisement.

Men that didn't think anything of me would be talking to women that have always wanted to get with me. There was no need to get mad at the men, for what they said about me. They were paid back in a different kind of way.

He will buy a woman drinks all night, thinking she's the one he's going home with. By the time the club was about to close, a move will be made.

I'll just walk over to the woman and say, "how about giving me that date you promised me."

We'll go home together, just to make the other man mad.

After that, another problem was faced.

Then women would be telling other women about me, or every time we seen each other, they'll think something is going on between us.

It's not hard to be rude, when you don't want to deal with women.

Especially with the one's that you really don't like.

Never told them the only reason we kicked it was to make the playa haters mad. The drinking excuse would be my ticket out.

Guess that's why, it has been over five hundred women accounted for.

That's probably not an unusual number for a person my age. And probably half of them were only done as a favor.

When my name was really ringing, over a hundred women were with me, in one year alone.

Yeah that's nothing nice, but prestige and being in the center of attention is what it was all about.

It's more of the women's fault, than it was mine.

If they had kept what we shared between us, then one third of the five hundred women wouldn't have happened.

It's cool to tell people you had the best time of your life, but you don't have to give the name of the individual that gave it to you.

Some women would even tell people we slept together, and there was no knowledge of it.

There were a lot of drunken nights, and one night stands, but I knew who was in the bed with me.

May not have remembered years later, but these accusations would be told to me, shortly after it supposedly have happened.

Didn't know whether to accept the fame, or say something to the women, that was making these false allegations.

Sometimes it got carried away.

Women started putting babies on me. Not from a realistic view, but from a playa haters point.

If one woman knew the woman that was dealing with me, and they didn't like each other, rumors would spread, about me having a kid by them.

One day, whom ever the woman was, called this woman that was dealing with me. She told her to tell me to start taking care of my baby.

There were no kids on record from me at the time. Not to my knowledge anyway.

The silly game women play, and because of jealousy, it makes no sense.

Don't know if it's because you won't sleep with them, or they just like to keep up hell.

There's no ways to prove your innocence, because of the life style people know you live.

Women are some of the biggest playa haters around.

One day this girl called the house.

Wasn't dealing with her, and had never dealt with her.

She was my girlfriend associate, and would make little flirting comments to me.

We had known each other, before my girl met her, but never knew she liked me. We would make little comments at each other, but it never went any farther.

After my girl and she became friends, the comments from the girl were stronger.

She would often comment on when she is going to get what other women were getting.

Guess she must have been talking about the way a woman would feel, after we're done.

She was asked about how she knew.

She told me how other women have commented, and my girl tells her things about our personal relationship.

I'm not trying to deviate away from the phone call story, just want to show you why a woman should never tell her friends about her personal life.

If there is a conversation about it, a woman doesn't have to go into deep details about what goes on behind her closed doors.

That leaves her friends in curiosity, and having them thinking about what was said. Then their friends are thinking about getting with your man. It happens all the time, because it happened to me.

Would wonder why the girl and others would say, "I heard you got it going on."

Never went into details about it, just looked at them like they were crazy.

What made me mad was they would say "oh your girl told us about you."

A man doesn't have to worry about the people on the streets spreading his business, because his woman will.

Any ways, let me get back to the phone call.

My girl and I were sitting on the couch watching TV when the phone rang.

She answered it, and from the words being said, it was woman talk. My girl kept saying "yeah, um hum, and he is."

Was about to get off the couch, because her answers made me think she couldn't talk, because of my presence.

When she got off the phone, she said "guess where you're at." My reply was "what do you mean?"

She said, "you're at the nigga park around a lot of women."

After she told me whom it was telling the lies, I couldn't do anything but shake my head.

Here's her friend saying how much she wanted to sleep with me, telling lies on me.

I'm glad we were home at the time, because my girl would have probably believed her friend.

Women will go through great lengths to make a man look bad. I'm not saying the opposite doesn't happen it was never done by me.

You never see me going around telling men their girl is out there messing around. Primarily because it was me she was probably messing around with.

There were women that didn't mess around with me, but was messing around with other men. They never heard of me, telling their men on them. It didn't benefit me, so why be a playa hater.

A lot of times I didn't sleep with a woman that didn't benefit me.

I'm not talking financially either.

I'm talking about the men that didn't like me for no reason, or if they had a reason.

Their women were either attracted to me, or wanted to get with me. That's another reason why a lot of women were added to the count.

Their men were never told about them and me. Girls will tell other girls, and never guys. Their man knew about me sleeping with several women, but would comment to me, on their woman.

They would make innuendo's like "my girl will never have you," not knowing we have already been together. You can hear men in clubs talking about how faithful their women are, and not knowing we have been together.

I never told the men, about being with their women. Never was I that kind of person, and still won't tell right to this day.

It was the same with women. Never told women about their men sleeping with other women, even when it was true.

But was never a playa hater, even after being offered to tell.

Men envied me.

The lifestyle, the clothes, the way women responded to me was a way to make me feel good.

Only wanted to get what was coming to me out of life. Nothing more, nothing less.

And I received everything that was wanted.

If it called for me to starve, just to save money to get what was needed, then so be it. If it called for me to get over on someone to get what was wanted, then so be it. No matter what it was, whether it was needed or wanted, was obtained.

That's the way life goes. People get over on others, everyday of the year.

It was a tit for a tat.

Get over on me, and it will be returned by me, or some one else.

As mentioned earlier, innocent people may have been a victim, but I was a victim also.

Later in life, a person comes to realize every one is not the same.

When someone did something to me, it wasn't a thought of who would be paid back.

As long as things got even, nothing bothered me.

Thought to myself, that person may not have done anything to me, they have done something to some one else.

It wasn't a good way to think, but who can think, with all the dirt that was being done by me.

Hated the lifestyle, but loved it. It seemed as though there was no out.

Seeing the same things over and over, and doing the same things over and over, wishing that it were a better way.

The dope game was playing out, and the same amounts of money weren't being made as when the game was first started.

The personal customers that still bought from me, was enough to somewhat make it. A lot of them would eventually fade out.

Was still living with moms, but needed a way out.

The different women kicked it with me either had a man living with them, or to many kids.

I'm not putting the kids down, it's the way their mothers were raising them.

Have much love for the kids, but could never build a relationship with the mothers.

Then hated it when women would hang out in clubs, some in brand new outfits. Then go to their house and see the kids looking like something off 'feed the children campaign.'

It's none of my business when women go out, but take care of your home and kids first.

Women need to go out and relieve some of the stress kids may cause, but have them looking the same way you would, when you want to step out.

Then you have welfare. Have never disrespected women for being on welfare, but let's be honest, how many of them, do well by the money.

Would just never want to date a woman on welfare, because that takes from the children.

And the lifestyle that was good to me, welfare wasn't enough to help me out.

It bothered, when women talk about how they are going to get their check, and what negative things will be spent on it.

How many of you all have heard women say that.

Now how many of you women, are guilty of that.

And because of my love for kids, couldn't have a relationship with the mothers.

It hurt when money was accepted from women with kids.

Sometimes I would only look out for me and for me only.

If the women wanted to give me their money, who cares where it came from.

That ended quickly, even though another man would probably end up getting the money anyway.

But crack would still be sold to women.

They would get it elsewhere, if it didn't come from me

Some of the women had kids, but they weren't getting anything free. They got no sympathy from me.

And if I didn't make the money, they would buy the crack somewhere else.

Food stamps and all would be accepted. If they cared anything for the kids, at least they would have spent the food stamps on grocery.

Some of the women did that. They would buy crack with half the food stamps, and groceries with the other half.

When the crack was gone, and they had no money to get high on, then they would sell the food they had bought earlier.

The kids were the ones suffering from it all, but once again, you're not concerned with that.

There was no control of what the parents were doing, but I had to live also.

A different lifestyle was wanted, and society wasn't about to let me have one either.

I'm not blaming society for the way life was being lived, because they didn't know a change was about to come.

A lot of brother's would like to escape the harsh realities of life, but need a reason.

People would often ask me why church was never on my schedule.

No one ever gave me a reason to go to church.

No one ever gave me a reason to get off the streets. That change had to come about on my own.

Didn't know of anyone dying in a church, but death was the order of the day in the hood.

After being shot at several times, being shot once, and a couple drive by's, it was do or die for me.

Eventually, my death was going to come about on the streets, but never knew when it would happen.

Had nothing to loose, but the life that was never asked for, and didn't own it either.

Was on a suicide mission, and the smell of death was in the air. Was never a person that was suicidal, but every once in a while, it crossed my mind.

I guess you could say there were suicidal tendencies.

It was tried a few times. Was just unhappy with the way life was lived, and wanted it all to end.

Was already taking Valium for my nerves, and the doctor was always increasing the milligrams, and the dosage.

I had been taking nerve pills since nineteen eighty-five or eighty-six. The pills worked fine, but the more problems with my nerves, the more the doctor increased the milligrams.

First started out with Triavil or something like that. It was suppose to help me with my nerves. The only thing Triavil did was make me sleepy all the time.

That didn't work, so the doctor put me on Valium. The Valium was supposed to calm my nerves, but that didn't help.

With nowhere to turn, and no one to turn to, death sounded lovely.

I was depressed one night, and you can say my life was ready to be ended.

On the way home, bought a forty ounce of red bull, private stock, and "olde english 800".

Had several flash backs of my life, and it all added up to nothing.

The only thing that was accomplished in life, was finishing high school, and spending one year in the military.

Was twenty-two and had no goals to achieve.

Chapter 11

It was almost summer of ninety-ninety, and I was still suffering from the gunshot wound in April.

Figured the only way out was to take the life that was being leased.

I started to remember all the bad things that were done to people. My mother, my sisters and brothers, and the one person that was hated the most, was myself.

That's why I probably could never truly love any one, because there was never any love for myself.

I started playing 'sign of the times by Prince.'

The song depressed me every time it was played, but the lyrics were true.

When Prince would say the lyrics "man isn't truly happy, until a man truly dies."

After the lyrics were heard, about five more Valium was taken.

I had already taken about five Valiums on the way home.

It said on the medicine bottle, do not take with alcohol.

That is exactly what was done. I took about ten Valiums with three forty ounces of the strongest beer on the market.

It was a Friday night, and the last thing that was said to myself, was 'good night world.'

Drifted off into a deep sleep, and knew it was the last night for me alive.

I was unconscious for two days, and didn't even know it. Moms said she kept sending Tara and Fran to the basement to check on me, and they didn't get a response.

Eventually woke up, but it was Sunday night.

Two whole days had passed me over, and didn't even know it.

I was not supposed to wake up again.

My family never knew the reason for me sleeping those two days. They didn't know the things that were going on in my life, and never suspected me wanting to commit suicide.

Life didn't end, so it was back to the same lifestyle, with the same problems.

It was about two months later, before Susan found out that she was pregnant with Little Joe.

That caused more confusion in my life, than anything that had ever bothered me.

The problem was Susan was white.

Didn't like white women for relationships, only to take their money.

Fran introduced me to Susan, and that mistake, is still being paid for to this day.

I was really ready to blow my brains out over that mistake.

Susan told me that she couldn't have anymore kids, because of some complications with her first child.

My dumb ass fell for the oldest trick in the book.

Don't ask me why it was believed when she told me that. She was trying to trap me, but I was to busy trying to juice her for every dime she had.

She claims it was the first time she had been with a black man. Yeah right. She was trying to get pregnant on purpose.

She knew my dealings Marcelle, Janine, and a few others that have to be kept anonymous.

Fran had introduced me to Marcelle also.

Marcelle and Susan didn't like the ground each other walked on.

Don't ask me why.

Marcelle knew Susan couldn't have any kids, so she taunted her.

She would always throw up in Susan's face about how we were going to have kids together.

Susan started to get big over a few weeks, and people told her it looked as if she was pregnant.

She went to have a pregnancy test done, and it came back negative.

That should have told me to be on the look out.

Never asked her to show me doctor papers, to validate what she was saying, about not being able to have anymore kids.

Had found a job in early August, and was doing well with it.

I went to work one day feeling really sick.

Was in the bathroom throwing up, when my supervisor came in.

After finishing throwing up, the supervisor called me into his office.

He said "Joe I can't tell you what to do on you own time, but you can't come to work with hangovers."

Told him that wasn't a hangover, my body didn't agree with whatever.

When the work day was over, went straight to Susan's job, and told her to go get a pregnancy test.

She went to the crisis center and took a pregnancy test.

We had to wait a few days for the results to come back.

When she did get the results back, my heart prepared for the worse.

As soon as she seen me, the look on her face gave it away.

She gave me this paper with the results, and it said positive.

Told her not to bother me again, and she boasted about paying me back some day.

Typical white girl threat, when brothers say they're going to leave them.

Showed the paper to Janine, and she was tripping. Don't know why, because she couldn't have any kids to give me.

Marcelle found out, and you could have thought we were married, the way she reacted.

None of that fazed me.

Just kept to doing what came natural to me, selling dope.

It was the end of September when Deb and I met. Saw her bowling one day at Spring lake Lanes.

Had never seen her around before, and wanted to find out about this mysterious woman.

Spring Lake Lanes had this club called Stryker's on the inside.

That's where we could get glasses of beer for a quarter. I went there on Thursday nights, the same night Deb would bowl.

Showed her to the fellas one night and they didn't know her either.

That puzzled me. Thought every woman in Battle Creek was either seen by me, or met me.

I was always the one to get approached by a woman, now the tables had turned.

She always saw me staring at her, but she showed no interest.

One night after bowling, Deb came into Stryker's, and my move was ready to make be made.

She was with a lady friend, so two strawberry daiquiris were sent to their table.

After a minute or two, finally made my move to the table she was at.

We conversed for a short while, and then got a beep to make a delivery.

We met up the next week and talked for a while. She was telling me about her job had relocated, and laid the employees off.

She was in the midst of moving back to her mother's house, because her unemployment check's were about to be depleted.

All her bills were shut off notices, and my guess was, she didn't have any money.

None of that concerned me, because my concern was with her.

I had to pull out my strongest game ever. Things that were said to her probably would have made Shakespeare jealous.

After all that were said to her that night, her only response was, "sounds good, but you're too young.

Deb didn't look a bit over thirty, so when she found out about me being only twenty-three, she really wasn't interested.

When she told me she was almost thirty-two, my mouth dropped.

It wasn't about giving up, since my specialty was dealing with older women.

Deb wasn't buying any of what was being said.

Maybe it was because of the situations she was in.

Each week we talked, and it seemed as though her situations were getting worse.

She was about to give up her apartment, and move back to her moms. She was offered money, but didn't want to take it.

Must have really liked her, to give away money, and didn't want anything in return.

Gave her a thousand dollars and had not been on one date with her.

It was so strange, because she had to be forced to take the money.

Then, we didn't see each other for two or three weeks after that.

She didn't take the money and disappeared, I didn't come her way.

Then, when we did see each other again, she told me there were too many women in my life.

Things must have peeked her curiosity, because she went from me being too young, to having too many women.

We eventually agreed to go out on a date.

When we did finally go out together, it was cool.

After we eventually got together, another satisfied older woman.

Didn't have any idea, we were going to be together seven years.

Deb was the kind of woman that my life desired to meet, at the time.

I moved in with her a couple of weeks later, without telling her my plans of doing so.

Was scared to ask her to move in, so me and some of my goods showed up.

She didn't object to the idea, and it made me feel wanted, without any conditions.

Besides moving in, I finally got a chance to do something that never really happened in my life.

That was to watch TV.

Deb would trip when shows like the Jefferson's, Sanford and Son, or Good Times would be watched.

Never had a chance to watch TV, because of my loyalty to the streets.

Didn't think they had anything good on TV, until cable was brought to my attention.

When we did learn about cable, to me it was for rich people.

Then Deb was going to get the cable cut off, but there was no way she could take my new found love of TV shows.

She needed help with bills, and the five dollars an hour job, with the part time drug dealing, wasn't going to cut it.

So the job had to be let go, and the dope game was back in full swing.

Deb never questioned me about selling dope, but she didn't like it.

It had been a while before she found out about me selling dope again. Guess real men do move in silence.

After a while, she was concerned about the possibility of me getting caught again.

I was already on probation, for a previous charge.

Sometimes she would question my future. She would tell me how smart I was, and needed to use the talent towards something positive.

No woman had ever come to me in that way. I had finally found some one that cared for my future and me.

The mentality Deb had was astounding. She received, many props from me, for being the kind of woman she is.

Instantly fell in love with her. She would be followed around, like she was my mother.

Never had a childhood, so it was like growing up all over again.

Never had any real love from a woman, not even my mother.

So she was like a mother, and a mate, and she gave me that kind of love my body was so desperately seeking.

It was fun to have someone you can share everything with.

It was almost like a dream came true.

Deb and I were together seven months, before Little Joe was born, and she became a mother to him instantly.

After he was born, I didn't want to have anything to do with Susan. If he was mine, he was going to be raised by me only.

I didn't want her no where in the picture of raising Little Joe. She could visit him, but not that family kind of relationship with her.

After he was born, she didn't let me see him. She claimed he was sick.

Told her if he was sick, the hospital would have not have let him go.

It was her prejudice ass mother and family talking her into not letting me see him.

He was five days old, when the chance came for me to see him. After he was seen for the first time, she wouldn't let me take him. So he was taken regardless.

She started hollering, and her red neck mother was screaming "call the police."

Then this red neck man ran in the middle of the street to stop me. He was hit so hard, you couldn't even see him in my rearview.

But saw him, when he hit the ground, and there was no need to stop.

Turned into the apartment complex where I lived, and the police were there waiting for me.

They arrested me for kidnapping, but later dropped the charges, because Little Joe and I had the same name, and that wasn't kidnapping.

Neither one of us had legal custody of little Joe.

They had told me earlier, that it was the man's fault, and they wouldn't charge me with hitting him.

Now, since the kidnapping charges could not be filed, they charged me with felonious assault.

They offered me a plea bargain, in exchange for a lesser charge.

By then, Susan had filed for full custody of little Joe.

My last dollar would bet it was her mother's idea.

Someone even talked her into changing his name, to Dustin Lee.

Would you like to take a guess at that one?

Dustin Lee. What in the hell kind of back woods, country ass, and redneck name was that?

I found that out by getting together his records to file for joint custody.

Went downtown to get a copy of little Joe's birth certificate, and they had no record of it.

They gave me the names of babies that were born on that day at Community Hospital.

When they said Dustin Lee, and who his mother was, someone had hell to pay.

Like he was really going to be around me with a name like that.

He got his name changed back to mine in no time.

Her mother had something to do with all of that, like she always did.

And to say she loves Little Joe. How can her prejudice ass say she loves my son, that is considered black, and hate me?

How can you hate the father and love the son. It makes no sense to me.

How can she be prejudice when her man or husband caught her in the bathroom with a black man?

Guess she hate the race, but love the body.

Anyway, enough of those nobody's.

Deb helped me raise Little Joe in the beginning, because Susan was no where around.

And that was the way it should have been.

Susan wasn't there when Joe was crying through the night, needed to be changed or fed.

She wasn't there when he got off the diapers and bottle.

When she came to see Little Joe, he would call her by her name instead of momma.

And when Deb came through the door, Little Joe would call her momma.

Then Susan would get mad, because of little Joe's reaction to her.

How in the hell can you get mad, when Deb is all Little Joe knew and saw each day?

I had to take care of Joe, while Deb worked to take care of everything else.

Dope was still sold on the side to help out, but more money was needed.

There was a need to get away from the dope game and start building a future for me, Little Joe, Deb, and her kids.

There were no problems with knowing how to raise kids.

Had already helped raise my niece, and women kids that were dealt with from the past.

People questioned Deb on why she chose someone as young as me.

Little did they know my mentality was the kind older men wished they could have had?

My age was young, but had probably seen and been through more than a forty year old man.

There was never a doubt in Deb's mind, after we got together, that from me, she could get what an older man couldn't give.

In fact, if an older man could have given her what her nature desired, then there would have been no need for us to meet. So erase the age mentality.

Women were never turned down from me, because of their age. Women were turned down by me based on their living arrangements.

If she has nothing going on in the inside of her head, how can she help me out, or help the both of us.

People had questioned the older women that were dealing with me. It was like the blame was put on me, for the condition the woman was put in.

That made me realizes that when an older woman did come along, she would have to have herself together.

I was tired of hearing that statement, "he's too young." "What can he offer you and your kids?" or "I don't think he's right for you."

What they should have been saying was "you're not right for him."

Deb's mother was skeptical of my age at first. Never knew if she accepted, or just dealt with it.

Some of Deb's friends made it look as if she didn't know what she was doing. Like she couldn't do any better, than having a younger person in her life.

As if she was desperate to be with me.

The guy she called herself dating at the time we met wasn't handling his business properly.

But he'll be the one people choose.

Deb knew opposite than what they knew.

We would talk about the future, on what was wanted out of life.

Would always tell her how business minded I was, and always wanted to pursue that career.

The dope game was fading out. Not in a sense that the money wasn't there, was just looking for a better way.

And the only better way was to get out the dope game.

One day, Deb came home from work, and we talked to about me going to college.

College had always crossed my mind, but never found the time to go.

That was the excuse I used, but in reality I thought I could not cope on a college level.

There was time, but there was money that needed to be made.

Jail never frightened me, so dope selling would come easy.

Slacked up only after Little Joe was born, because he needed to be cared for.

So my mind was made up to go to college.

Figured if Deb cared enough about my future, and no woman ever had, why not go.

Went and filled out the application to enroll.

They looked at my high school records and were wondering if college was ready for me, instead of me being ready for college.

High school records don't show what a person is capable of doing.

Could have went through high school with high honors, but it was no need for me to do that. Yeah high school was hated, because of what was being taught.

Who wouldn't be tired of year after year, hearing about how we were slaves, and never contributed to anything to the advancements of civilization.

All lies. Let me give you a synopsis of what we have contributed.

Inventions included: the elevator, the automatic gear shift, the traffic signals, the electric trolley, the street sweeper, the pencil sharpener, the fountain pen, the type writer, the advanced printing press, the post marking, the hand stamp, the letter drop, the lawn sprinkler, the lawn mower, the air conditioner, the heating furnace, the electric lamp, the lantern, the automatic cut off switch, the dust pan, the comb, the ironing board, the clothes dryer, the refrigerator and the cell phone.

Where would this world be without us?

Anyway, told the college about me being ready to take the test.

They figured if the test was taken and didn't go well, that would convince me not to enroll.

After the test was taken, they had me to take it again.

The reasons were unknown.

And when they did have me to take it again, I was by myself, and in front of some staff members.

While taking the test, it hit me as to why they wanted me to take it all over again.

Must have done well, and they assumed cheating was going on, since we took it as a group.

Passed the test again, and started classes January nineteen ninety-two.

Classes were cool, but still didn't like to go.

Transportation was not at my disposal and walking in the middle of the winter was not about to happen.

The bus system was not a choice of mine either. Standing in the cold, with two feet of snow, and waiting for a bus, was never my cup of tea.

The days when there was no need for me to go, Deb would always say things that would change my mind.

Thought about what she would say for a few minutes then drag myself to the bus stop.

On the way to the bus stop, thoughts about how Deb cared for me going to school, when my own mother wouldn't say anything.

School would be skipped a lot, and Deb wouldn't even know it. Not that anything was trying to be hid,

Didn't want her to think I was giving up.

The reason for skipping is because attending classes were not mandatory.

You had to attend, but it didn't make any sense to sit in a classroom, when test could be passed without being there.

The classmates would be envious of me.

When test time came, students would have sat in class, and studied extra hard, would get a lesser grade than I would receive most of the time.

A lot of the tests were common sense, and there was no need to sit in a classroom all semester long, to get an A.

My teachers would tell me, if classes were attended a little more, the honor roll would probably be made every time.

If a student gets the honor roll and graduate, and I just graduate, what's the difference.

My associate's degree was obtained a year and a half later.

It was cool, because it was another major accomplishment in my life.

Brothers that started at the same time were not present in the auditorium, came graduation day.

It hurt.

The first day made me happy, because more brothers were seen than just me, in the classrooms.

But what happened to them in the end.

You have to learn about not giving up. No one had ever seen me give up on anything, but life.

Yeah there were thoughts to give up school at first, but Deb was constantly on my case.

She wasn't nagging me, just didn't like going to school in the Summer time, when you have waited all

Winter long, for some warm weather.

I was already working a second shift job, for two months, at an auto parts manufacturing facility.

It was April nineteen ninety-three, and the last time a real job was held was December nineteen ninety.

Yeah you guessed it Deb suggested the dope game needed to be ended, even if it was part time.

Heed was taken. The dope game was ended, and after almost four years, was back in the workforce.

Went to school from eight a.m. to one p.m., then off to work from three p.m. to eleven thirty p.m.

That was in the Summer time also.

I didn't have a life and the problems started between Deb and me.

I'm not saying getting a job caused the problems we just had no time together.

When I was at work, she would be at home, and vice verse.

I graduated June ninety ninety-three with an associate's degree in business management. And it was one of the better highlights in my life.

Dope selling was constantly on my mind. No need to lie.

Yes the easy way out was always wanted, because nobody likes difficulties.

I'm glad school was in the morning, and work was in the evening, because it kept me off the streets.

That kept me from being in the streets both day and night. People were still paging me constantly, looking for dope.

The urge to get back in the game is gone, but the desire was still there.

If only a couple thousand dollars could be made again, then I'll quit.

The desire for getting back into the dope game grew stronger and stronger.

College was done and I was still working, but was itching to get back to the streets.

Deb knew my desire to get back to the streets, so she talked me into going back to college.

I enrolled in the fall classes to get a Bachelor's degree in administration.

There were no breaks, since the first day of college had started January nineteen ninety-two.

Got off the streets, but needed someone there, to make sure that didn't happen again.

And Deb was there. She was like the mother that was never in my life. No woman had ever taken a personal interest in my well being like Deb did.

She didn't care about the money, even though she never asked me for anything.

That's another good thing about Deb that turned me on. She never asked me for anything.

Even though the chance was given to her, she was not a materialistic woman. She would receive jewelry, clothes, and whatever else that was in mind that would be nice for her to have. She was the first woman real money was spent on.

A lot of women were jealous of Deb. They would ask her constantly, if we were still together.

That would piss her off a lot, because it made it look as though the women were in line waiting on me.

Women caused a lot of problems, in the relationship, between Deb and me.

I still remained friends, or better yet an associate, with the women that were in my past. There was never any bad blood between the women I dated, that caused us to be enemies. That's why it was easy for me to communicate with them.

Me being over friendly, as Deb would often say, made it look as though something was happening, with my female associates.

That is a topic that really doesn't need to be talked about.

I wouldn't want to incriminate myself, and those, who are involved.

There's a lot Deb really doesn't know about, and she doesn't need to know.

Always wanted to shed the light on a lot of things that's in the dark, but that's not important.

Once again, because of the people involved, revealing any of the secrets would not be ethical.

I have always been real like. Too many people out there would be exposed, and that is not needed in my life.

Like the beginning of any relationship, things are great until the novelty wears of.

Deb and I would go every where together, and did everything together. The love we had for each other was real. Had never had a conscious until we met, and never cared about the way people felt, or what was said or done to them. There was one thing missing, in the relationship, from the start. Trust.

Chapter 12

No woman was ever trusted by me, it was not about to start.

That was one reason, for the several relationships, that went on at one time.

When several women were being dealt with at one time, there was no room to fall in love with every woman.

I was hurt by a lady name Tracy that lived on the East side of town. All I can say is I so called fell in love with her then she disappeared without a trace. But that didn't stop me from distrusting women it made me realize something can be erased at the drop of a dime. Tracy left me and that was the end of that.

The real distrust for women started with the relationship, with Mindy.

I called myself doing everything for this woman. Mindy had my nose all the way up in the air. It wasn't the first time a woman was ever told, "I love you" by me, but this was different. And it was different with Tracy.

Mindy was at the mall, when we met in November of nineteen eighty-seven, the day after Thanksgiving.

Her appearance was outstanding. That look she had instantly turned me toward her direction, and we exchanged phone numbers. We hit it off instantly.

We started seeing each other, and it was love at first sight. Haven't we heard this all too many times?

Had never really did anything for a woman, women had always done for me.

Mindy received everything from me. Every dime was spent on her. Everything that was hustled went to her.

She dressed well all the time, and always cared about the way she looked.

Christmas was right around the corner, when we met and, and every since then, it had been.

Bought her everything she wanted, and what I felt she should have.

Then her birthday is January 9th. She was still getting Christmas gifts from me in January, so when her birthday came it was more gifts.

Was either blind to the fact, or truly in love, because miles would be walked just to see her. Just like with Tracy.

You know winters in Michigan, in January, are not anyone's favorite. Mindy lived clear across town, and the walk to her house every day was treacherous.

I never cared about getting splashed with ice on my way over there, because the warm thoughts of just making to her house made me feel hot.

When the visit was over, had to journey all the way back home that night, wishing she would have asked me to stay.

Then, when my destination was reached, we stayed on the phone the rest of the night.

Our relationship was going great. No problems or no arguments.

Was still having problems with moms, but always stayed at Mindy's house, from sun up to sun down. Then, would stay on the phone with her all night, without worrying about what mom's said.

Mindy knew the problem's that were going on with my family. She was also having problems with her family.

Her brother's would fight her. Her mother would call her bitches and whores. Mindy's pain was felt, because I was facing the same experiences.

Then on top of that, her mom's boyfriend was molesting her. She would tell her mom, but it didn't do any good.

You know how it is when women care more for a man, than they do their own kids.

It hurt me to see Mindy go through that. It seems, as though, the only person that would believe her was me.

Everyone else thought she was making up stories.

It all became the truth in the courtroom. It was sickening to hear the things that this man had done to her.

He was free on bond while the trial was going on, under the condition he stayed away from Mindy.

But that didn't stop him. He would still stalk her, despite of what the court said.

One day he was following her, and good thing she had me around to protect her.

He didn't fear me, and there was no need to fear him.

So, when he was seen following her, all hell broke loose.

My aluminum baseball bat was close at hand, and he didn't have a chance to think.

When it was all said and done with, he suffered fractured ribs, a broken jaw, and what other ailments he may have sustained during the brutality.

The police came and of course arrested me. I wasn't worried, because the guy was in the wrong.

The police found out, he was not suppose to be anywhere near Mindy, and they let me go.

After the trial, the guy received thirty or more years in prison.

Things were fine when that ordeal was over for her.

A month or so later Mindy got pregnant. It was one of the happiest days of my life.

Tara was already pregnant, and Mindy having a baby made the occasion more special.

Moms had already put Tara out the house for being pregnant.

With Mindy being pregnant, the rift had widened with moms, and the military was my only way out.

That was a choice, that didn't have a choice, but it was no other way out.

I joined the military for my baby and Mindy, only to be used in the end.

Mindy left me after a week of being in the military. Don't know when she lost the baby, but those were the most painful days in my life.

Now, women were just being looked at as objects, because the pain was to excruciating, for me to have another woman that could be trusted.

That incident with Mindy caused me to act harsh toward every woman.

Deb knew about the situation with Mindy. About how she left me and, and me thinking she got rid of the baby.

She threw it up in my face, when we would argue. It didn't help any, because when we met, the feelings for Mindy weren't completely gone.

A replacement was needed immediately, and finding Deb was the key to being sane again.

Yeah that changed a little, but in my heart at the time, Mindy was the person for me.

Would think to myself, was Mindy wanted again for a relationship, or was it for just pay back, for what she had done to me.

Deb suffered through it, even though we went places and did things Mindy was always on my mind.

That eventually faded a few years later.

By the time my feelings for Mindy were gone, a new set of problems had emerged with Deb.

Women were still playing an active part in my life, only because of the accusations Deb would claim.

Yes I wanted the relationship to grow between Deb and me, but it was over from the start of the problems.

Deb knew about the women that were cool with me, even though we had a past relationship.

Deb didn't say anything in the beginning, because she was always being followed around like I was a lost child. And that was evidence enough to let her know that we could somewhat make it.

My boys were even cut loose when Deb and I met, because you would want things to workout, in the beginning.

Mindy was out of my life.

But hey, Deb and me were opposite attracts anyway. We could never agree on anything, and the thoughts of having things to go my way were there.

We never compromised on anything, and shared different taste in foods.

Our ideas were different, and she didn't care for material things.

She put a price on everything, and we had different a viewpoint about the way kids should be raised.

You're probably wondering why we stayed together, for so long, if all that was going on.

Deb was the most caring woman that ever came across me, and one reason was, she wasn't a street runner. She cared about my well being, and she was always there for me. Every time the police arrested me, she would either help bail me out or she bailed me out.

Her insecurity kept us at variance with each other, and she never trusted me from the start.

She was never given a reason to distrust me; especially not at the time of her accusations.

When she started accusing me of the things that were untrue, we started to drift apart.

I started spending less time with her, and more time with the fellas again.

I had this motto about the fellas that Deb didn't like. 'My boys were there before we met, and I'm sure they will be there long after we're over'. That became true.

When the problems got out of control, a way out was needed. It truly was needed. There was no need to continue a relationship that was going no where.

We would stay in the same household and wouldn't speak for weeks at a time. Would sleep on the couch down stairs, and she would sleep upstairs.

After that, there was no need to continue a relationship. We had stopped going places together. We couldn't go to the movies without arguing, and couldn't go out to eat without arguing. Every where we went, we couldn't get along.

One day we talked about how the relationship should end. She asked me not to go, so I stayed with the hope of things getting better.

Things weren't getting any better, because of the same problems. She's always accusing me of cheating, so there were inclinations of doing so.

Figured, if you're going to get accused of those things, why not make the lie become the truth.

The lie almost became the truth one day.

Marcelle Johnson, a girl from my past, said Chantiece was my daughter.

Had to tell Deb about the situation and that brought on extra problems.

Knew it would bring problems, but there was nothing to hide.

Friend of the court called and said a paternity test was needed, because Marcelle labeled me as being the daddy. I'm not 'just her babies daddy.'

The baby was four years old, and they were talking about child support.

Didn't ask about me really being the father, and didn't ask if there could be a possibility.

They told me to come down and sign for the child.

Told them hell no, I'm not signing for no child that that was not mine.

They said the guy that was supposed to be the father, blood test came back negative.

Like that was my problem, they couldn't find the baby's daddy.

They said either sign the papers, or take a blood test.

My veins were already tapped, and a blood test was agreed.

When the lady was putting the needle in my arm to draw blood, she told me it wasn't a nervous look on my face.

Thought she was talking about the needle going into my veins, she was referring to the baby being mine.

I told her that didn't worry me at all. And my arm is not going to be the last one stuck, concerning the paternity of Chantiece.

Deb was the only one worried.

And there was no need for me to be worried, because the blood test came back negative.

After me, neither Marcelle, nor friend of the court knows who the father of the baby is.

My boy would call friend of the court, 'friend of the whores.' This is not disrespect, to the women that truly need friend of the court, to intervene in some of their affairs.

Thought he was wrong for saying that, until the situation came my direction.

Was paying over a hundred dollars a week child support, and Joe was living with me, and he was on my medical insurance at work.

Tried to tell friend of the court, but they didn't care. They told me I would have to sue, before they could stop taking my money.

Susan was still getting welfare for Joe, and he was living with me. Even when Joe was living with her, dam caseworker said as long as Joe was in the household, she could receive.

How in the hell can they make a woman take welfare, if the father agrees to pay for everything?

On top of that, the four hundred plus dollars they were taking from me each month, she was not getting half of that in welfare.

That's another way women get back at men. If they are receiving welfare, the father will be the one suffering, and the mothers don't win either.

Friend of the court is the one that wins. As long as the mother is angry with the father, friend of the court likes that.

If women would let the true fathers take care of their responsibilities, friend of the court would go broke. They don't really go after the one's they know won't pay, so they over charge the brother's that will pay.

And the women don't receive but a portion of what they take from the brothers.

It should be like this.

If a man is paying for his child or children's medical and dental expenses, buying the child clothes, and spending time with them, friend of the court should not intervene.

If a man is not doing that, then friend of the court should take him for what he's worth.

But they drain you for every dime you have. They take my income taxes, and don't even owe back child support.

My son lives with me, but she was getting ADC, so I have to pay it back.

They told me it should have been reported that the mother was getting ADC, for a child that is not in her home.

How in the hell is I suppose to know, go to her and say "Susan, are you getting ADC for our son?

And Deb couldn't get a dime for her kids, even though she tried.

Tamela father is a crack head, and can't stay out of prison if his life depended on it.

Leonard's father is an alcoholic, and rumor has it a drug user also.

They can't get a dime from them, and have been owing money for years.

Me, they will try to juice a brother for everything he owns.

But there was a problem, when other men didn't look out for their children.

Deb had help from me looking out for the kids. Her mom raised them, but we added that little extra touch.

Tamela was my girl. There was nothing in this world that wouldn't be done for her. Was hard on her, and made sure she did a good job in school, and wasn't out in the streets.

She respected me, and she got what she wanted. I'm glad the experience came for me to know Deb kids. I loved Tamela and Leonard from the beginning. They became my kids, since their fathers had no dealings with them.

I had trouble with Leonard in the beginning. You know how it is when you're not a child's father, and they feel you can't tell them what to do.

Yeah that caused problems with Deb and me, because hardheaded children are hard to deal with.

Later on through the years, Tamela started scheming on Deb. That was a dislike that caused problems with Deb and me also.

Tamela would lie about going one place, and end up in another. Let her use the car, she's late picking you up, with the most unusual excuses you ever heard of. Tamela grew to be real sneaky, and that drew a dislike from me about her.

But yet, Deb would let her do what she wanted to do. Tamela knew that her schemes didn't go too far with me, but as long as Deb let her do it, she felt it was ok.

Knew then, if a woman couldn't control her children, there was no need for me to be around.

Tamela respected me more than Deb, for the simple fact, she didn't get by with anything.

But there was a need for her to respect Deb. If Deb couldn't get the respect from her own kids, then maybe she deserved it.

The kids didn't do anything she asked them to do. And when they did, they did it when they wanted to, or they didn't do it at all.

It may sound as though I'm putting them down, and that's not true. There was love for Deb and the kids, more than anything. It was the first time a woman and her kids were loved, and it was a family I could call my own. They were called my children, and they accepted it.

Well Leonard didn't really accept it he just ignored me most of the time.

Tamela, she did more than accept it. She called me dad, even though it was never asked of her.

Chapter 13

I have never wanted to take the place of no kid's father.

The kids are loved more than the mother, because they need love the most.

Never had true love from my mother or father, and that's what was given to every child.

Was dealing with women at a young age that had kids almost my age.

I gave every woman's child love, even after a relationship would be over. The father was no where to be found, and if he was, he didn't take the time to spend a day with his children.

Then they would get upset at me, when they see their children with me.

How in the hell are you going to get upset with me, for spending time with your child, and you don't?

Then when the children are bought clothes or shoes or something, the father's would leave word not for me to be buying them anything.

They don't buy them a pack of bubble gum, and going to tell me not to but buy their children anything. They can go straight to hell.

Those things are not done to replace the fathers. Kids need that kind of love, other than from just the mothers, when the biological fathers are absent.

If a man is in the household and truly love the woman and her kids, he will treat them like his own.

Then chances are the child won't turn to the streets. When the streets get your kids, chances are, you'll never get them back.

While men were trying to tell me not to do for, or do with their kids, they should have been there for them.

Plus, if men had treated the kid's mothers the way it should have been, there would have been no need for me to be there.

So men don't playa hate me for your kids loving me more than they love you.

Whether I'm with their mother's or not, I'll still make sure they are on the right track.

That's from knowing what it like when the streets get kids, because they had me.

Mothers and fathers, you fall a sleep too much on your kids.

Always be there, when they need the questions answered.

There's nothing wrong with learning something about the streets. If your kids have questions about what goes on out there, you can be able to tell them.

That's why I'll teach my kids and others about the streets. To let them know about the harsh realities of life, and what the streets have to offer.

The streets are a bad place to be, but if the kids know about it, they'll have an idea of what they're facing.

If they did know about the streets, no one out there can misuse them. But always make sure education and spirituality are their priority.

Kids can make it in both worlds then. The street world and the so called real world.

That gives kids balance. If they go out in the streets, and know how bad they are, then they'll know what not to get into. People can't easily influence the children's decisions, because there is no peer pressure to think about.

I know what it was like to be influenced, by street smart people. They were smart people that know one understands. Smart in ways that will make tycoons on Wall Street look foolish.

It may have been done in negative ways, but what if they changed.

You have fine doctors, lawyers, and accountants, right now, on the streets, and in prison.

They just needed the right kind of guidance, but now, most of them, their lives are over.

Kids serving life in prison without parole, for murder, dope, or whatever the crime may have been.

That's the way society likes it. They like the three strike law. The law likes it when kids get three felonies, so they can put them behind bars, and they will never have to be bothered with them again.

I'm not blaming society, because kids are in jail, or getting murdered.

Society hates it when kid's starts to change. If kids change the way they think and live, there will be no need to build prisons.

Parent's, change the way you think, then help your children change the way they think, and you won't have the kind of trouble that this world is offering.

As long as crime is happening, construction workers have jobs. Guards have jobs. And that is the best job security for anyone. Start doing the right thing, and watch how many guards loose their jobs.

Prisons get more money to house criminals, than schools get for students to learn.

Prisoners say they would rather be dead, than to spend the rest of their life in prison.

They would say it cost the system thousands and thousands of dollars a year to house them, but a few cents to kill them.

That's a hell of a way to think. But think about that, for a minute.

For the prisoners that have life in prison that want to die, the system doesn't want to do that. They can give people the death penalty for crimes that most of them are innocent of, but they won't honor prisoner's request to die.

The system wants that money to house the prisoners for forty, fifty, or sixty years.

Being in Battle Creek, there are at least ten youngsters that I know are serving life without parole.

And men my age are serving life sentences without parole.

These boys and men reach out for help before they get into trouble, but the mothers and the fathers are not recognizing it, until it's too late.

All these boys and young men want help, but no one has the heart to rehabilitate them.

Mothers, your kid's need you. Fathers, your kid's need you.

Mothers are mad at the kid's fathers, because they are not with them, and with another woman.

Fathers are mad at their kid's mothers because she's with another man.

The kids can't go to their fathers, because the mother's paints a bad picture of him.

The kids can't go to their mothers mate, because he feels they're not his children so why be bothered with them.

Now, the kids turn to the streets, because there is no one in the house to confide in.

Then the parents wonder what went wrong with their kids.

Kids are in jail for life, and never had a real chance to see what life was all about.

No chance to have a family of their own, to love and take care of.

Kids dying at early ages, before they get a chance to develop into men, that they may change their life and do better.

No fathers around to show them love and a better way. No fathers around to throw a football or baseball with them. No fathers around to teach them how to be a man, so kids are becoming men, before they exit child hood.

Young men age eighteen and under are having kids before they are out of high school. Babies having no hope in life, and they're the innocent ones that gets punished.

Young men are dying before they get a chance to see their kids grow up. It's enough to make you want to cry.

Every time you turn around a funeral is in procession.

No one is sad but the family, and a few friends, because people would talk about who are the next one's to go. And most of the time, the guessing is correct. We are guessing who will the next one to die, go to jail, or become a drug addict. Instead of helping the individuals, we don't say anything, because we want to be right, so we can say "I told you so."

People loosing their lives every day and we tend to think it could never happen to us.

And chances are the life style you're living and are accustomed to, it will happen to you.

There was a definite need for a change, through me. Life was short, and death was imminent. The bad things that were done to people, made me realize there was no need to live, and face the chastisements GOD is going to deliver on us.

But anyway, we need to help our kids make it through childhood, so when they are faced with tough obstacles, they will know how to overcome them.

Kids walking past the casket, not knowing what's going on. Not realizing that is the last time they will see their father.

A lot of times, it's the first and only time of seeing their fathers, because of the constant animosity between the mother and the father.

Often wonder what would have happened, if my life had ended, after being shot.

The forty-five seconds to a minute, was an uncomfortable situation.

Besides feeling the hot barrel on my temple from the second shot, it was an instant moment that my life was about to end, and that would be my last breath.

With my eyes closed, the twenty-two years of my life flashed before me.

Did I want to die like it was often asked, or was it just bluffing.

It would be asked frequently to die in my sleep peacefully, and not painfully.

As you can see that never happened, and it pissed off my adversaries. They would have to contend with me even longer.

Word was going around that I died, or got killed. Can't remember a time, when people celebrated the death of anyone, as much as they did mine.

The people that were happy acted as if the guy that shot me did them a favor. If people wanted me dead so bad, why they didn't do it themselves?

Guess they weren't as ready to die as they were ready to kill. At times I was ready to kill, but my enemies were not ready to die.

There was no reason to hate people, and people had no reason to hate me. Some of the people were asked why they hated me.

I had not done anything to them or their family. If you are mad at me for some thing that happened to one of your homeboys then let me and your homeboy settle it.

If you hate me and want to fight for no reason, we can do that. You will never see me fighting over a woman that's not mine, no territory, no dope customers, or fame.

If you want to fight just for the principle of it, then we can do that. We can tangle if that's all you want to do.

Since there was no recollection of me loosing a one on one fight, I'll let you work the anger off.

Then we can be associates, despite who win or loose.

Not many people wanted to do that. They would rather wait like cowards for their boys to gather, then, act like they want to fight.

For those of you who that have known me knew that it was hardly ever a time when a fight was backed away from. Whether it was one or ten, there was no thought of running. I'm not going to run from you, I'm going to run to you.

It was also times I ran, and you can call that scared if you want to. Was either drunk or in enemy territory, when the chase was on, and there was no time to scramble.

Couldn't go anywhere with out running into an enemy. Some of the associates, not the true fellas, would bail out on me leaving me hanging to do battle on my own.

But that was ok, because coming into this world by myself, made me realize it will be left by myself.

Death means nothing to me, because we were only born into this world to die.

Never had a problem with giving back what didn't belong to me.

Didn't ask for this life, so what happens to it makes no difference to me. This life has to be given back to the creator one day anyway.

My thoughts may be harsh, but how can a person such as myself think any different.

Would talk harsh to people, because there were no feelings for them. Harsh things were done to people, because they would try to do the same to me.

I would think that all the things that were done in life, only death could compensate for it. Whether you kill me or my own life is taken, people would be happy. My death will be more important than my life.

The way people were treated wasn't like I had a split personality. My family treated me bad; they were treated badly in return, so we treated each other bad.

So why do they call me crazy one day, and a loving person the next.

If I was so bad, why was the center of attention always focused on me? Why did people emulate me? Why were so many women on a list, to see if I was this great person, other women perceived me to be?

Took the name CAJ (pronounced cage/crazy ass Joe), and tried to live up to that as a street person, and took the name Joe, and tried to live that name as a good person.

Half the people would say my life would end by me being a lonely old man.

All the attention that was given to me, and people really didn't receive anything in return, would come back to haunt me.

It didn't bother me that they spoke those words, because there was never a thought to live past forty anyway. I mean you are looking at over twenty years from now.

Were people really treated that bad, that my life would end up being lonely.

When Deb convinced me to stop selling dope, convinced me to go to school, convinced me to get a job, and convinced me to get off the streets, why was there still flack from the people on the streets?

Because people hate to see you change your life.

Why were women still telling Deb, they would see me here and there with different women, and she would know my whereabouts?

Had disassociated myself from the gang banging, and stopped drinking at one point in time. Why were people still against me?

Was looking for permanent change, but still had to battle in the meantime.

Enemies, as well as people that were close to me, were still envious of me. Did they want me to change, or did they want me to die in the streets, where it all started.

I am not, I repeat, I am not the same person today that I was yesterday, and tomorrow will be different.

I don't care what your race, gender, or religious preference is people will still tie you to all the bad things you have done in life. They make sure you or they don't forget. I mean we all have done bad things in life but what about this forgive and forget mentality.

I mean I would want people to remember how I use to be, and then say that was many, many, many years ago.

But people act as though it just happened yesterday.

Is it designed to always brings up the bad and either forget about or not bring up the good in people.

People can or some of us do change.

Remember that.

Those thoughts would come about often, even though a change was yet to come. Figured I will end up dying trying.

A truce was wanted with the gang members. I wanted to forgive and forget the things people had done to me, and what was done to them by me.

I wanted to forget how they tried to take my life, and how theirs were almost taken.

To them, it was too late for change. They still had nothing to live for, while the nice job was found, it did me some good.

Realized then it was a better way out there than selling dope, hanging on the streets, or gang banging.

The nice cars in the parking lot, the nice clothes in the closet, and the money in the bank meant nothing to me.

What was missing was the happiness that came with the material things that had accumulated.

It all came to me one day that the only way a complete change would happen, and be happy, was that if Deb changed also.

She needed to start trusting me. She needed to let go, of the things that plagued her mind. I didn't want to tell her the accusations being said that some of them were true.

Some of them only became true after the accusations were brought down.

The accusations were not used as an excuse to do the things that were done.

Figured, the lies may as well become the truth.

So when the change came to me from Deb, there were no excuses, because my life was ready. When the change came to her from me, she half-stepped.

Yeah I was young when we met, but was all she wanted in a man. Her insecurity caused her a lot of pain. Didn't want to cheat on her, but pressure from her caused me to do it.

You can say 'yeah right, that don't cause a man to cheat.' You're right, but it was more to it.

Deb called me names that didn't I deserve.

The last three or four years we were together, the mental abuse came from Deb. There was no name calling or abuse from me.

She would do all the arguing, and the name calling.

Was either a sorry this or a sorry that. She would often say she will find a man that will treat her the way she wants to be treated. We'll see. After me there will be no more.

Even after my life was starting to be something, she still said it would be nothing.

If she received all of that abuse from me, why did she want to stay with me?

And don't give me that love is blind junk, because if that was so Helen Keller, Stevie Wonder, and Ray Charles should be the most loving people on earth.

Went along with what she was saying, but little did she know it would only hurt herself, in the long run.

See that's the point we're missing. If I'm this evil person she or anyone else perceived me to be, why have or want a relationship with me.

Even with me changing, things didn't get better between Deb and me.

The name calling continued. It didn't bother me when she called me names, but she would put Little Joe in it also.

When we separated, we talked about the lies that were told on me, and why the name calling continued. She claims it was all done to make me mad, because my reactions to the allegations would be nonchalant. Who had time to put up with childish games?

She knew my life had taken a turn for the better, and she was making it worse.

A went through a lot being with Deb. She would often tell me there would never be a woman, in my life that was better than her. Ok we'll see also. I say you won't find a man better than me, and you say I won't find a woman better than you.

There was belief to a point, because there was no one else that met the qualifications required. I'm talking about qualifications that meant compromising, trust, and respect.

At first there was no respect for Deb and no one else, because there was no respect for myself.

When the change started, I fell in love with myself again. After that, Deb could be loved, and anyone else.

Some uplifting was needed at the time of the change, and I didn't know where to get it from.

You're probably saying to yourself "you should have gone to church".

I had never put a church down; it was the leaders behind them that caused me to have issues.

Chapter 14

The problem with church is the misrepresentation I think the leaders bring to it.

You have pastors and preachers sleeping with young girls, and unmarried women, in the congregation. Telling the flock they should not commit adultery, should not fornicate, should not drink, and should not do this or that.

Then will have the nerve to prepare for a Sunday subject, to talk about the wrong people do. You wicked hypocrites.

How can they be men of GOD, while this type of indecency is going on? You can't blame the little girls for that, because they trust and believe in the preacher, and think what is going on is right.

The preachers are supposed to be a guide for them coming up, and now the pastors are taking little girls virginities.

Then when the little girls are grown up and realized they have been deceived, they don't want a man anymore. Now a woman is on their list, because now men are dogs.

Such sick men of GOD even turn little boys out. Then boys grow to be men, and now they want men. They have a sick encounter with someone they trust, and when deceit set in, the trust has been tainted.

Not wanting a relationship with a woman, because the woman has been so misunderstood.

A man that don't want the responsibilities of true manhood; say he's better off with another man.

No children's diapers to change. No waking up, in the early part of the mornings to feed a crying child. No responsibilities to run from. So a man with another man looks like it's the easy way out. Or a woman with another woman justifies the outcome of a life that was deceived.

You preachers need a preacher.

Why are you having these people to give up all their money for nothing? Why are you telling them that they are stealing from GOD when they don't pay tithes, or all the tithes?

Let me ask you preachers something. Was Jesus of two thousand years ago talking about giving up ten percent of workers gross earnings, or was He talking about ten percent of wealth, food, or time spent helping the needy?

What did people know about gross earnings two thousand years ago?

Please someone show me in the Bible where it states you have to give money as a tithe.

Then some churches are still having building fund drives that have been going on since my childhood days.

Why are you building a new church, when you need 'to go to church?

I'm not a Christian, but I still pay tithes. It's called having a job. It's called the federal government. They take taxes from me to pay for welfare and criminals to receive free food, free medical, and a free place to stay. That's paying tithes.

Quit telling people they need to do this to help the less fortunate. If you emptied the store house every harvest season the poor, and the needy would be in a better predicament.

You are bigger liars, drunks, adulterers, fornicators, and hypocrites around, and trust to tell the people not to do these things. How hypocritical is that?

Yeah liquor was consumed by me everyday, I just didn't like to see preachers leaving the pulpit going to the liquor store buying it. The Bible said 'be not drunk with wine or strong drink.' Then hypocrites say "Jesus drunk wine", and though Jesus was walking around drunk. You say that to justify your drunkenness.

I feel that these things are forbidden by GOD, but hey, if you feel its right then more power to you.

I never cared what color Jesus was. It is his message and mission that I love.

Why would I walk around with a WWJD(what would Jesus do) button, bracelet, bumper sticker etc., doing everything he would not do.

That is a nice quote but how many are really living up to it?

Think about everything you do on a daily basis and ask if Jesus would do it.

You should be ashamed of wearing it.

Also I didn't like to go to church and see a blonde hair, blue eyed Jesus on the wall, when the Bible said He had hair of lamb's wool, eyes of flames of coal, and feet of burnished brass.

But you'll say 'none of that matter.' To me it does. I don't want to be one of those that transgress, but I understand we are not perfect, though we should strive toward perfection.

It says not to bow down to images and statues, but you have pictures of a make believe Christ, all over the house and the church.

People are always talking about other people, like they are so holier than they are.

People are broke, cigarette smokers, crack smokers, alcoholics, and hypocrites.

And you say you love GOD, and Jesus, when they do none of that.

Hey but God still loves you but hate your ways.

You are lying wicked hypocrites. My words may be harsh, but the truth is the truth.

How can there be some uplifting from preachers, when they need some uplifting themselves.

And let me get something straight right now.

This does not pertain to every single person.

I mean this is a true case of 'If the shoe fit wear it'.

The uplifting that was needed for me was coming in a few months. The Million Man March was on October 15th, 1995.

That was something needed to make the change worth while.

The Million-Man March was the most spiritual connection I ever had with myself. It was people there from different walks of life, whether it was from the streets or a different country. I saw Christians, Jews, Muslims, and some that didn't believe at the March.

All looking for the same desire, and that's to please God and God alone.

I can now look at everyone and love everyone as one human family.

And every one got along with each other.

Wouldn't say a change came instantly, but it changed drastically.

Left the Million Man March with a change of heart, and wanted peace between every one that had animosity with me.

On the way from the March, I wondered if the people from the streets were willing to accept a true change.

Chapter 15

It wasn't two months later, the most devastating thing in life happened to me.

My youngest brother was lost at age sixteen. There was no mention of him until now, because of specific reasons to keep him concealed.

Really don't know how to introduce him, but he was, and is the closet person I have ever known. He was somewhat similar to me coming up, except for moms being close to him.

She did let him get by with a lot of things that she would have never let me get by with. She let him drop out of school at an early age. She didn't know until later, about me dropping out of school. She let him drink and smoke in front of her. We could never do that. He would curse at her, when we could never say dang around her. She said that sounded too much like dam.

Older women were attracted to him, like they were attracted to me.

No one really understood him, except me. He knew what it was like, to be in a confused situation. He tried to please every one, just like me.

Moms was always on his case, just like me, and he always caught hell from me. We would often fight, because of him disrespecting moms.

In a lot of ways, there was no blame to Peanut, the blame is to her. Peanut would not have turned out the way he did, if moms would have kept him in school, and put a stop to the disrespecting.

If she had stopped him from smoking and drinking in the first place, he would have respected her.

Letting him do that, and not putting a stop to it, caused him to turn to the streets.

He would always tell me how he wanted to be like me. I would tell him to finish school, and make a good life out of what you do.

After the Million Man March, I wanted Peanut to be like me. The changing was coming, and I wanted him to follow in my foot steps.

But the streets had him.

Tried to get him to change his mind, but it didn't work.

Was on him every chance, as the father role had to be played. Would pick him up after work, and kick it with him. He was my video game partner, my baby sitter, and my friend.

I didn't want to come at him like a brother. I wanted to come at him like one of the enemies on the street.

That was to let him know, that if your family will do you in, the streets are even worse.

He was shown the harsh realities of life. He had already known some of the things that were totally unaware to me.

Thought if he seen and remembered the things that were shown to him, he would not be out there.

But a fighting battle was lost, because moms had already given him a head start.

He figured how he could listen to me, when moms let him do whatever he wanted.

I can understand him always wanting to be in the streets. There was some understanding as to why he disrespected moms the way he did.

Satan did all of that to moms. He would call her bitches and whores. He would tell her how much he hated her, and wanted to kill her.

Satan did inhumane things to moms, so Peanut started to do it.

I guess you can say if she would have put a stop to it when Satan started, Peanut probably wouldn't have started it.

Satan hated Peanut guts. Peanut had never done anything to Satan for him to hate him that way.

Satan thought Peanut was always getting favoritism from the rest of the family.

He would pick fights with Peanut for no reason.

Plus, Satan smoked crack and that didn't help at all. People that know Satan, think that the crack has him acting the way he does.

Satan was in the condition he's in long before crack.

He has done things that will make me look innocent. He was smoking weed at seven. He broke into two houses in one day at six or seven.

I don't know whether you would say he is demonic or invincible.

He has no heart. He has no life. He has no soul. He has no respect for moms, or anyone else. He has no respect for the law. He has no respect for GOD.

Nothing hurts him.

He has done things, not on purpose, that makes stunt men look foolish.

He was cursing moms one day, and I started chasing him. We were living in a two story house, and he tried to run upstairs. He had on shorts, with no shirt, with no shoes and it must have been about two feet of snow on thc ground outside.

He started to run up the steps, and I figured he had no place to run.

He was chased into one of the rooms, and then the fool jumped through the window.

Didn't even let the window up to jump out, he went straight through the panes.

The window had two panes, and a tree was outside.

He hit several branches on the way down.

When he hit the ground all he said was 'oh shit!'

Moms was like "the fool has killed himself."

Of course she sends me out side to check on him.

Went outside, the fool was on the curve, in the snow, sucking his thumb.

Walked towards him to see if he was ok, he started running.

It scared me so bad that all kinds of thoughts were going through my head.

Like wondering if he was human or not.

When he finally came back into the house, he didn't have one cut or scratch on his body.

When people were told about what happened, they thought I was on dope or drunk.

We started paying more attention to the crazy things he were already doing.

Had a dog name King, and he was not your ordinary dog. Had never seen a dog eat fish bones, or onions, or whole potatoes.

We had pizza one day, and threw the cardboard out, so King could lick the cheese and meat that was stuck to it.

The dog ate the cardboard, as though it was all food.

We would feed King, and teased him like we were going take back what we gave him.

He would growl and charge at us like he was going to bite us.

We can feed King, and Satan would get on his hands and knees and eat with the dog.

I'm talking about actually eating and chewing.

King never growled at Satan.

His insides and nature must be that of an animal.

He bit Tara on her thumb one day, and the bite got infected. She had to go to the hospital and get a shot. And if my memory serves me correctly, she had to get the pus drained from her thumb.

The doctors thought a dog bit Tara. They could not believe a human had bit her, and infected her the way it did.

They didn't know that Satan is not human.

He reminds me of Michael Myers in the Halloween movies. No matter what you do to him, he gets back up and walks away, as though nothing happened to him.

He was arguing with moms one day. She had a tire iron in her hand. She told him if he cursed her again, what she was going to do with the tire iron.

Satan didn't stop, and she hit him in the knees with the tire iron.

She drew all the ways back and hit him. The hit hurt me from just looking.

He stood up and said, "that didn't hurt" and walked away.

That is one reason I quit fighting him. It did no good but made me tired.

Now there were reasons to understand, why every mental institution said there was no hope for him.

They did everything to find out what was going on inside his mind. I think.

After being in mental institutions for over ten years, the government finally gave up.

The last words from them to us were "may GOD help and bless you all."

We have needed help since he got out of the institutions.

Peanut was the one who caught the most hell. Satan hated Peanut so much that telling him that actually made him feel real good.

He would tell Peanut how much he hated him. Peanut would ask him, "why do you hate me so much?"

Satan never had a legitimate reason.

Peanut would say "You left when I was four years old; I never did anything to you."

But jealousy caused Satan to do lots of ill things to Peanut.

It wasn't like Peanut was given everything. We had nothing, so what was the jealousy about.

Was he jealous to the fact that Peanut got along with people? Was it the fact that Peanut would go places with me, and he wasn't invited?

When he did go places with me, he embarrassed me every chance he got

He hated the whole family, so it couldn't just be Peanut. He had a different kind of hate for Peanut.

The kind of hate that, if you passed away, someone would be glorified.

Like the people that were happy when they thought someone killed me.

Satan is always in and out of jail, and Peanut started to follow his footsteps. Peanut went to the juvenile and that didn't seem to help. Like juvenile really helps kids.

Satan was already hanging in the streets from day one. He hit the streets hard when the mental institution in Detroit couldn't do anything with him.

It seems as though it made things worse.

When he left Detroit, he was smoking crack. Some body in Detroit must have turned him out.

Can you imagine a mental patient on crack?

Taking medicine and smoking crack is like gun powder, and a struck match.

The medicine they were giving him didn't help. As the doses got stronger, Satan got crazier.

But Satan has the kind of crazy that he knows what he does.

He knows right from wrong, but pretends to people that he is really 'crazy.'

When he would curse moms out, he would get broke down for it, and people would say "you should leave that kid alone."

They don't know all the hell and chaos he's caused us for years, and they have the nerves to say leave him alone.

When they did find out how sick minded he really was, they would say, beat him down. Never speak up on anything, or anyone, when you don't know the deal.

He would take medicine and smoke crack. One drug battling with the other.

We got sick and tired of Satan stealing from people, and blaming it in Peanut.

People would come to moms house and ask for Peanut. Then they would say Peanut stole this or that from them.

They would threaten Peanut for no reason.

Some dude got his dope taken one day, and Satan said his name was Peanut.

Peanut seen the guy, but he didn't recognize Peanut as the one who took the dope.

Satan was in jail at the time, when the guy wanted to get them both together.

Don't want to talk about this, because there is still a lot more to it than what we know about.

Satan got out of jail on December 11th nineteen ninety-five. It was a Monday, and I will never, as long as my days are on this earth, forget that day.

Peanut had been staying over to a friend of his for a few days, and moms didn't like it. She accused me of taking Peanut away and hiding him from the family. I didn't even know where Peanut was at, at the time he was staying out.

When he did get in contact with me, he was told to go home, because moms was tripping. He didn't listen, because he already had a taste of the streets, and there was no turning back.

Plus he said Satan was getting out, and he didn't want to be fighting with him.

His pain was felt.

Moms had accused me of having Peanut out on the streets selling dope. Don't know where she had got the accusations from, but they were all false. She claims Tara gave her that crazy information.

One night, went and got Peanut from over his friends house, to let him tell moms I didn't have him selling dope. He told moms that whatever he was out there doing, it was his free will.

Moms still didn't believe him.

Peanut was ready to go back to where he was when moms told him "that's ok, my baby got out of jail tonight, and I don't need you any more."

Peanut looked at moms like he wanted to cry. He was probably saying to himself 'all of what Satan has done to her and me, she still choose him over me.

You have to be careful of what you say to people. You never know when they will leave this earth, and you regret what you said. Then it's too late.

Moms didn't know those would be the last words she'll ever say to Peanut.

Took him back to where he wanted to go, and gave him some crack rocks I had bought to get some food stamps from whomever he could get them from.

When we made it to the house where he was getting dropped off at, I told him don't fuck me around on the food stamps.

Didn't know that would be the last time we would have words with each other.

I just wish it could have been a better choice of words.

Two white girls were waiting on the steps and told Peanut, the guy he knew was looking for him.

Drove off, not knowing that would be the last time I would see my little brother alive.

Two days had passed, and we hadn't heard from Peanut, and that was unusual.

Got his friend's name off the caller ID and called.

The guy told me Peanut left a few days earlier, and he hadn't seen him since.

Moms hadn't heard from him either.

Thought maybe he was over to a friend's house staying, because of Satan being out, and he didn't want to be bothered with him.

We looked for Peanut for two days, and then decided to call the police.

They thought, since him and Satan didn't like each other, he was staying away, and didn't want to be found.

We knew something was probably wrong, because Peanut would at least keep in touch with me.

Two weeks had passed, and no word from him.

The police had put his picture on the news, and asked if anyone had seen him, notify the police department.

People called in and said they had seen Peanut either here or there.

We checked every lead, but nothing turned up.

It was time for me to go to Mississippi for Christmas vacation. We had not heard anything from Peanut, so we left.

Didn't know whether to go, or stay until we at least heard from him.

Since people said they had seen him around town, we went to Mississippi anyway.

Called Michigan regularly, to see if the family had heard anything.

Still nothing turned up.

When the vacation was over, we made it back to Michigan, only to find out that they still didn't find Peanut.

Now the police were seriously involved. They were asking me questions I didn't understand.

My family started asking me if what was being told to them was in fact the truth.

It didn't dawn on me that they were implicating me, in the cause of Peanut being missing.

The media started saying I had something to do with the disappearance of my brother.

Because there was nothing for me to talk about, the police said it was no cooperation with me in the investigation.

We were sitting around one day and the phone started ringing.

Thoughts of it being some good news or some kind of hope were in everyone's eyes.

Someone called and said Peanut was in the Kalamazoo River dead.

We gave the information to the police and nothing turned up.

We don't know who called, but it was an ignorant thing to do.

News was just coming on, and Peanut was the first to be talked about.

The news anchorperson showed Peanuts picture, and told the viewers that if they had any information on his whereabouts, call the police or the family.

I couldn't help but to cry, when my missing little brother was shown on the screen.

The person that meant a lot to me was missing. Would say to me "why hasn't he called to let me know he was all right"?

We thought the reward we had out, was going to bring someone, to tell us where Peanut was at.

It was the New Year, and we still had not heard from Peanut.

Twenty days had passed, since the last time I heard or saw him.

Was so worried, that when I did see him again, he was going to get a big hug, and tell him not to do that again.

We found out that Peanut supposedly had owed this guy some money.

Moms knew who the guy was. He was the same one that the white girls told Peanut about.

Found out where he lived, and went to his house, and asked him about Peanut.

He made some indication that Peanut owed him four hundred dollars.

He wouldn't tell me what it was for, but said it was all taking cared of.

Told him the money would be paid back to him, if he would tell us where Peanut was.

He looked at me and swore he didn't know where he was.

Left his house went and told moms the guy had nothing to do with it.

We never gave up on looking for Peanut.

The media and the police were having a field day implicating me.

Probably wouldn't have been any implications, if moms and whoever else in the family were not spreading rumors.

They actually thought I had something to do with Peanut being missing.

They would say things like "you were the last one to see him, and talk to him."

So what.

Should have sued the newspaper for printing lies about me.

Not once did the newspaper ask me questions in relation to Peanut whereabouts.

All they were printing was "the brother was refusing to cooperate."

My own mother was saying that I had something to do with Peanut being missing.

That hurt me more than anything she's ever done to me.

Moms asked Satan if he seen Peanut around. Satan said, "his ass is probably somewhere laid up, shot up."

Moms told him he shouldn't say bad things like that about his brother.

Little did we know, Satan was telling the truth.

We should have known he knew something, by his demeanor.

He showed no remorse, about Peanut being missing.

He hated Peanut, but no one thought he hated him that much, to wish something would happen to him.

More and more things were surfacing about that guy that Peanut supposed to have owed the money to. The same guy that told me, he had no knowledge of Peanut's whereabouts.

Found out him and Satan did time in the county jail together.

Also found out that Satan took the dope from the guy and said his name was James which is Peanut's name.

The guy that Peanut was staying with came and picked Satan. Then took him back to the same place where I had dropped off Peanut earlier.

Things just didn't add up right. It was hard for us to put two and two together, with what was going on.

Went back to the guy's house and asked him about Peanut again. He was giving me this off the wall story about what was going on.

He was talking about whatever was going on at the place Peanut was dropped off at, it was causing problems for his business.

He was saying the police had the place mapped out, and he couldn't go back to the house.

Anyway, it was a Sunday morning, woke up feeling good, because I had a dream that we found Peanut, and everybody was happy.

That good felling didn't last to long.

It wasn't a few hours later, the police had went to the house where Peanut was dropped off the night of December, 11th nineteen ninety- five. It was now January 15th, nineteen ninety-six.

It puzzled me as to why they were there.

Was at home when Tara called me and said the police found a young male body in the garage.

She said they didn't know who it was, but the feeling was not good.

Asked GOD, if it be HIS will, don't let it be Peanut. And if it is Peanut, give us the strength to pull through.

Tara called me back, and told me, it was Peanut.

They had finally found him after being missing thirty-five days.

He was found in a garage with trash over him. GOD please rests his soul.

That was the most devastating thing to happen to me in life.

It was worse than me getting shot, and worse than a friend passing away.

Moms had to go identify Peanut at the hospital. She couldn't take it. Tara had to also identify him.

Wanted to go and see my little brother, but the police said only two of the family members could go for identification purposes.

Tara told me, it looked like he died with his hands in the air. She said it looked as if he was begging for his life.

I cried and cried and cried, until no more tears could be formed.

Life was meaningless, from that day on. Suicide was on my mind constantly.

No one knew the pain and agony that was going on in my life. It seemed as though my body had suffered a nervous breakdown, and no one knew.

Chapter 16

My little brother died that my life might be saved. He passed away at sixteen, and moms said I would never live to see past sixteen.

He had told me constantly, that he wanted to grow up and be just like me.

He often did things just to see if it would be approved by me.

All could be said was why, why, why.

Answers were wanted and needed, as to why my sixteen-year-old brother was taken from us.

He was not only a brother; he was a friend, a baby sitter, and a video game partner.

He was little Joe's favorite uncle.

Days went by and, like always, situations had to be handled by me.

Asked GOD for strength, to have my little brother placed away decent.

His body had to be shipped to Mississippi for burial, and all of the funeral arrangements, had to be handled by me.

God gave me the strength to handle things, and to keep my composure.

We buried my little brother January 21st, 1996.

Would often think to myself, and wondered if it would have been better that we found Peanut dead, or that he stayed missing forever.

It bothered me that he was found at the same house he was dropped off at.

Information had started to surface from everywhere.

We found out that he had died at ten o'clock, December 11th, the same night he was dropped off.

He had been dead thirty-five days, before we found him.

It was also the same day Jason got out of the county jail.

Things didn't add up the way it was put together.

Peanut was shot four times. Once in the back, once in the temple, once in the forehead, and once in the back of the head.

How could anyone do such a thing to a child?

The only enemies Peanut had were the jealous neighborhood thugs. They only disliked him, because girls responded to him.

That wasn't enough to kill him for it.

We found out who was responsible for killing him.

They were the ones he called his friends.

Didn't know the reasons until more information started coming through.

They had this guy name Scum in custody, but didn't have enough evidence to bring others.

The people that called the police were friends with the person they had in custody.

He had told Russell, his friend that he had killed the kid everyone was looking for.

Scum showed Russell how he had Peanut in his garage. Garbage was thrown all over him, like he was an animal.

Russell recognized a picture of Peanut that was circulating, and he knew me and Mike from around the way.

Scum had asked him to help cut up Peanut's body and dump the evidence in a river, somewhere in Ohio.

Russell had probably asked his father about what he should do, because it was bothering him.

So Russell called the police, and told them what he knew.

We were hoping he didn't change his mind about testifying.

Moms couldn't handle it, so she went to a shelter.

It was so ironic that she went there, because she met this lady that was friends with Scum's girlfriend.

Moms was talking to her about Peanut, and the lady started telling all what she knew.

She told moms that Peanut was begging and pleading for his life, and how much he needed us.

She said they ignored his request, and shot him anyway.

Right to this day, still don't know why my little brother was murdered the way he was.

Some people that know about it say that Satan took the guy's dope, and said his name was James.

The guy wanted to put both of them together and get the truth, but Satan was in jail.

And when Satan did get out, the guy got both of them together, and from the information we received, an argument ensued.

This is where the mystery comes in.

My brother was shot four times and one person was charged with the murder.

The night Peanut died, Satan came home with blood on his clothes.

Moms asked him what happened, and why he had blood on his clothes. He said it wasn't blood, that he got drunk and used the bathroom on him self.

If he used the bathroom on himself, why did he burn the clothes?

We found out that Satan was there when Peanut got shot. He said he might have been there. How can you be somewhere and not know it?

The disturbing part is that what was Satan doing there, and why did he have blood on him?

Scum's trial date came in July of nineteen ninety-six.

I found out later he had already been in prison and was released less than six months earlier.

The prosecutor said it was best if we weren't in the courtroom, while the witnesses were being called.

Maybe I'm wrong, but I think Satan truly had something to do with the death of Peanut.

Despite the fact that the police had implicated him in the murder; Satan has said on many occasions he had something to do with it.

Don't know if the police had enough evidence to try him, but it will all coming out in the open.

Have heard him with my own ears say he was involved. He has told moms he was involved, and she acts as if she doesn't believe him.

They accuse me of having something to do with the death of Peanut, but find out Satan was really the one.

They still, right to this day, have not apologized for implicating me.

My family had the audacity, to say I had something to do with the disappearance of my little brother.

This is to you Aaron, my oldest brother.

Will never forget the day of the funeral, you did all but say, I killed my brother. The threats you made towards me, it will never be forgotten. Why say to me that you would have something done to me, because of Peanut?

It doesn't matter if you spent only one day with Peanut his whole life, but Aaron, you didn't even know him. He was almost three when we originally left Michigan, and he died when he was sixteen. You didn't know anything about him, to accuse me of inflicting harm.

You didn't know what he liked, or what his dislikes were. You didn't know what was always going on in his mind.

Your biggest mistake was, when you accused me of harming one of the greatest people in my life.

Greater than a woman, greater than money, or anything of value.

Often times, there are thoughts of going to the site, dig his grave up and see him again. Just to talk to him, and see what's been happening, catch up on things. Then reality set in.

And you had the nerve to say I would harm him, without know anything about our relationship with each other.

You have never said, Joe I'm sorry for the threats that were made. You have never said Joe I'm sorry I listened to the rest of the family, when they blamed Peanut's death on you.

And you are supposed to be a so called preacher.

They know Satan is guilty of what was accused of me, but they justify it.

Satan, Peanuts death will not go unanswered or unpunished.

Moms can treat you like royalty all she wants to, that's her guilty conscious bothering her. She knows Peanut is not resting.

Can understand if it was rumors being spread around, but everyone knows the truth.

The evidence is overwhelming.

Being there when it happened, coming home with blood on your clothes, knowing Peanut was dead for the thirty-five days, and saying he is glad that Peanut is dead.

He would often say that he was going to get rid of Peanut, so he could take over moms house.

All of that, and Moms still let him come around her.

He even tells her, he going to one day kill her.

Since he really doesn't like me, he has threatened me on many occasions.

Another reason I know he had something to do with it is he's constantly telling me I'm next.

He has drawn a gun on me in front of moms and little Joe.

Really wanted to do him in after that, but he is not worth it.

He will get what's coming to him, and one finger will not have to be lifted.

May GOD forgive me, but if something bad happened to Satan, there would be no emotions from me.

That is a harsh way to think, and who really cares.

Believe in an eye for an eye, a tooth for a tooth, and a life for a life.

Don't believe in taking a person life anymore, but what comes around, goes around.

For every action there is an equal and opposite reaction.

You reap what you sow.

So if he, and anyone else, had something to do with the death of my little brother, beware.

Don't beware of me.

Beware of the ONE that we call upon that control the Heavens and the Earth.

He is my SUPPORT, He is my PROTECTOR, and He is my DEFENDER. This is why even though I walk in the valley of the shadows of death there's no evil to fear, because GOD is with Peanut, and me.

Satan, GOD has been asked not to forgive you for such a morbid crime.

HE'S ever returning to MERCY, but there's hope HE will answer my request.

Satan, if you ever read this, you will never be forgiven by me.

I believe in GOD so much that nothing is feared but HIM, and, that is not enough to make me want to forgive you.

GOD has been asked, over and over to help me understand why you would want to do such things, to your own family.

Moms, if you ever make it to this part, how could you let Satan finish what we never had, as a family. Unity.

He has brought the family so much grief, since the first day he entered this world.

You know what he said he did to Peanut is true. How can you expect us to just ignore the situation like you have?

Moms, Peanut needs you more now, than he ever has. He's not resting knowing that you uphold Satan for what he said he's done.

We come to visit, and you're holding something of Peanut's crying Satan is lying on the floor sleeping comfortably. He's at peace with himself sleeping, while you are trying to recover.

He tells you Peanut got what he deserves, but you act as if nothing has happened. He tells you how much he hated Peanut, but for what reason. He tells you how much he wants to kill you, or some of the other family members, but you don't take heed to those statements.

When we come around, he's calling you bitches and whores, and destroying your things.

When something is done to stop him, you say leave him alone. Moms what's up?

Are we supposed to sit back and let him harm you, like he and the others have harmed Peanut?

Hell no we are not going for that.

We don't get along moms, but you are loved more today than you were yesterday. We as a family need serious help.

Peanut died that we should come together.

Since his death, the family has gone father apart.

That's not the way Peanut wanted it. We all battled for his love. He gave all of us love, but we took it for granted.

Moms this is for you.

Those last words to him from you will never exit my mind. How can you tell him to go on, and that since Satan is out of jail, and you don't need him anymore?

The look your baby gave, after you said that, hurt me more than the words. I felt the pain Peanut was feeling, because he didn't want to fight with Satan.

He told me he was tired of Satan trying to jump on him everyday. So don't you ever forget those last words you told Peanut when he was alive.

Peace is wanted between the family, and you will never give it to us. We haven't had any peace, and we will never have any peace, because there could be no peace.

As long as Satan continues to threaten you, and rule your household, how can there be peace.

How can you continue to feed him, and take care of him, knowing he should be ostracized from the rest of us? The only thing that bothers me is he has not once said he was sorry. He's not sorry, because he's constantly reminding us of how he hated Peanut, and glad he's gone.

If he said he was sorry, I wouldn't believe it, or forgive him.

Why?

It wouldn't be legitimate. He doesn't believe in GOD to begin with. He likes satanic cults, and always getting the writings from somewhere.

He will never change, but that is your headache, not mine.

He would have to repent to GOD first, because I have no power to do anything to him.

By asking GOD to forgive him, he will have to be sincere about it.

Satan, you need some serious help. We all need help, but you are on a self-destructive mission.

Can't understand how you rob people, go to jail, and then get out. That is the way the system works.

Satan, you smoke so much crack that every time you speak, smoke come out of your mouth.

Then moms had to contend with her husband, and two other sons smoking crack.

But she could never tell me that she was sorry for all the times she's accused me of being on drugs.

She should have been paying attention to the ones that were smoking crack and trying to conceal it.

Moms would deny the charges when people told her Greg (her husband) was on drugs

She just took it for face value when he said he wasn't, and ignored the facts that people were telling her.

But in due time, she came to know all.

Chapter 17

I feel my mother was sometimes blind to the truth, and believed what she wanted to believe. It reminded me of being in Mississippi when people told her Greg be fooling around with punks.

She knew it was true, but in reality, didn't want to accept it.

Like when Greg was messing around with a friend of ours Timmy Lee, in Michigan.

He told moms it wasn't him. Moms believed him, until Timmy confronted him with it to his face, and even told him about his body parts.

Now moms have a husband that fools around with punks.

She knew he fooled around with punks when we were in Mississippi. She knew he was hanging out at this bar called Mill and Oakley, picking up punks.

If she likes it, I love it.

She knows Satan messes around with punks, but tends not to believe it. She uses women wanting to talk to him, as a cover up to conceal his preference of sexes.

She knows Mike messes around with punks, gays or bisexuals, or whatever they choose to be called, but tends to ignore it.

Don't know where Mike came off on dealing with the opposite sex from.

The rumors that would circulate made me wonder.

This guy we were enemies with, said he seen Mike in the back seat of a car with our cousin, on homecoming night.

Thought the guy was spreading rumors, until I heard it from the horse's mouth.

Still couldn't believe it until one day he went to Mississippi.

This white man he would call boss man, would come by the Ave., or wherever Mike was at to pick him up. This man would come by every other day to pick Mike up.

About forty-five minutes to an hour later, Mike would come back with a nice amount of money.

He would say he worked for the man doing this and doing that.

We never thought anything of it.

Then Mike moved to Mississippi, after a hit on the Hart Hotel, and we would see the man still coming around.

Figured Mike didn't tell him he was leaving, so it was like an opportunity knocking at the door.

Figured I could make the money while Mike was gone.

The man came around one day asking for Mike, and I told him he moved to Mississippi.

It was a lie when he was told Mike wanted me to take over his job.

A strange look was on his face looking at me as though I was crazy. He was like, "are you sure"? Then let me in his car and drove he drove off.

As he was driving, he was asking me if Mike told me what they did. I played it off like he did, not really knowing what to say.

Should have known something was up, when he kept asking me, "are you sure Mike told you about us."

I was like "yeah he told me."

So the man said "me and Mike are bisexuals" and we do things to each other.

I got out of the car immediately and never seen the man again.

I told moms and it was no response from her.

Wondered to myself, if any of the things other gay or bisexual people were saying about Mike was true.

One of his friends told me how they were involved in different kinds of sexual things.

Timmy Lee, the one that was with momma's husband, said him and Mike use to kick it.

Timmy was good. He had the stepfather, and the stepson.

How in the hell could Mike be that way, when we would have all the neighborhood girls hanging around us?

That was in Mississippi. When we moved to Michigan, I don't know what happened to him.

I continued to run after girls and Mike continued to run after whatever.

Can understand if one or two people may have said that they did something with Mike, but four or five.

He's not gay, I guess he's not. He has kids and so did the white man he was kicking it with.

The girls must have been a front, to the real life he concealed.

You're my brother, and there are not any thoughts of me thinking any less of you.

It makes me wonder, when we had to sleep in the same bed.

Hope you didn't try anything to me, while I was sleep.

I say that with humor, because you wonder what went wrong, during whatever transition you were going through.

It makes you wonder who turned him out, or was he born to like the both sexes.

Don't think GOD makes men or women to like the same sexes. Don't think we are born into this world with gay tendencies.

GOD destroyed a whole nation in Sodom and Gomorra, so he wouldn't make a people that he would again destroy, for their gay actions.

I'm not against my brother or anybody else, for their choices, but you have to be careful of the outcome of it in the end.

Some people may have been abused as children, by a loved one that makes them turn out the way they do.

Mike, you can't say you were born that way, because we never seen anything coming up, that would have made me wonder. No one really paid any attention to that anyway.

You must have been turned out in Michigan, by some one.

Still have much love for you anyway, just don't get caught up like your cousin.

You know he died of aids and the things that he said about you and him should make you more aware. That should have been a warning to you about being careful, on the things you do.

It was also a warning to me. Not in a sense that I'm a different kind person, because I'm straight heterosexual.

I'm speaking of the five-hundred women that have slept with me. I know you're probably wondering where all the numbers generated from.

It began around age eighteen, when the names of women, were starting to be written down, after we slept together.

Would cheat at first, not intentionally, by writing down the same names twice. I realized that one day while reminiscing on past females experiences.

Then it became a game. Would see how many women in a week, or a month I could sleep with.

Actually it's more than five -hundred, because women were sleeping with me before age eighteen, and that's when the counted started.

The challenge became overwhelming, as the numbers increased by the weeks.

I was finding myself sleeping with women for money, or just to get drunk, or just to keep the numbers increasing.

Sometimes it scared me, the next day, because there was no protection used.

Then as a cop out, blood would be given to see if a disease had been acquired.

That is a sick mentality, when you sit back and think of it.

When you're on the streets, you don't care about the outcome. It bothers you about catching a disease, or getting aids, but you do nothing to prevent it.

When you find out there is nothing wrong, the thought is, it could never happen to you.

I slept with over five hundred women, and never caught a disease. Guess you could say that was luck, because people would get diseases after loosing their virginity.

GOD was with me, and not luck.

Would be drunk and sleep with who ever offered, or whatever looked good.

No protection was ever used.

Think about five percent out of the five hundred plus I used protection. And a hole was bit in the tip of the rubber, so that it could slide up, and you wouldn't loose that feeling you was looking for.

Started getting scared, after people that were close to me started contracting aids, herpes, and other kinds of sexually transmitted diseases.

Some of them died, and that scared me even more. Yeah I slacked up tremendously, but that didn't totally stop me.

It only takes one time to catch something, and to me, there was no time to see who had anything. It was done by statistics.

Went by who was known the longest or who was sleeping with whom, and a crazy solution was thought of.

Now when looking back at a lot of the things took place, GOD should be thanked everyday. Something could have contracted along the way, and was too silly to realize that.

Eventually I quit sleeping with many women, and held some what of a monogamous relationship.

The thought of wanting to settle down, and be with one woman, was on my mind.

The motto that was lived by, (I'll sleep with half the world, before getting married, then sleep with the other half, after getting married). That's if I ever do decide to get married and being under twenty-one is no time soon.

Chapter 18

The relationship was shady between Deb and I, at the same wishing things would get better.

I was approaching thirty, and never had somewhat of a future planned.

I just wanted to have fun in my twenty's, and Deb somewhat hindered that.

Not saying she made me stay in a relationship, that I didn't want to be in. After the problems first started, the intentions were to go, but stayed in it, for the love of the kids.

Then the problems started with the women, and the accusations grew wider.

Sometimes I wished we could have held off from being in a relationship, because I was young.

Yeah I knew what was going on, but didn't know what was wanted.

Had always said, the best times of any ones life, is twenty -one through thirty.

After you turn thirty, then life becomes more and more serious.

That is what I wanted. To have fun until age thirty, then settle down.

The problems with women, and the accusations from Deb started to increase.

Jealous hearted people saw a change coming in me, and really tried to undermine my relationship with Deb.

Then it hit me in the beginning of nineteen ninety - seven.

Told Deb, our relationship wasn't going to last, as long as we were in Michigan.

My thoughts were to leave Michigan, and take her with me.

We had been to Mississippi, Christmas of nineteen ninety-six, and it was cool down there. A lot had changed in a short period of time.

It was nice and warm, and people were wearing shorts in December. That was my first thought of moving back to Mississippi.

Told moms my plan of moving to Mississippi and Deb was like "go right ahead on and move I'm not going."

That answer hurt a lot and then, it was just cloud talk about moving to Mississippi. I wanted to make it with Deb, so my apartment was given up, to move back in with her.

That didn't seem to help with all of the people still playa hating, and interfering.

I went back down to Mississippi for Spring break April 7th, nineteen ninety-seven, with Big Rod to check it out again.

When we made it back to Michigan, my mind was made then that Jackson would be my home. Went back to Michigan and told Deb about my plans to leave.

Gave my job a thirty day notice and prepared myself for, the biggest transition in my life.

Deb was asked on several occasions to come with me, and she refused every time.

She would always use me being close to my mother as an excuse not to go.

It is reasons to understand why she would feel that way.

She didn't want to leave her mother and be with me, where me being close to mine.

Didn't want to live in Michigan with her and not be close to mine. The time had come, for me to go.

Left Michigan May 18th, nineteen ninety-seven, two days after my job ended.

I left everything in the apartment and pulled out of town at three in the morning.

For all of the people at I.I. Stanley, there's still love for you all, and you're still missed often. Still remember the days at the Christmas parties, and tripping at Springbrook Lounge. I will never forget the ones that remained loyal to me from the beginning to the end.

And for the ones that didn't like me, for whatever reason, 'I ain't mad at cha.'

It was a Sunday, when my journey was started, to start a new life in Mississippi.

Thought long and hard, if the right decision was made or not.

Was it worth leaving a job and the people that loved me?

My job had even offered me to go on a six month to a year leave of absence, to make sure if that's what was wanted. They were still turned down.

Was thinking, was it worth leaving a lady that had been there more than anybody in my life. More than my mother, more than my daddy, or even sisters and brothers. And that is in spite of the issues we had.

The thought's plagued my mind the whole trip. Thought about what Deb would always tell me about not being able to meet anyone better than her. Thought about the times of being in jail and she was there, to bail me out. Thought about how she got me to stop selling dope, then influenced me to go to school, and then talked me into getting a job. Thought about how she was there when we lost Peanut. Thought about how she stayed by my side, when she caught me in the bed with another woman.

Started to turn around and go back to the woman that was there for me through thick and thin.

Then it hit me that, we could never be happy as long as we were in Michigan.

It was too many enemies on the streets that didn't like me. Too many jealous people that were envious of me, and still had to deal with that.

It was too many people running to Deb and telling her places they would be, and she knew my whereabouts.

If Deb loved me the way she said she did, why didn't she come to Mississippi with me?

Was selfish, in a since, that things always went my way. And for the first time in life, I didn't get what I really wanted.

The sun was shining beautifully that Sunday afternoon around three. Jackson Mississippi was finally reached.

When my destination was finally made to moms house, Satan was cursing her out.

I was like "oh boy, here we go again."

He sees me, and takes off running. Moms didn't know about me coming, so when he told her he sees me, she didn't believe him.

She didn't mention anything about why was he cursing her out.

Told her everything was going to be all right, and Satan was not going to be around.

That's what I thought.

Don't want to spend anytime on Satan, so I'll make it quick.

He would terrorize moms everyday, and when I went to get him, she would say leave him alone.

He was still calling her bitches, and saying he was going to kill her.

I couldn't take it any longer. Asked moms why she let him curse her out, then let him in the house and feed him.

She would always say that he was her child and she did what the hell she wanted to do.

There was still intervention when he cursed her out. She may tell me to stay out of it, but who could stand by idly and watch their mother get threatened.

Police would come to her house almost everyday looking for Satan. He will rob any defenseless person, and elderly people were really preyed on.

He was on crack harder than ever, and got a social security check every month, that went to the drug dealers, before he could spend it.

Crack would be given to him on credit, and then he wouldn't pay the people.

Moms end up having to pay the dealers on numerous occasions.

When I moved to Mississippi it really bothered him. He would try to get back at me. He knew how gang members and drug dealers hated the JPD(Jackson Police Department).

He told the neighborhood people that I was a police officer that just transferred from Michigan to Jackson, to arrest the drug dealers and gang members.

I would wonder why people would stare at me funny when I drove by.

I went down the street from moms to the laundry mat one day. As I was walking through the door, people started hiding the beer they were drinking. Then they started looking at me rolling their eyes.

Had the slightest idea what was going on.

I had never known, until one of them asked me if Satan was my brother.

I said "yeah, why"

They said "you are the policeman that came from Michigan."

Told them no, and who told you that.

After they told me what Satan said, I knew then was out to get me.

He had hated me for years and years, and right to this day, still don't know why.

Moms would always call me and say come over, Satan is tripping again.

One day, he was really tripping.

Got over to moms house and the fool had taken her gun.

Asked him for it, and he pointed it at me. He was saying how he wanted to kill me anyway. So I slipped away, and called the police.

He still wouldn't give me the gun. Little Joe was crying and the thought of me getting my hands on him to kill him was great.

The police came and he tried to run. He put up a good struggle, so they sprayed him with pepper gas. They handcuffed him from the back and put him in the car.

The police had to do what they had to do. While they were spraying him with the pepper gas, moms was in the police face saying "leave my baby alone."

How in the hell is that your baby, when he had a gun on me a few minutes earlier?

As the police was talking to me, he had broken the handcuffs, and kicked the back window out.

They didn't catch him either.

The police in Michigan hated him, now the police in Jackson hated him.

Satan can rob whom he want to, get caught, and be out of jail a few days later. It makes no sense to me.

I knew then the mistake of leaving Michigan.

Was suppose to come and protect moms from him, but she was upholding everything he done.

I ended up moving back to Michigan two weeks later, only to be miserable again.

I spent about two weeks in Michigan, before moving back to Mississippi.

Hated being there but was missing the fellas and the family I left.

Found myself going back and forth from Michigan to Mississippi, Mississippi to Michigan about three times a month.

I was so confused that suicidal thoughts were there all over again. I needed the valiums all over again to calm my nerves.

Would often cry through the night, wondering why times could not be better for me. Was never happy, and at times, it made no sense to live.

The woman that was met in Mississippi, things didn't work out, so we ended up just being acquaintances.

Sherry was ok, but what she wanted out of life, could not be delivered from me. She helped me out a lot, by taken in me and little Joe.

Even after what we had, for the short period of time ended, she became little Joe's GOD mom. Sherry and her cousin Shun was there when someone was needed in Mississippi. They gave me money, and made sure me and Joe were fed. They always looked out for us.

One of the reasons Sherry and I didn't get along was because, of Deb. There was no healing involved, and Sherry was the one that got hurt most of the time. And there was no need to continue hurting everyone that was met after Deb until the emotions were over.

Deb was missed so much that there was no where for me to turn. Even though Deb had not changed, and would still do things that were not agreeable with me, she was still missed.

Why didn't she want to move down here? I would always ask myself that question. Now I'm somewhat of a changed man, and was going to treat her the way she needed to be treated.

We could have made it together if she would have moved down to Mississippi with me.

We had agreed on moving to Atlanta, after Tamela started college there.

That hope failed, after Tamela got pregnant. I knew then, when Deb said she couldn't leave Tamela, it was all over.

Tried and tried on every occasion, to get Deb to move to Jackson or even Atlanta.

She would use me not finding a decent job, and starting over, as reasons not to move.

Also she indicated leaving Tamela while she was pregnant was not an option.

So I exercised my options and left.

I could understand what she was talking about. It was hard. Who would want to go from making almost a grand a week, too barely two hundred?

The employment agencies would send you to hell, to work for the devil, if he needed help.

All this work experience and education, but working at temporary services. Yes it was a start, but a finish was needed.

It wouldn't have bothered me, if the jobs would have been office oriented, but they were mostly dirt and sweat related.

Ends couldn't be made, if two points were put together.

I was trying to please people in Mississippi, and trying to please people in Michigan.

Everyone was getting pleased but me.

I had just left Michigan again, and moved back to Mississippi a little before Thanksgiving nineteen ninety-seven.

Back unhappy again in Mississippi, then moved back to Michigan a week or so after Thanksgiving.

In Michigan all that could be done was stare out the window, and look at the snow.

Yeah it was an unhappy situation in Michigan, so two weeks later, moved back to Mississippi.

Are you getting bored yet?

On the way back, a voice told me if I stayed content in one spot, everything was going to be all right.

I didn't know which one spot to be in, and that made matters worse.

Running back and forth confused me more, but it saved my life.

The true reason for me running back and forth was to keep from committing suicide in reality.

The thought of ending my life went from, wanting to do it, to planning to do it.

Think it was a few days after Christmas nineteen ninety-seven, I had planned to go back to Michigan.

Was tired of running, so it became evident, that my life had to be ended. This time, there was no turning back.

A bottle of pills was in one hand, and a pencil in the other.

I anted to take the pills so bad that, the smell of death was really in the air. A voice told me to go talk to Tara.

I did and we talked about it. She had friends over that talked with me also. It seemed as though the hope that was wanted in life was being brought to life.

That was the most emotional time I had shared in life with someone other than Deb. Deb would always be told about the intentions I had, and she would tell me things that made me feel better.

Would always think of Peanut, and that would only hurt worse.

Suicidal thoughts had plagued my mind, more and more, after Peanuts death.

The closeness we had, there was nothing left in the world to live for.

He was the heir apparent to my life, and I wanted him to be. Now all of that is destroyed.

It seemed as though there was no one left in the world but Little Joe. Deb wasn't moving to Mississippi, and getting a decent job was no where in sight.

My whole life was coming to an end.

Must have been in a different zone, because it didn't bother me about telling all the things in my life that was plaguing me.

GOD must have sent them to talk to me, because there had never been a more serious thought about suicide, as that night.

Even though Tara, Regina, and Michelle took me to the hospital, the words they told me were inspirational.

There was instant relief after the talk.

In the hospital, that same voice that told me everything is going to be all right come back to me again.

It said "go home, change the way you think and act, then you will have no worries."

People thought I was really going crazy.

I listened to the voice that was talking to me. Heed tends to be taken when you hear voices that would talk to you.

People would call that 'strange phenomenon's.'

That was GOD telling me everything is going to be all right. HE is trying to give me another chance at life.

Since life was hated, and the way people were treated by me, death meant nothing to me.

Suicide didn't even mean anything to me.

All of a sudden, the desire and a want to live had resurfaced.

I was still confused, in a sense that no direction was set in place.

The thought of always wanting to settle down was imminent, and needed to be set in motion.

And to be the kind of man that a woman would love and respect was also imminent.

Knowing how to make or create love from a sexual point was simple. Knowing how to love from a spiritual point of view was obsolete.

If there were to be a change, the woman that would be chosen, would have to be the chosen one for me.

I wondered if Deb was the chosen woman for me, or if the woman of my dreams, would be found.

The voices that was heard, would often visit me.

Chapter 19

You may think of me as being a crazy person in reality, but the voices were as real as you are reading.

We tend to ignore the deep inside spirituality. The spirit that tells you to do one thing, but we tend to do something else.

I'm talking about doing something good in faith, not in evil.

I feel that when people take money, and go and try to win money, whether it was at a casino, bingo, lottery, or whatever game of chance it may be, is wrong in the eyesight of GOD. And they should not put GOD in it.

And when a person is told that, they want to argue with me saying, "oh it's a blessing from GOD."

DID YOU HERE ME WHEN I SAID, "I FEEL IT IS NOT RIGHT IN HIS EYESIGHT" I am entitled to my own opinions, like you are entitled to yours.

People can be gambling, and a voice can tell them to wager all the money they have on a certain number. They put the money on a different number, other than what the voice was telling them to.

Then they loose all the money, and say "one mind told me to put the money on such and such number."

That's not the way GOD intended for the spirits to be. People go to the casino boat and gamble, and will win. Then will have the audacity to say that "the Lord told me to go and play so I can win." Stop lying on GOD like that! God is not a gambler, and would never influence His people to do so.

I would only listen to the voices that would tell me to do bad things. But now the voices have changed into a more positive thinking.

All that was needed was some spiritual guidance in my life. I'm not the one that claimed to be this way, in the eyes of people, and then live opposite.

Who are these people fooling, thinking they are getting over, by having you believing one way, and GOD knowing how they are?

And for the ones that conceal their evil practices, something is much more in store for you.

They forget that GOD is always looking, always listening, always knowing. Even in our good times, GOD let us have our moment.

Then HE will come to claim what was giving to us in the beginning. The life we have.

I never understood the purpose of me being here.

I would often ask myself, "how did we get here, and how was the world started?"

These questions plagued my mind.

There was never a purpose for me being here, as long as the bad person was still there.

My thoughts were, if you came into this world a good person, you go to heaven.

Then, if you came into the world a bad person, you go to hell.

Everyone come into the world a bad person. It's up to you to live right or wrong, good or bad.

When those thoughts entered my mind, my purpose was then discovered.

GOD intended for everyone to be a good servant to HIM, but HE knew better than we did.

As earlier stated, in the writing, GOD knew the things that were going to be done by me, good or bad. Though HE had the upper hand, that no matter what, I lost.

Later realized, and understood, that GOD gives you the choice to be the person HE wants you to be.

Not the person you yourself want to be. If you want to be a bad person all your life, GOD will not force you to change and do good things. Judgment day, you will only be rewarded, for what you earned.

GOD gives you the freedom to get all messed up in the world, then when HE'S ready for you, take heed to the call.

That's what was felt, after the call was heard. GOD was telling me to quit doing the things that were being done. And not to go back doing the things that were previously done

He preferred that we start from the beginning praising him, but my life had already taken a turn for the worse.

The conscious that was never there, started to surface. The desire to learn about GOD, and change my ways increased more.

Help was needed with overcoming what my mind was going through. I was thinking of going back to Michigan to be back with Deb. Had made my mind up that it was now time to change, all the way.

The voice told me that was not a good idea, that Mississippi would be my home.

Asked Deb several more times to come and live with me. I was still unsuccessful each time.

Communications were kept open between Deb and me, as a way to try to make it through the days.

Eventually, we parted company. She went on with her life, and my life was still going about a change.

It was a painful experience to go through something like that.

We didn't have the best relationship in the world, but it was painful to leave someone after seven years.

You grow fond of the kids, like they're your own. Then, we you leave, all of you leave.

Memories are supposed to be good for the mind, but in my case it wasn't.

I was on a serious mission to change. To change the way I thought, live, and acted.

It was something Farrakhan said one day. He said if you want to change you actions, you must first change your thoughts.

Changing my thoughts didn't happen easy.

Could no longer look at one side of a coin.

It was no longer heads or tails. It was heads and tails then the best solution was chosen.

My mentality had started to excel. Always assuming what people do or did, was the first part of the thinking that was changed.

People were stereotyped. My own people to be specific.

If a brother were seen with a nice car, I would say to myself, he must sell dope. The fact is he probably graduated and had a good job.

If a black man was seen cutting grass in a nice neighborhood, I would think he worked for somebody white.

Not knowing he may have already paid for the house in full.

If a brother was seen with big muscles, I thought he probably got that way in jail. When a white dude was seen with big muscles, thought he probably worked out in a gym. Not knowing the brother may have been in a gym also.

That was just a synopsis of the way people were stereotyped.

I am not the only one that would think like that, so it's a lot of guilty people out there.

We need to quit assuming people are the way we perceived them to be.

We think of people of being one way, when they can be totally opposite.

People see me dress like a "thug" and swear I am a thug.

Then, when they see me dressed in a suit to go to work, people would say "you look so different, I thought you were a bad person."

People assume me as being one way, but they don't know about me having a few college degrees and is somewhat smart.

How to make it in the street world, and in the real world, were already known.

It bothered me that people didn't see me, as a person looking for a change. They only assumed things about me, in the past, were still going on.

The people that know me, they won't speak against me, except for some of the envious ones.

As for the ones that don't know me, they will take heed to the rumors of the he say she say garbage.

That goes for old people and young.

For those of you who listened to the garbage that was spread, why you didn't come to me for yourself?

You like to keep up hell, just like the one's that was doing the spreading.

And for the people that know that a change has came about, you know I'm not that kind of person anymore. Why you didn't stand and tell the people that, when they spoke against me? Why didn't you defend me against my enemies? That's because you are the same jealous good for nothing nobody, that have people fooled, as though you are living right.

See it's easy to spread lies to keep the heat off your back. But wait until the truth does surface. Are you ready to be condemned, as you are so ready to condemn?

Yes there were bad things done in my life, that when it was time to reap, there was no reason to stick around. Yes suicide was going to be a cop out, instead of trying to ask for forgiveness.

The more changes that came for the better, the more alone my life became. The ones that were supposedly to remain loyal are gone.

That's ok, I came into this world alone and more than likely, I'll leave it alone.

That's the scary part of life. Who wants to leave this world alone?

It's already lonely in this world, so why does a person have to leave alone.

Every since my little brother passed, I would often wonder what he's doing. Have heard how his last words were spent pleading for his life.

No one was there to console him. No one there to tell him that everything is going to be all right. No one was there to even die with him.

We often talk. He's being constantly told, "Peanut, you're not alone."

He should have not been there alone, especially when he had a so call family member there.

GOD knows my wishes were, it should have been me, instead of him.

Moms would always tell me that my life would never see past sixteen, not knowing her youngest son was going to be the one.

It scares me that he is in reality gone, and alone. He has no one that grew up around him. He is a stranger to the ones that surround him.

When my day arrives, "I don't want to die all alone." Company will be needed, or someone to join me.

Who is willing to die with you? People will tell you that they are with you through life, but what about death.

Don't tell me that you will die for me when I want to know who will die with me.

How afraid of death are you. Death means nothing when you have lived a life of hell.

To some, my death will be more important than my life. Oh well, kill me if you still want me dead. This body was meant to go back to the ground anyway. And I hope you are as ready to die, as you are ready to kill.

People said my life would eventually end, being a lonely old man. Never intended for my life to go the way it did, but that's life.

I have changed dramatically, but people don't like the man I'm trying to become. People are always trying to keep you from rising

As mentioned earlier, if you were born into this world doing bad things, you will die a bad person.

But why did I want to live? Why do I want to live? Why do I want to change? Why did I change?

I don't want to die a bad person, so a change had to come. Change would come at a subsequent time; it just had to be over a period time.

When the dope game was over, that was the biggest change of it all. The gang banging stopped. I had to give up my Vice Lords membership to live a little longer or to keep from going to prison the rest of my life.

Then I went to college, got a job, and eventually made the same amount every week, as selling dope.

It was hard to go from a thousand dollars a week selling dope, to a minimum wage job.

But how can you tell a child that wants the finer things in life, to quit selling dope.

I'm not condoning dope selling, but kids feel they have no other way out.

They can't get Air Jordan shoes or Boss jeans, on a Burger King or McDonald's salary.

Society, have made it where a child knows no other way but the materialistic world.

So now dope looks easy to kids. It's hard to convince a kid to stay in school, and leave the hustle alone.

Then you have these sick mind people telling kids to stay in school. Why should the kids listen to you, when your life is in worse condition?

It was, in a sense, easy for me to quit selling dope, because there was a need, for a definite change, in my life.

No one was behind me, when a change was needed.

My own peers that were close to me, started to be envious. My own momma and family could not relate to the changes that were needed.

When it became a choice to go to college, it was only a few people behind me. And the few that were behind me, made it seem as though no one was behind me. But those few were enough motivation to go.

College is everyone's preference, if they want a better job in life. You may never use the education, but employers only look at, did you go, and did you finish.

People would say my enrollment in college wouldn't last one semester, and I would just drop out and go back to the streets.

No one ever said, "Joe that's good what you're doing". It was most of the time "don't go today, let's hang out and kick it" or, "you are wasting, time and money".

The money was wasted, but the time wasn't. Yeah classes were a lot, but that was never a reason for me to drop out.

During my days in college, the streets still played an important part in my life. It was to understand that because you start to change, don't forget where you came from.

I didn't want to act like there was a difference, even though my thoughts began to be different.

The streets were my life, and I couldn't just give them up. It was like an old habit that was hard to break.

Didn't want to forget what caused me to be where my life is today. The streets put me in the predicament that I was in, and it caused me to be where I am headed.

There would probably be no college if it weren't for the streets. There would probably be no understanding of what it felt like to have hard times, if it wasn't for the streets. There would probably be no life, if it weren't for the streets.

I know what it was like out there, so there is no need for me to continue being out there.

Kids don't know what it is like to make it on the streets. They join a gang, get a sack of dope, and get a gun. That's all they know.

That is not survival.

Survival is when you have to eat out of garbage cans for a meal. Digging through ice and snow, for food or looking for bottles and cans all day for a few dollars.

Pilfering through dumpsters for meat and other rubbish we considered food.

Who knows, someone could have done something to the meat or goods that we were eating. The food could have had all kinds of bacteria in it. We didn't care, because we were happy to eat.

Going to the goodwill or salvation and put on clothes or shoes to keep from looking ragged. Coming in from the streets and going in to a home with no heat, when it was thirty degrees below zero out side, and thirty-five below inside. We all are sitting on the inside with our coats and gloves on to watch TV, or try to keep warm.

Having to dress at night, in the cold, with the clothes you were going to wear the next day. Then we had to lie down on a cold bed, and hope you could have a good night worth of sleep. Every night we were sleeping in coats, hats, and shoes to stay warm.

And when we did iron the bed to go to sleep, the warmth didn't last long.

Anyway, that is survival.

Put the average kid on the block, and take what he calls his survival kit, from him.

Take his gun, his dope, and his gang initiation from him.

Then set him free, and tell him to survive. He wouldn't last a day. He'll be asking, "What do I do now?"

He would be too proud to eat from the garbage for a meal, or walk miles and miles for bottles and cans. He wouldn't know how to defend himself without a gun.

See all of that was known by me by the time I was thirteen years old being on the streets.

Long before it was decided enough was enough.

Kids today think because they only know how to sell dope, be in a gang, and carry a gun, that there is no other way out.

Kids, I'm here to tell you, it is a better way out. Kids are tripping over the material things in life, when I knew nothing of it. Yes with the stealing and the hustling, a few things were bought at a young age. But look at what the kid's wants today. They don't know any other way to think but materialistic.

Just think of the days like me, when you had two black and white TVs. One you could not see, and one you could not hear. Put them side by side, and enjoy.

One TV with a half of picture tube, and that was still fine. You didn't like it, but you had no choice.

We didn't have Nintendo, and Sony Playstation. I'll even go back to the old school. We didn't even have Colleco-vision or Atari1200. We didn't have Air Jordan tennis shoes, or Boss jeans. No Fubu or Karl Kani to sport.

Kids have went from playing dodge ball to dodging bullets.

Some of those trinkets were bought when I was older, but the rough days are not forgotten, and no dope will ever be sold by me, to get them. People will tell you little crackpot stories to get you off the streets, and quit selling dope.

I'm not going to tell you to listen to those that don't know anything about the streets.

How can they tell you what's out there, when they never been out there?

That's like me telling you how to fly a plane, and I'm not a pilot.

You have these probation officers and counselors, telling you how to behave and leave the streets alone.

Notice a lot of them have nice jobs, live in nice neighborhoods, and have a future. Ask them if they were in a gang, or sold dope, or ever carried a gun illegally.

Most of them will tell you no. My daddy was a lawyer, my mother was a nurse, and we had all the finer things in life.

Kids don't need to hear things like that. They need to hear about how you were in the ghetto, living rough, made some bad choices in life then changed.

If kids knew about that, then some of them may think they have somewhat of a future.

Pay attention to the news sometimes kids.

They are building concentration camps all around America, and they know who the tenants are going to be. Jail is the only place that can be over crowded, and you can still make a reservation. Call any hotel, anywhere, anytime during a major event. They will be booked up, and you couldn't make a reservation for the bathroom no matter how much money you have.

Commit a crime anywhere, anytime, and it doesn't even have to be an event going on. They will tell you, we're over crowded, but we can still make room if we have to place you in a closet.

They know in a little while, your house will be finished being built, and you can close on the deal at anytime. The jailhouse is what I'm referring to.

Now you don't have to worry about a home, because you're stuck there, for the rest of your life.

Don't you see they are making laws that you would be locked up for the rest of your life. The three strike laws were made to lock you up, for the rest of your life that they will never have to be bothered with you again.

Imagine the cost to house an inmate for a year. Now imagine if society took that same money and sent an inmate to college. Then help him get a job with the education he has just obtained. Chances are, he won't go back to criminal life, now that he has one leg up on a future.

Do you think they will do that, probably not?

What I'm getting at is brothers quit waiting for something to be given to you.

Go get a life, an education, a job, and live peaceful. Believe in GOD, and all that HE can, and will give to you if you have faith.

And give back a little something to the community. I give as much as I can back to the community, because it's where life really begins.

I'll hold neighborhood basketball tournaments, where kids could win money and trophies. It's my way of thanking GOD for the job, the house, and the money, HE has blessed me with.

I take my money and put little money making ideas into practice, so that the kids can have a few dollars without having to use dope as an excuse.

I look back at the way my life was twenty to twenty-five years ago. And even as recent as a few years ago. If my life had not become spiritual, I would probably be dead or gone crazy, or even in jail.

Kids, please stay in school, and for the ones that are out, go get a student loan if you have to. At least it's a start in life for you.

Yeah jail is easier, because you don't have to pay for that, they will pay you.

They will pay your rent for the rest of your life. Pay for your medical and dental expenses, for the rest of your life. They will even pay for your three meals a day, for the rest of your life. This is all in exchange for you staying in one of their suites, for the rest of your life.

They have to do what they have to do, and you have to do what you have to do.

I have been stabbed, shot at, shot, sold dope, did b&e's, been in gangs, used illicit drugs, been to jail, and have done whatever inhumane things you can think of.

If it's bad, chances are, I did it.

The whole point is kids don't give up on a future. You take one step towards GOD, and HE'LL take two towards you.

I had always believed in God, but never thought there was a reason to serve HIM.

Why serve something you have no knowledge of.

When good things did started happening to me, it was because of the change.

I'm not saying bad things don't happen to good people. We need to erase that kind of thinking.

What if you are a bad person and something bad happened to you. The first thing people will say, "if you had GOD, it wouldn't have happened.

What if you're truly, a GOD fearing person and something bad happened to you. What will people say then? If you didn't have GOD in your life, it wouldn't have happened.

We don't realize is something bad happens to the best of us. We don't know when, or if something bad will happen to us.

If circumstances occur like that, we need to be ready and keep the faith.

I'm more so ready now, than ever, if something bad happened to me. I am not the same person as yesterday, and tomorrow it will be different. I'm constantly looking for ways to enhance my life spiritually.

Don't do a lot of the things the Bible or Quran say not to do. I don't smoke, don't eat pork, don't drink, nor do I steal, gossip, or claim to be that I know I'm not.

I try to live everyday like it's my last, but I also live everyday like I'm going to live forever. That's because tomorrow is not promised to us.

So kids, please don't give up on life, like I had many of times.

Don't be afraid to bow down and pray to GOD, hoping that HE'S listening. GOD is always hearing, always listening, and always knowing.

Without GOD, we can do nothing, and with HIM, nothing is impossible.

And don't be afraid to loose a few friends, while you are changing. Not everyone will agree with what you are trying to accomplish.

My own family does not agree with what is trying to be accomplished through me.

If they did, they would be for me, instead of against me. I try hard to get along with my family, but the people on the streets, have treated me better.

There will be some people that will even try to hinder your progress.

If you're in a gang, get out. Some of your boys won't like it, but get them to understand that there is a better life down the road.

Make peace with your enemies. Let them know that you no longer subscribe to gang banging.

It doesn't matter if you claim Vice Lords(Peoples Nation), Disciple's(Folks Nation), Bloods, or Crip's, being affiliated will land you in jail or hell.

Believe it or leave it alone.

Kids, I have no reason to lie to you. If you like to be shot at, banged up all side the head and body with a bleak future then continue your quest towards death.

The best thing is not to join. They will sugar coat everything as though gang life is so glorious and lavish. And you accept this because you didn't want to do what you were told to do at home. So now the gang leaders make it look like freedom on the other side of the railroad.

Then when they feel you are committed, the worse is yet to come. Now that they have suckered you into rebelling against your family, and join them, all hell breaks loose.

Now they make, not ask, you to put in work. For those of you that don't know what put in work mean in street and gang terms it simply means to do whatever they make you do. And this requires staying up long hours selling dope for them. Staying up long hours being on the look out for police to make sure the other dealers can do their thing. Then you have to fight for territory or respect when you don't want to or know how to fight. And if they see you not participating you get beat down when the crew makes it back to the compound.

Then you have to beat up innocent people whether man woman or child and you don't have the heart to do it. So you get beat down for that. And after getting beat down so many times for not participating in brutal activities, you give in.

This is what they want you to do to become heartless. You know you are not that way but you joined thinking it was all fun and play. Welcome to the real world.

You cry in the night so much until you think about killing yourself rather than go through another day of gang life.

When you don't show up they send the wrecking crew to locate your where about.

You tell them you want to get out of the gang and they tell you it's over your dead body.

So now your family can't help you out because if you go tell you are now labeled a snitch and that will get you to hell quicker than an enemy will.

And for you young ladies that also like to join gangs please reconsider.

Unless you liked to be ganged raped, treated like a whore, slut, or prostitute then you need not join.

These people mean you no good. After you are treated like a dog getting used and abused they put you out on the curb like weekly trash.

Then you have this label and town that will make you wish you were dead when you may as well be.

I spent years trying to figure out why I quit doing all these things.

A very special lady told me these words.

She said "Joe it's because you wanted to live."

So simply put, but yet very true.

Kids, if you never finished school like most of us, go back. Don't ever think, or let anyone tell you it's to late. You can even go to college if you want to. If it's a dream of yours, like it was a dream of mine, leave the streets alone and do something positive with your life. I could have fulfilled the dream earlier, if there had not been negative people in my life.

(Thanks Deb for influencing me to go to college).

Start doing positive things that will continue to give you life, not negative things to end it.

Believe me I know what it's like to have a gun pointed at your temple. That is not a good feeling. Even though there was no care about dying, death was stared in the face many times.

That's the way a person thinks, when all they have are the streets. Now that my life has been changed, the way I think and feel about life, I'm much happier.

The only sad part is, my family thinks I'm going crazy. As long as I was on the streets wreaking havoc, it was ok. It gave them a reason to say bad things about me.

I would get drunk, and argue and want to fight them all the time. Alcohol played a big part in me acting foolish.

Some times it alleviated pressure, but most of the time it did harm.

I would wake up drinking then lie down drinking.

Breakfast would be Seagram's Gin or Paul Masson with a glass beer.

It got to the point, where there wouldn't be no eating for days. Would only drink, and drink, and drink.

I would often throw up, because no food would be eaten. It would only be alcohol.

It scared me that, when I did throw up, I would cough up blood.

I didn't like to mix the liquor, because it was washed down with beer.

Another part of my change was to quit drinking. Being an alcoholic, and knowing it, was one of the reasons it was easy for me to quit. There was never any denying. Since my first sip of beer was taken over at six years old, there was no turning back. I didn't instantly become an alcoholic. Wasn't like Drew Barrymore, life ate up at thirteen.

Chapter 20

When I join the military, drinking was a way of life. We were partying from sun up to sun down, every day of the week.

Was stationed in El Paso, TX, and Mexico was only five minutes away. At the time, in Mexico, a half-gallon of gin went for under five dollars.

You could only take a certain amount across the border. So you had to take a person that didn't drink, buy liquor for you to take back across the border.

When my military days were over, drinking straight liquor was easier than drinking water.

Spending three to four hundred dollars a week on liquor was easy. You're out selling dope, kicking it with the fellas, buying liquor all day everyday. Then go to the club and finish the night out.

One day, April 19th, nineteen ninety-eight, I decided to give up drinking. I had been drinking since age six, so Seagram's and Budweiser should give me a pension.

I just out of the blue decided this would be it for me.

One day I bought liter of Seagram's gin, and a six pack of Blue Bull. Got drunk and that was the last time a drink was taken.

People often ask me how drinking could be instantly stopped. Even though I was an alcoholic, I had drinking, drinking didn't have me.

All you need is faith and belief in yourself. That goes for anything you want to accomplish in life. People don't need rehabilitation, they need faith and GOD.

Cigarette smokers don't need the patch, or go through any kind of treatment. Just quit.

Drug addicts don't need rehabilitation, they need faith and GOD. Drug addicts never get over the craving, so rehabilitating them never rehabilitates them. It only relinquishes them from the drugs a little while.

Then they go around people that still use drugs so they get turned back on to them.

Those are weak mind people.

I'm around people that drink all the time and they sometime offer it to me. Most of the time they are playing, but they are waiting for me to break.

There's no desire for it. My mind is strong enough to turn it down. They try to pressure me into getting it on with them.

Once you make up your mind to do something, you don't need any reassurance from yourself.

You don't need to think about it, nor say, should I do it or not. You just don't do it, after you stop.

It's been years and I don't even think about taking another drink.

People need to believe in themselves first. There was no need for alcoholics anonymous.

How could it be anonymous, if you're telling everyone "hi, my name Joe and I'm an alcoholic?" What is so anonymous about that?

If you want to quit drinking, smoking or using drugs, just quit. You don't need anyone to tell you to quit if that's what you want to do.

You spend money to become an alcoholic then spend money to go to a rehab. It makes no sense. That's like when a person becomes overweight, then want to go on a diet.

You paid for the food to get you overweight then you pay for ways to loose it. It makes no sense.

Whatever you set your mind to do, do it.

You don't need anyone to baby sit you, to make sure you on a right path.

Chances are the same ones that are trying to help you out need some help themselves. They are always trying to be the benevolent one's that take the credit for your success.

Take control of your own life, and you won't have people saying "I solved so and so's problem."

You can solve your own problems if you believed and respected yourself enough.

People go to the doctor to complain of ailments, when they already know what's the problem is.

If you smoke and complain of ailments, the first thing the doctor will tell you is to quit smoking. Or you may go complaining about high blood pressure. The doctor will tell you, leave the swine alone.

The point's that's trying to be made is you don't need a doctor for the problems you already know you have, and the answers you'll get, when you go.

Nike couldn't have made a better slogan when they used the term "Just Do It."

If you want to quit drinking, quit smoking; quit using drugs, or eating swine, "Just Do It." If you don't want to go back to doing the things that plagued your life "Don't Do It."

You don't need to pay a doctor for medical expenses, if we just stop doing some of the things that affects our health. Simple changes in our lives are all we need.

With the Doctor I have, there's no co-pay, and since there's belief in Him, my deductible is met.

All the changes that are going on in my life, there's an excellent feeling about myself.

No one affects me anymore. It seems as though I affect them. I'm not out there to envy anyone. If anything, I will rather help you than hurt you.

For anyone that has ever thought about giving up on life, your pain is felt also. It was many days and nights there were thoughts about ending it all. When your family is against you, people on the streets are against you, it makes you think GOD has forgotten about you. When in reality, we forget about him. I'm glad life did turn around for me.

Thought if you put your life into GOD, it won't be any fun again.

Knew drinking, getting high, and tripping was fun, but you couldn't do that and serve GOD. The getting high and drinking, were given up, and there is still fun with laughing and tripping. So you can have fun and serve GOD.

But sometimes, there are thoughts of being back out there on the streets. You reminisce of how it was.

The way the homeboys would all hang together laughing and tripping.

But you also think about the numerous brothers that you know that's either dead, in jail, or on drugs.

Some of them you know have no hope of ever walking the streets again. A lot of them won't be able to take their kids to the zoo, or share an ice cream with them.

And the young ones that would ask me for money coming up they have life without parole, and never will have a chance to raise a family.

Brothers, where did we go wrong in life? Why was it so easy for me to leave the streets alone? Was it because of the many years that were spent on the streets? Was it because reality set in, that there is a better way?

To my brothers that are in jail, turn your life to GOD, HE is ever returning to Mercy.

Some of you may not be able to walk the streets again, but you have someone to walk with you, the rest of your days.

Brothers, I can not plead enough to you, that you can make it without the material things. When you realize that money means nothing to your freedom, everything else will fall into place. A few brothers were asked by me two simple questions. "Would you rather have everything in life for five years, then go to jail for the rest of your life?" Or, "would you rather be broke for five years, go to college, get an education, and then get an entry level job. The ending response was that they would take the money for the short period of time.

That's enough to make you want to go crazy.

There are periods of frustrations that set in, to make you want to have a drink. My mentality is stronger than that, so the thought quickly relinquished.

I still ride through the rough neighborhoods to remember how it was before. Seeing all the run down houses, looking at how people don't have to live the way they do.

Some are in situations like that, because they have no other alternative. The rest live like that, because they want to.

So when people live the way they do, you wonder if there will ever be a change in their kid life.

The cycle has to be broken some where in life. My sisters and brothers don't want to live the way moms is living.

Moms have always lived in the hood, when there were better choices.

Really think about this. The hood is all good for nobody.

We had never seen or lived in anything better than the hood, so there were never any thoughts to leave.

I liked the sound of gunshots and the smell of gunpowder. When that is what you are exposed to all your life, it's hard to wonder if there is a better way.

Then, if a better way was shown, you know it could never happen to you. I was wishing everyday for a different way of life and that's what dreams are made of.

Ride around the hood and see how people just sit on their porches from sun up, to sun down. Not doing anything productive in life. That's not the way life is supposed to be.

Moms sit at home drinking coffee, and smoking cigarettes all day.

Then Fran is doing the same. With a talent that Fran have, many people dream of. There are hair stylists and beauticians out there, but the way she does hair is unbelievable. But she would rather sit at home all day and drink coffee, and smoke cigarettes. A cosmetology license in my opinion going to waste, and she have the nerve to get the license renewed when it's time.

Now opportunities are being presented to me, because there were limitations being put on my life.

There are no longer the thoughts of "I'm nothing and will never be anything."

Now that there is success in my future, moms wants to take credit for it. Moms you can't take any credit for this. You claim you're so proud of me, but where did the influence come from. You thought it was always going to be like the days of old. Moms wake up, there is a GOD. We are only in these bad conditions, because of the choices that are made.

Our past generations did not prepare us for the future. Moms you didn't prepare a future for us. This is all new times for us and me in particular, to rise up. You know what it's like to be down, and moms, you're still down. This is not criticism, just actual facts.

I knew what it was like to be down, and now there is a rise. Moms you feel I am all of that, because there are no running the streets, no more drinking, no more trying to smoke weed, no more drug selling, no more gang banging, and no more arguing with you any more.

I'm no better than any one else, other than wanting to be a person of change. And have never acted that way. Moms, you are supposed to be happy for me.

You suppose to honor thy mother and thy father.

There's much honor to you, and to dad, even though I don't know him.

Moms you have spread so much untruth about me, that now you can't face it.

When my name is mentioned, you have negative things to say about me.

The question is do you really know who I am?

Have you ever sat and talked with me, to see what kind of man, your son is becoming?

Let me answer that for you. No. You tell people that there's no love from your kids, and me in particular.

There's more love for you today, than it was yesterday. The disassociation with the family is not an act from me.

When we were at each other's throat, we stayed together as a family. Now that the foolish ways have been dispelled, why not come together as a family.

If we got 'along', as enemies, why we can't get along as a family with truth and spirituality behind it? There shouldn't have to be a truce called, between family members. We are not rival gang members, even though we act that way. You are my mother, and the foolish thoughts are gone.

There's no thought's of me wanting to kill you anymore. I wanted to kill you, for the times you pulled your gun on me, but refrained from doing so.

And also for all the scars that are left on me, thanks to you. I thought about it, I would have to kill a lot of people that have a left a scar on me, but my mentality was senseless to even think that way, so please FORGIVE me moms.

There are no more thoughts of getting rid of you, for all the times you blamed me for being crazy, or on drugs, when you know none of it was true.

The thoughts of how we lived, when we didn't have to live the way we did, is now a memory, and not a grudge.

My life was a product of yours, so take another look in the mirror. Now the difference is a change has come about on my behalf, but what about you. The same Valium the doctor gave you to take for your nerves, then got me hooked, another DOCTOR relieved me of them. That was a major relief, because the doctor put me on the Valium, when I was seventeen.

What do we, as a family, get in return, segregation? You keep us divided. You hear about how joyous it is, when families are getting together to forgive each other, but what about us. Then there's peace that follows.

It has been many times when everyone tries to get along with each other, and you break it up.

Mothers are not supposed to be that way.

You can say one thing, and then change the story around.

You tell one family member something, knowing they are going to tell. When confronted, you say you know nothing of it, or we misunderstood you.

How can you have some of your kids angry with you for your behavior? You need some serious help. I love you moms, but in this day and time, we could never be a family until you participate.

A lot of things would not have to be written, if we could sit and talk.

But it always has to be about the money that is owed to you. Moms, it do not bother me that you tell everyone, probably the newspaper to, I owe you money.

Did you tell everyone that your sister owes you money, and you don't drill her for it?

Why try to make me look bad? I know this sounds childish, but it's painstaking.

See you fail to realize that it doesn't bother me anymore. You still call me names like a little child. Grow up. Please start telling the truth about the money.

What bothers me is that, there is no truth being told behind it. It started out being 500 hundred dollars that was owed, but in reality it is one hundred.

Two hundred dollars was borrowed from your brother that said he could be paid back anytime.

Who asked you to pay him?

Two hundred dollars came out of Jason's check, when he was locked up, so the money is owed to him.

The last one hundred dollars came from Peanut's insurance check.

You got five thousand dollars for that, so you should have given me the hundred dollars.

You was only out of your pocket one hundred dollars, and trying to discredit me for that. It's not my business, but how could you spend five thousand dollars in less than a year, and have nothing to show for it.

Then you bitch and complain about your kids not giving you money. Moms, you are over fifty years old. Have you ever had a job, in the last thirty years? We never seen or ever heard of you having a job. If so, where and when was this job?

Fran is going to grow old like you. You all just sit around drinking coffee, and smoking cigarettes day in and day out. Not doing anything to enhance your life. It's almost as though you have given up on life. You can be more productive out of life, instead of always waiting for a hand out.

Moms you're always talking about you need money for rent, or bills. You smoke almost four packs of cigarettes a day. That is the equivalent to seventy dollars a week, two hundred eighty dollars a month. If your rent is two hundred seventy-five dollars, you smoke more than what you pay for rent. And if you only get five hundred dollars a month, you smoke over half of your check away in cigarettes. Even if you cut smoking in half, you could save one hundred forty dollars a month. Now you think we are supposed to take care of you.

It's hard for us, and you think we are obligated to take care of you.

You have pushed everyone away. Even your own sisters and brothers, say they don't like coming around.

Your own husband was driven away, because of money. You took his money in Michigan, and he left you.

He was asked him to move back to Mississippi with you. So much for thinking you was going to treat him right. He was better off being in Michigan. Of course he left again. Then, moved down here and you were lonely again.

That went on for over a year, until I went to his job and asked him to go back to you.

Why were you drilling him for money? He was making only two hundred dollars a week and giving you half.

You were not satisfied with that, so he left again, and now you are not getting anything from him, because he's gone forever.

Lonny was trying to do better, but every time he got a job, you drilled him for money. When he was out on the streets smoking crack, you didn't argue with him about money, or getting a job. He wasn't giving you anything, so it should have not bothered you, about how much money he was handing out, when he did find a job. You nagged him about money, so now he's gone, and you're still without.

You claim no one is going to be living off of you for free. Greg wasn't around, then he was talked into coming back, and you weren't getting not one dime.

So you should have appreciated, what you were receiving, while he was around.

One day, you were complaining about the money he was giving you, and he straight up told you, "Half Pint, if I wasn't here, you wouldn't be getting anything."

And that is what you are getting today, nothing.

If Greg and Lonny were giving you one hundred dollars together, you would have had four hundred dollars a month extra. But you were not satisfied with that, and you're still without.

Satan was getting a social security check every month, and would get dope on credit.

When it was time to get his check the following month, he owed it to the dope boys, and you received nothing. But you issued his check out to the dope boys, like you were his financial broker.

Guess you figured, every time he went to jail for two to three months at a time, you spending his check, was your pay.

When he was getting his check, you received nothing, and you did not complain to Satan. You still fed him, bought him cigarettes, and gave him a roof over his head.

He curse you out on a daily basis, talk about how he wants to kill you, and us, and you still let him come around. It makes no sense to me. Neither Greg, nor Lonny, has been accused of harming Peanut, or being mean to him.

Look at the evidence that surrounds Satan. Moms, is it about money, or do you want to keep people away, for a specific reason.

You have no one to come around, but everyone is the problem. You talk about we don't come around, but you live across the street from your own momma, and can't get along with her.

You talk to her, like she's a dog, and you never heard bad words come from my mouth to you.

Bad words may have been thought of, but you never knew about it, because the respect was much greater, than my hate for you.

Moms it's not too late for the family to come together. It has started with us, and need to end with you.

How can we come together if all are not participating? Even though everyone was told, I'm sorry for the things that were said and done to them, why are you still putting me through hell?

There's no arguing with you anymore. You still curse me out, and make it appear as though I'm the real troublemaker.

People would look at me as though, I'm some deranged lunatic. Now they are beginning to see the light. After you curse me out, call me names, talk about me to other people, errands are still done for you.

If you considered me as being such a bad person moms, why do you have me to pay bills, and do things for you?

There is no animosity in my heart for you. There is no hate for you anymore. Yeah moms, there were hate feelings for the things that were done to me, by you.

The scars that are on my lip and jaw are constant reminders of the cruelty you displayed.

I remember the times you pulled your gun on me, as though you were going to shoot me. You shot your own husband, and Satan's daddy, what makes me think you would not have shot me?

The extension cord marks are finally gone. All the brooms and sticks that were broke on me, and us as a family, are still remembered. Like it was mentioned earlier, the hate was strong enough to kill you. The way plans and plots were contemplated, but never carried out.

Remembering those incidents, are always on my mind. The grudge was held for years, but now that is gone. Forgiveness has already taken place, and you won't return the favor.

All these health problems that are plaguing you, is a sign for you to change. You take medicine to keep you awake, and medicine to make you sleep. You take medication for your nerves, heart and asthma condition. Then you smoke three to four packs of cigarettes a day.

Only GOD is keeping you alive.

Have there ever been thoughts of changing the way you live. Maybe that's why GOD is keeping you with us, is that you may answer the questions that we have to ask.

Every time the truth is presented, you get mad, curse me out, and tell me to leave. All was asked, is that you listen to my side, because you are not always right. And you know the truth is being told, but you want it hid. Those that know the truth won't speak it to your face. That's because they are two faced. When you tell them untrue things, they agree with you. Then, behind your back they talk about you, and me, and everyone else in the family. Moms, your time is up. You can no longer keep the truth hid, nor can you keep telling lies.

We, as sisters and brothers, are going to make it. Even though, to this day, we don't get along, but we'll find a way. We need to stop telling lies on each other, and find the real enemy. There will be a day when we will be sisters, and brothers, and mothers and fathers, as a family.

Tara won't be spreading lies about me, telling people about my past, when she knows that's done and over with. There will be a day when she won't use me to get money from people. Yeah Tara, that was foul of you to tell people I was living with you, and did not contribute anything to help you out. Then they would feel sorry for you, tell you to put me out then give money to help you.

To justify the lies, you try and put me out anyway, knowing that was wrong. People telling me "you should not do your sister like that." Like what. When a job did come about, Tara you was given 99% of my paycheck to help you out. You were close to me, in one point in life, but I was always close to you. So close that when moms would be on your case, I defended you then she would accuse us of sleeping together.

I always looked out for you, even when we were little. Always took up for you, when moms was against you. When you got pregnant, moms put you out, who was there. When you and Fran had your differences and moms was on Fran side who was there?

When you had your baby, who quit their job, so you could work? Who paid your bills for you, and went to the store, and did EVERYTHING you asked despite making me look like the enemy to the people you knew.

What did I ever ask you for? What did I ever ask you to do for me? Despite the lifestyle you lead, did I ever disclose any of your business? No, because it was none of mines. You would tell people, you were tired of helping me out. Tara stand on truth, and answer this.

When did I ever ask you to do something major for me? I do things for you, but you're like momma, make me look like the bad person.

You don't like to tell the truth, so you make up things to justify your accusations. But the good part about it is I'm not mad at you. We are a product of our parents, and the cycle needs to be broken.

We see that moms, in particular, have shown favoritism to Fran, and kept the rest divided.

Even the grandchildren see the favoritism in Fran's daughter.

Mom's will keep Fran's daughter, when she, at times won't keep the others. She calls to Michigan to speak to Missie, when she won't call local to speak to the other grandchildren.

But we can't hold that to be justifiable. Let us come together as a whole family, and the ones want to know the truth get whatever is ailing them off their chest.

Tara, Fran, and Mike, we are the victims of the latter part of the disintegration of the family. We need each other more so now than ever.

Rochelle and Lonny, whatever animosities you have, relinquish them through truth. I'm not afraid to stand up to moms, or anyone else.

Come face me with the truth, and make me out of a liar. A lost soul is now found.

No one wants to deal with the truth, and what it stands for.

People are all stressed out, doing so much evil, that they are gray haired before their time.

I am growing and evolving into a man that no one has ever witnessed before. People may look at me, as though my life is meaningless, but it's worth more than what you think.

GOD used me that even my family should be trying pattern their life after.

But you'll say, 'how can GOD use a person like you, with the way your life use to be.'

See the key word is 'use to be' Yes I was at the lowest point in my life, but witness my rise, before your eyes.

You call me the devil, but how can I be the devil, if all the bad things have been relinquished from my life. The devil doesn't want you to rise, so where are my devilish ways.

Take a look at your own life, no matter whom you are, and ask yourself questions.

Be truthful with yourself, and see how many good verses bad, you come up with.

No I'm not perfect, but am striving to perfection.

You wonder why so many people die from stroke, high blood pressure, stress, and everything else that is associated with worrying about life.

See, that is why nothing worries me. I don't go through life wondering how a bill will get paid, or where my next pigs feet dinner, or cigarette will come from. I don't worry about where my next drink, or joint, or crack hit will come from.

I don't worry about my family, or anybody else accepting me.

In the end, no family, no preacher, or no friend will be there to save you. My reliance comes from ALMIGHTY GOD ALLAH, and HIS CHRIST, and no one else is needed.

Even you reverends, and preachers, and deacons, and ushers, and who ever sits on the rostrum, please look at your life.

You are so programmed, and have others programmed, that when real truth is presented you nor they, don't want to hear it.

This guy Willie Benson told me one thing. He said 'Joe, the things you say are the truth, but people would like to think that they are living right".

Now imagine that. If you think that you are living right, and people start pointing at your faults, you don't want to hear it.

When people pull the coat off individuals, they don't want to hear it, because now a real change has to come about. People don't want to change, and do the real things it takes to be righteous.

They want to stay programmed, and have people to think they are doing right.

Let's tally up our faults, and go to the scorecard.

Make one tally mark for good, and one tally mark for bad.

Include things like do I gossip, back bite, lie, cheat, steal, connive, deceive.

These are just a few of the things GOD doesn't allow us to do, but people are the first ones to criticize you for other wrong doings.

This is not being disrespectful to anyone or anybody. Just look at your own life first people, and never criticize anyone for what they are doing.

Now let's talk about sins, since the one's that think they are righteous, are not.

Before continuing, let me say this. Someone said my truth offends people, just because I bring out their faults.

People bring out my faults and the majority of the time if I am guilty of it, I'll try and correct myself.

They tell me, "you're sleeping with a woman, and not married to her, and that's sin." O.K., I know that, so there's no denying it.

Look at the percentages of men and women that lived together, before they got married.

And you are one of them to, so don't play like you're dumb to the fact. Some stay living together twenty, to thirty years, before they are married. Then, when they become married, they want to chastise others for doing it.

Now later on in life you run into couples that know it's wrong, but have ambitions to do better, but you put them with this religious rhetoric. "The LORD doesn't like what you are doing." The LORD didn't like what you were doing all those years either, so now who are you to judge?

Sin is sin no matter how you look at it, and when you did it.

And one sin is no better than another one, meaning there is no measurement.

But look at the sins you are committing, while you are trying to put others down.

People going to church, thinking they are holy and all, putting people down for the same sins they are trying to conceal.

Some are so bold that they don't hide the sins they do, but still get on others for committing sins.

Now I'm no scholar in religion, but to me, sin is something that is not pleasant in GOD eyes. Now that's settled.

Some are still intoxicated from drinking all night, and then sit in a church Sunday morning with a hangover.

We can be guilty of these things, while putting down others for different faults.

I did a lot of things years ago, but you don't see me putting people down for doing them.

Could really care less what you do, because there's no way you can be saved by me.

People may not see us doing evil, but why do we conceal it, as though man is so powerful, he will punish us, instead of God.

Forget about man, and remember GOD. He's always looking, always listening, always knowing.

I'm not perfect, and there are things that are done, that are not pleasant in God's eyes.

HE sees me, so to hell with what man, or preachers has to say, because you can't punish me, nor save me. Your criticism means nothing to me.

Whatever you have to say, keep it to yourself, and quit fooling people into thinking they are living right, because they are programmed by you.

I have known preachers to tell members of their congregation to stay away from my kind. What do you mean my kind?

People that know the truth and are not brainwashed. People that are not programmed nor have a slave mentality, like you wish we had.

The kind that will pull the coat off your wicked doings, that you think you are hiding.

You are wicked hypocrites. Nobody is trying to change the way you conduct your flock. If that is what they believe, then let them believe. Didn't Jesus say you shall know the truth, and it will set you free? Then Pastors, you need to set your flock free.

People committing sins all their life, and now they are ready to die, and then want to act like they are saved.

Then they will see people that know they are not doing right, but are on a path to change.

And they say to them, "The Lord don't like what you are doing"

The Lord didn't like what you were doing, so don't come to me with that.

At least there's no denial in what was being done by me, so why should there be advice to the next one.

Then, you have some of these, that are suppose to be loyal to me, waiting on me to take a drink, gamble, or eat a piece of swine.

Instead of you all following suit, you are sitting back waiting like vultures, for me to do the things that were in my past years ago.

You are at fault so bad, that you would like to see others that are trying to do well, go back to doing bad, so it will equate to your evil doings. You are wicked hypocrites.

Anyway what was being said before the emotional tirade?

Oh yeah, it was about worrying.

I saw a quote and it said "Ain't no sense in worrying if you ain't gonna pray, and "Ain't not sense in praying if you gonna worry."

There's no worrying about the next day, because it wasn't promised to me. There's worry about the hereafter, and seeing my family and close ones again.

That is why my life needs to be in order and straight, before this short life ends.

My mission is almost complete, but without an unconditional compliance with the family, everything is meaningless.

Well not meaningless, because if the family don't come together, GOD is there the beginning of the way, as well as the rest of the way for me.

Moms and Satan, you two need some serious help. We, as a family need help, but GOD has mercy on the two of you.

Once again, moms, there's no hate for you anymore, so why is there still animosity.

You still keep up hell with us, but the good thing about it, now we know the deal.

It wasn't our fault that we hated each other, it was your fault. Even though we are grown, you still interfered with us coming together.

You feared, that what you did to us, we would in return, do it to you. We don't think that way anymore. Being a family is what we are trying to accomplish. That is all I have wanted, since we lost Peanut.

Now more than ever, we need each other. What ever truth your sisters and brothers said you need to tell us, forget it.

That's not important to the family or me anymore.

Maybe that's why you want me divided. I stressed about learning the truth, until you have made me look like the enemy. Then, people will look at me at though I am a troublemaker.

You know that's not me. Why you didn't stand up and tell everyone, all I'm searching for is the truth. I'll tell you why you didn't. It's because you don't want us to learn of certain things that occurred in your life. And once again, I don't care. Forget about everyone else. Let us have our own family reunion. At this present time, we can't even get three of the family members to come to dinner together.

Something is seriously wrong. We need to really analyze why no one can get along with each other. Offers have been suggested about getting everyone together, but all won't volunteer.

Moms, Mike have seen you sporadically, over the last five years, with at a least a four plus years gap. Why haven't he been down to see you?

You have been sick, in the hospital, and he's been asked to come see you, on others expense. He blames everything from the parole people not letting him go, to not having money. When he was released in January nineteen ninety-eight, his parole officer said he was eligible to go out of the state in six months.

That was over a year ago. I have offered to pay his way, so he can't say he would have been out of anything.

Where's the love at, that your son haven't seen you in all these years, and now have an opportunity to do so, won't. Something is definitely wrong with this picture. Let us come together. Let's do it before time depletes us all, because moms, 'I don't want to die all alone.'

Chapter 21

I can see it in your eyes momma something is not right. I continue to ask, but what do you say, other than I'm ok. No one will believe me when I tell them you are sick, because you act as though nothing is wrong when they come around. Well you act that way around me also but I can sense something is wrong moms.

Well at least I'm glad we are closer now than we have ever been. The visits to your house are now more pleasant, because I don't bring up the past anymore.

Guess I just had to realize that it is best to just leave it alone, though it would have helped me to understand myself, and where I'm going.

And plus with a new woman in my life, I don't want her to think I am disrespectful towards my mother.

I have never been intentionally disrespectful to any woman.

With a new woman in my life, all that I dreamed of accomplishing with my family begin to fade.

I had a new mission in life and that was to have someone special in my life, settle down, have a good job and just enjoy all the good things a decent person deserves.

I feel myself excelling now more so than ever.

Have you ever met someone that you continue to run from yet finding yourself running to them?

That's the way it is with Michelle(Chelle).

Now here's a lady I met while running back and forth from Mississippi to Michigan. I was on my way to Michigan Thanksgiving nineteen ninety-seven. I was at Tara's when she introduced me to Chelle.

It was no big deal. I spoke to her and was saying goodbye to Tara when out of nowhere said "Tara that is going to be my future wife."

And I left with no thought of returning to Mississippi soon.

Of course that thought did not last long. I was back in Mississippi a week before Christmas.

This was also the time when nothing was still going right in my life, and I was still contemplating suicide.

I told you earlier Tara had her friends to talk to me and Chelle was the one that prayed for me and with me so long that I thought it was church services.

And Chelle held my hand and gave me a hug and said everything was going to be alright.

Then it became apparent to me who she was.

She was the same lady I met before leaving for Michigan a month earlier.

I was impressed by her concern and consideration for me.

Though I learned later she has concern and consideration for a lot of people.

That's extraordinary.

I tried to talk to Chelle after that ordeal was over, but she was not interested.

She indicated it were things going on in her life that she was battling.

She had a baby that was less than a year old, and a four year old daughter.

I had always said to myself after Deb, there would be no more relationships with women that had small kids. Or even kids in the home for that matter.

Chelle at the time was living with Tara until she found her somewhere else to live.

She was on the verge of getting a divorce and had decided to move out until it was over.

I was dealing with Sherry at the time but it wasn't working out.

That brief encounter was going and went no where fast. But I at the time wanted to just be Chelle's friend.

No matter what I said or tried to do, it didn't faze her.

She would always say "what do you want from me?"

I would say nothing but to be your friend.

After bout a month of bugging her she felt like talking.

This is when we began to see a lot of similarities we shared and a lot of the same issues in dead beat relationships.

Soon after we started to become friends and be close. Though her family and others around started to doubt we actually had a friendship.

We were truly friends, but because we were close, they thought otherwise.

Our closeness caused a concern amongst those associated with us.

This caused trouble for her especially since she was going through a divorce.

She felt our friendship was hindering her divorce and people assumed we were an item.

She asked if I would go to Michigan until the divorce was all over. Even though she did not indicate this meant we were going to be together, she felt it was best for my safety as well as hers.

I agreed and the fellas were down for the Fourth of July, so they took Lil Joe and me back with them.

I was so miserable being in Michigan until it drove me near insane.

Chelle and I constantly talked and she was missed daily.

I had never felt so close to someone so quickly.

It was a month later when we decided no one was going to dictate our friendship and cause us to be going through hardship.

That little vacation ended as quickly as it began and little did I know it would be the last time I would choose between Michigan and Mississippi to live.

My journey back to Mississippi was as pleasant as leaving the first time.

This time it was someone waiting that we could go places and share a lot of our pain.

After moving back that August of ninety-eight, Chelle helped me find a job at Saks Corporate Office in Jackson.

This was in October, but I was already working slave labor jobs digging ditches, working in heat factories pressing steel, and playing errand boy running parts damn near all over Mississippi.

This job was simple. All I had to know was how to help people that called in from Saks retail stores, corporate offices, and distribution centers. It was cool because I was making close to the same money as being at Stanley in Michigan.

See it's cool to know someone that knows someone in the job world.

Now before working at Saks, I had applied there numerous times. I know they seen my applications everyday, because the first fifty were mine.

Then come along someone Chelle know that work there takes my application and resume then bypass Human Resources, and it goes straight to the manager.

Then during the interview we talked about nothing pertaining to the job.

It was about Michigan and Iowa or Minnesota.

I'm assuming that's where she's from.

After the interview, I knew the job wasn't mine.

I felt the guy only asked the manager to give me an interview to boost my confidence.

That was in early September of ninety-eight when I interviewed, but they called almost a month later and made me an offer.

It was less than in Michigan at the time of leaving Stanley, but a lot compared to what I was making currently assembling valves for a manufacturing plant in Madison, Mississippi.

And it was a whole hell of a lot that what this lady was making there after almost twenty-five years of being there. Making nine dollars an hour after a quarter century of work is ridiculous.

Hell that's bout as close to slavery as you can get.

That's more like involuntary slavery.

After accepting a job at Saks, my begin date was October 5th, nineteen ninety-eight.

This is a relief because it appears to be a permanent full time job.

While still working at the manufacturing facility in Madison, I got a call saying Chelle was in an accident.

They didn't tell me how bad it was at the time, but I rushed to the hospital to check up on her.

I couldn't see her at the time because of various reasons still on going with her divorce.

I mean the issue could have been pressed, but that would have caused more problems.

Since she was in intensive care, and the soon to be ex-husband wanted to play like he all of a sudden cared, I didn't bother going in to see her at the time.

She had a ruptured spleen, facial cuts and fractures, and bruises all over her body. The kids suffered bumps and bruises and I think Noah had a hairline fracture to his skull.

Prayer was all that could be done at the time, to ask the Lord to see them through this.

This I believe brought Chelle and I closer together even though her mom was there to help her out.

Some of her other family members were also there, and despite all the lies and rumors they heard about me, they looked at me in a different way.

Some of them did anyway.

And had it not been for my on family speaking bad about me, how would Chelle's family have had ill feelings about me?

I didn't blame them for feeling the way they felt.

Hell I wish my family could be as close as hers and care about each other like they care for one another.

Instead of just letting nature take it course and let me handle my own affairs, lies as well as the past was introduced to Chelle's family.

But the thing is, a lot of my past was already discussed with Chelle and it was nothing I was hiding.

She knew about Deb, and Sherry.

It's not like Chelle and I were dating. I mean true enough we were getting close to each other, but there was no commitment.

Besides, I have never been alone. After one relationship ended, it was always someone next in line.

This has been going on for as long as I can remember. Being alone was never my forte.

By Chelle being there after Deb, and the brief encounter with Sherry, she was the one chosen.

This was just not the time for me to be alone.

We really didn't know we were heading in to each others direction. The friendship was based on being there for each other. Consoling and comforting each other as the drama days were passing us by.

Eventually after living separately for a while, we decided to move in together to see if we could actually make something more out of the friendship.

My mother approved of the relationship with Chelle.

Even though my mother called Deb her daughter, she actually introduced Chelle to everyone, as her daughter-in-law.

This made me feel good to know that my mother had accepted Chelle, because it was a rocky start when they first met.

My mother had some harsh words for Chelle, when they first met, because of our friendship was growing and she had not got a divorce yet.

Moms thought Chelle was playing games with me and was not seriously about a divorce.

Wonder where she got this information from.

I don't think it was told to her to protect me but more or less as a gain for them.

After that had gotten straight between Chelle and moms, everything seemed to go well from there.

I even felt closer to moms. This has been the closest we had ever been and we have seemed to have made peace with each other.

There was still a concern about her health though.

Moms has lost a lot of weight and had been in the hospital several times, for several days.

The doctors wouldn't say too much about why she was in the hospital.

Other than the fact of her taking high blood pressure, asthma, heart and nerve pills, the rest of the family thought everything was ok.

Just to be on the safe side, I was in constant contact with the few family members that talked to me about moms appearing ailing health.

It was about to be a new year, and a new millennium and yeah I was worried about moms.

These are now the best times we have ever spent as me being an adult, and I know there's something wrong.

Fran was convinced to come down in February to judge for herself. This was to see if what was being said had some legitimacy to it.

When Fran made it to Mississippi some of the other family members assembled over to moms house. And the way moms was carrying on laughing and joking, the family just said there's nothing wrong with her.

I said ok, and Fran went back to Michigan. Everyone was happy because it had been a while since they saw moms like that.

Satan was still driving her crazy, so to see her in a good mood even made me think twice.

No soon as Fran could make it back to Michigan, and everyone was satisfied with knowing moms was ok, I immediate saw a drastic change.

Now I'm telling Fran this because of her and moms relationship.

I even now had accepted the fact Fran was her favorite, but this goes on in any household.

I was telling everyone something is up with moms and she's fooling everyone about her health.

The family was beginning to blow me off thinking this was some scheme to try and get us together.

Figured if we came together during this we can probably stick together after it.

I really did want the whole family to assemble and have our own little reunion. We had not done this since we lost Peanut, and this would be a good opportunity.

The family agreed the only way we could get the brothers and sisters, nieces and nephews together was to do it around spring break.

This way Fran and Mike could bring their kids down from Michigan even though Mississippi's schools spring break would already be over.

The date was set for April 7th year two-thousand.

Moms and I continue to grow closer and Satan was still being Satan.

I hated the way he continue to treat moms, but some of the smaller issues were over looked.

This was only done so Moms and I would not argue and put us steps backwards instead of continuing to move forward.

And with the family get together coming in several weeks, I didn't want to be the blame for messing things up.

Aaron had also got the news from everyone else about me saying moms was ill.

He, and I think some of his family members, were down a few days before everyone had assembled.

Can't remember who all were there but I do know an argument ensued between Aaron and me over some religious matters.

I guess by him being a preacher, there should be no reason for him to get all hot and heated over what someone says.

The argument got intense and everyone was trying to control the matter. By him being a Christian and me being a Muslim, I feel we can still talk about religion without being disrespectful to each other or get upset.

I mean we all bow down to the same God, and I know the Bible speaks of not getting angry. The Quran also states, "Invite all to the way (or word) of thy Lord with beautiful wisdom and preaching and argue with them in the best manner."

It may have said some things that shouldn't have been said, but his status is higher than mine. He should have been the example and let it go.

But no, what did he do?

He gets upset then tells moms, "I was under the impression that you are gravely ill, so I came to check on you."

Then he leaves.

What kind of crap is that?

Guess I'm the bad guy all over again.

It was a few days before the gathering and Fran was on her way down with her family.

Mike didn't make the trip again and that didn't surprise me or anyone else.

Chelle and I were going visiting moms a lot up to the time of the get together.

Satan was still being Satan, and I didn't interfere as much. This was only because moms and I were getting along for long periods of time, and I didn't want to end that.

When he would start to act violent over money, I would intervene.

Satan didn't care about the way he acted around anyone.

People in the neighborhood sometimes looked out for moms, when they would see him arguing and trying to fight her.

This upset me a lot, because he was a time bomb waiting to explode.

All I could think about was moms always being alone in the house with Satan.

But as long as she gave him money, he was ok.

I really don't know where she got it from being on a fixed income.

Maybe it was money she had stashed for many years and would give him a little at a time.

That way when someone come by and threaten Satan because he owes them money for dope or whatever, she would be able to pay them.

Satan knew this, so he would have people to go by moms house and say they were going to hurt him if he didn't pay them.

After she paid them, then if it were some dope boys they would keep the money and give him some dope.

If it were some regulars in the neighborhood, Satan would do the same but split the money with them.

How trifling is that?

He would also either steal clothes, or if someone else had stolen some clothes, sell them to moms.

He also did this on household items, yard items, or car items.

Anything of value he would sell.

Then if someone brought something to him to sell, he would always say "my momma will buy it."

They tell Satan if he was able to sell the items, the money would be split.

Satan would charge momma a higher price, then split the money with whomever.

This way he was able o get double the money off someone else's goods.

But they say he's crazy. What ever.

Satan became desperate about getting moms to buy things until he would bring junk that would otherwise make the Sanford Arms look like the Mall of America.

And of course moms would buy it from him for what reason is beyond me.

I still think it was to keep him from getting violent over money, because she was mostly alone with him.

That still didn't work because when whatever money she had was gone at the time he still acted an ass.

Then to add insult to injury, he would go back and steal whatever he sold to her, the resell it to her again.

She acted as though she didn't know he was doing that, but I'm sure she did.

Chapter 22

Well the day for the family get together has finally arrived. I mean this is a long awaited arrangement that hadn't taken place since we lost Peanut.

Little did we know this was going to be a joyous day for many years to come.

Aaron and his family were not present. He was probably still upset from the argument earlier in the week but oh well that's life.

Mike and his family did not show either.

With them not being there did not stop up from having what we considered the greatest show on earth.

Moms was in one of the happiest moods we hadn't seen in many years.

I mean can you believe daddy was there and they were in the same room together.

Now I had not seen this in all my life and it was nothing but family love and God present that day.

Moms did not even smoke while being there. This was the longest I had ever seen moms go without smoking any cigarettes.

One of the many highlights that day was when daddy told moms despite all that had happened long ago, and the absence of him from us, he still loved her.

So much love was in the air that moms even told Rochelle she loved her.

She may have told Rochelle that absence of us, but I had never heard her say it.

And I know with the animosity Rochelle still had for moms over what happened to daddy, and the way we were raised, it still meant a lot for her to her that.

Another highlight was me break dancing. I mean it brought back so many memories until I wanted to cry about it.

I know the happiest times in my life were when break dancing was popular. This gave us a lot do and not be on the streets doing negative things.

I mean we put a lot in to mixing music, dancing, having competitions, until just that moment of showing off made me emotional.

And I did my little dance routine, and went in to a little pose, I couldn't move.

I was to embarrass to tell people I was hurting and they assumed I kept the pose while the cameras were flashing pictures.

When they stepped away, I slowly and quietly limped away and rested my aching body.

The pain was no where near the enjoyment we were experiencing.

I can remember standing off to myself wondering what it could be like if we could have these constantly.

With Fran and Mike in Michigan unable to participate, it would be meaningless.

Not to say anything bad about the ones that are already in Mississippi, but it would just be even better with everyone home.

To bad the get together is coming to a close and everyone is still hyped up.

No one appears tired and that's probably because we don't know when the next get together is going to be.

I had a talk with Fran and several others about moms not being her self.

They assured me that everything is ok and I'm just being over cautious.

Yeah she was eating and had even picked up a little weight before the get together, but in my mind, and in my heart as well as in my soul, something was wrong.

It's like the more I talked to them about it the more frustrated they were with me.

I do not literally mean to be a nuisance but at least someone should take heed to what I'm saying.

I wish this was just my imagination playing tricks on me but a deep spirit just tells me otherwise.

The get together ended on a good note. No arguing or fighting from the sisters and brothers. And even though moms and pops were not together anymore, and had not been since I think nineteen seventy-two, they even got along.

This is something the family can hold on to for a long time.

Even the speeches from the ones that wanted to speak were emotional.

We called for unity amongst the family and a renewed vow to carry Peanut's legacy on. And that was to be a family all over again.

We had agreed that before something happened to the next one of us, at least we would all be in harmony.

We agreed we should have more family gatherings whether it was with a few at a time or all, at least as brothers and sisters we could exist.

This was something I believe moms also wanted to see.

After seeing her at the get together, my love and respect for her grew.

I knew then she could not bring the family together for something like this, it had to be one of her kids.

Ah hah, now it was becoming clear to me why it was such urgency to assemble everyone.

This was something that may seem trivial was put together by me.

And since I had individually told everyone in the past how sorry I was for whatever they suffered through me, this was a time everyone could quell whatever animosity they had.

And to see that moms and daddy made peace with each other, I knew then what we had experience as sisters and brothers were a microcosm of what they went through.

Now here are two people that married each other three times, then divorced, talking, laughing, and carrying on as though nothing happened.

I believe in my heart that day moms said she was sorry for shooting him, and since day one, daddy has forgiven her.

The family member that were there made peace with each other because I knew then what I had been tripping on all these many years now meant nothing.

My mother and father on were now on good terms.

The sisters and brothers were now on good terms.

This is what I had dreamed about accomplishing all the days of my life.

I mean this was history in the making.

Unconditional peace had now spread through my heart.

That night we all returned to our homes with a since of hope and can now live knowing we accomplished something that day.

Fran stayed on a few more days before returning back to Michigan. She was thanked for being a part of this because without her being there, moms would have not been the same.

I mean she still would have enjoyed her self, but when she's around Fran, a new life in her appears. I can now accept that because if that's what makes moms happy, then I need to get Fran here every year, every month, every week, and every day.

I know if Fran was here with moms, Satan would not do no where near the things he does to moms.

For some reason, he knows Fran will not tolerate it.

Why he upset moms when he's around us puzzles me, but when Fran is present, he acts like a different person.

I've had my share of clowning moms and other family members but the things Satan does are horrendous.

I can remember when a police officer told moms Satan was not crazy. Said he was aware of all that he does. He explained to moms that if Satan was crazy, he would not do things and hide from the law. He would not steal and try to conceal it. A person unaware of these things will do them as though they don't believe they are doing anything wrong.

After Fran left and things were still good with the family with the exception of Satan.

Moms started hinting around as though he be hitting her.

That Friday April 14th Chelle and I visited moms. When we showed up she had her screen door lever wrapped up with some sort of rope.

This was unusual for moms but I didn't pay it any attention. She indicated Satan had been over bothering her about money and was acting violently.

She asked if we could come over Monday to take her to get the tags for her car. We said yes, visited a little while longer then left.

That Saturday was nice warm, and sunny, as it had been the three years after being back. Moms called but I wasn't around. She left a message with Chelle asking if I could come over she needed a favor.

I told Chelle we can go another time because she already said she wanted us to get her tags Monday.

Chelle was like no she wants to see you so you need to go.

We ended up going, but moms was looking a bit distraught.

She said everything was ok, but I knew Satan had done something to her.

I told her not to let him in the house and keep her gun close, by just in case she needed it in a hurry.

She told me she was alright now and there was nothing Satan could do to harm her any more.

She was talking weird to me saying things like "I'm alright now, and yall look over Satan" I was like "moms everything is going to be alright and we are going to find a way to have Satan committed in a mental hospital so he won't bother you." She said there's nothing he can do to harm her anymore.

We talked a little more and she said goodbye. I told her we would be by there Monday to take her to run errands and she said ok.

Sunday was just like Saturday with the way the weather was.

It was a nice, sunny, bright, and beautiful day.

Chelle and I were just out and out enjoying that time together.

We were driving down State St. I think when Tara called me crying. I didn't know what was going on because she was hyperventilating.

It scared me because I didn't know what to say or think other than wait on her to catch a breath.

When she was trying to say momma something, all I could keep saying was "momma what, what's wrong with momma."

She caught one desperate breath and said "Joe momma is dead"

Part of me died then.

Everything happened so fast.

I thought it was a dream because ironically it was a Sunday Tara called me crying hysterically telling it was Peanut they found dead.

This cannot happen to me all over again.

I immediately lost it.

Chelle was trying to console me and all could be said was no, no, no not again.

My mother cannot be dead.

Chelle and I were just there yesterday visiting and she seemed ok.

This cannot be happening just a week after the get together and moms seemed ok.

To my dismay it was true.

The lady brought me into this world, and I just now understand my purpose in life is no longer with me.

What I had feared about her being sick, and would soon no longer be with us, had come to pass.

I made it to her house and the coroner was already there. We had to make a positive identification on her.

People from the police or fire department said only two of us could go in to the house.

It was more than two of us but the nice coroner lady let us all go in and say goodbye to the woman we so misunderstood all these many years.

I didn't know if she was killed or any kind of foul play was involved.

I didn't know if we were going to go in there and the place be ransacked from robbery.

All these thoughts ran through my mind, but all I could think about was how it will be once I seen her.

I slowly walked into the house and there she was on the couch looking as though she was asleep.

Everything in the house was intact. Nothing was moved or looked out of order.

It was one thing that puzzled me though. She had taken all the linen off her bed and folded the sheets, blankets, and pillows, then placed them at the end of the bed. Very strange.

What was also strange was that she had a bank Peanut use to have tucked by her side.

I know I'm jumping ahead but another strange thing is several days after we moved some things around, her gun was in some boxes or something tucked away.

Now I know moms always slept with the gun at her side, but why was it tucked away?

Did my mother know it was time for her to go? Did she give up on life and was tired of going through what she was going through?

My mother is now gone one week after we all made peace with each other and even dad.

Was this something that had divine intervention?

I mean was I used to warn the family something was wrong so they can be aware and come together?

These are questions that will probably never be answered.

All that matters now was laying my mother to rest, and to see how this will affect the family.

Was this designed to bring us together?

So many thoughts were going through my head.

Here's lightning striking all over again.

Now you see why I don't want to die all alone.

Who was there to help with Peanut?

Who was there to help moms?

Both of them died all alone.

You couldn't help but to think of what should have been different while she was alive.

Visit more often maybe, or not argue as much.

Should we just take things the way they are so everyone can feel comfortable?

I'm just glad we made peace long before her departure from us.

Believe me, even though it's been several years, she is not forgotten.

Today is the wake, and the people at the funeral home let Fran do her hair.

She looks really good and at peace. We were able to get some good pictures with her. Even her play sons came down from Michigan to see her laid to rest. Thanks Big Rod, Keith, Marshall, Jeffrey, Mitchell, Meshelay, Deb, and all that made that trek to see her laid to rest.

Momma we have made a vow to be a close family and not bicker and fight with each other.

We vowed to not let you or Peanut's passing go in vain.

Yes we said the same thing at Peanuts funeral momma, but hey, the tree that bared the fruit is no longer with is.

Maybe this will cause us to think twice about not being a close family.

After the celebration of her going home, she was laid to rest next door to Peanut.

Now he's not alone.

Moms you will truly be missed. I'll reminisce over the good as well as the bad, because that will help me to continue to become the man I have always desired to become.

I know you are ok because you told me you will be the day before you passed away.

Then I didn't understand, but now I do.

No more pills to take. No more suffering from the blow that caused you to have a collapsed lung. No more pain and arthritis from the broken bones you suffered through men. No more having to deal with me, even though we were on permanent good terms. No more worrying if we are going to make it as a family. No more Satan hitting and cursing you out.

And best of all, no more having to go day in and day out with Peanut constantly on your mind.

Bye momma. You will always be loved, despite all we have been through and hopefully I'll see you at the crossroads.

May Allah (God) rest your soul as I send you off in the Arabic words of peace.

Asalaam Alaikum.

Chapter 23

It's been almost a month since you leaving us moms and tomorrow is your fifty-seventh birthday.

We are still trying to cope with the loss as in most cases of death, it was unexpected.

I often cry because there was so much more ground we had to cover with our relationship.

After only three short years of being back to Mississippi to be close to you and the family, just like that you are gone.

I love you more today moms than I did yesterday based on me understanding myself.

I felt if there ever came a time for me to move to the next level in my life, the first would have to be me understanding and loving myself.

That's why I can look at the past, learn from it, and do what has to be done so it will never happen again.

Family is looked at differently. And no this was done before your passing moms.

I will keep my end of the bargain about what we said on the day of the funeral.

I will still continue not to argue, fight, or curse them out.

The family is still kind of close but as the days go by, you can see the drifting away again.

Moms, it's still arguing there, and I really don't want to go around some of them. Your brother is always telling me to continue to go as they may change, but I don't see it in their heart.

And no I won't talk about them in a negative way.

Hey if you want to gamble, go clubbing, smoke crack, marijuana, or even charcoal, hell that's your prerogative. If you want to be up day in and day out drinking and ruining your health, more power to you.

You all can do whatever you want to if that pleases you.

But don't get mad at me when I don't want to come around while you are doing it.

If I choose to then so be it. If I don't choose to, still so be it.

If you want to continue to say I just moved away to be with the white folks then so be it.

And by the way, my neighborhood has different walks of life in it.

I see nothing wrong with wanting to go somewhere that when you leave, there's a greater chance of you returning and it still be there.

There's nothing wrong with wanting your kids to go to a somewhat decent school that you know curb gang violence, drugs, and disrespect to teachers.

Then you wonder why so many kids are not graduating.

Start with momma. She did not graduate. Rochelle, Aaron, Lonny, Mike, the first four of momma kids did not graduate. I think a few of them did at least get their G.E.D.

Then you have what they called us when we were little 'the three little kids.'

This consisted of Fran, Tara, and me. We all graduated.

Then you have Satan and Peanut left.

Of course Satan didn't graduate because of being in and out of mental institutions.

And from the looks of things with Peanut, he had already been in juvenile and was not going to school.

So we can assume he was not going to get a diploma, but later maybe pick up the equivalent.

That's three out of nine kids not getting a high school diploma. Math computation configures that at about at about a twenty-seven percent graduation ratio we had.

Pitiful. But who's to blame for these low numbers?

Let's see if it's a cycle here. Let's start with the oldest kid to the youngest on how their kids fared or where they are at this present time. Aaron, the oldest sibling has three biological and one step-son.

I do know probably two of the biological graduated but not the real figure.

Rochelle has fours kids and neither graduated. I do know one did go back to get the equivalent. They should be thanked for being the only one out of that bunch that at least wanted the equivalent.

So that' a zero percent graduation ratio.

Lonny has no kids on record. Mike has four kids. So far, according to my sources, say they are no longer in school. The other two are active in school and the last is too young to attend at this time.

Fran has one kid and keeps them very active in school and make sure they attend. We don't know the future so we won't be prejudice and say yeah they will graduate. I have one on record and he attends school daily. When I say daily, I make sure. He's already received several perfect attendance awards among others because education is stressed daily. He may not be a rocket scientist, but I'll be damn if he becomes a loser while living with me. And I can speak for mine when I say yes he will graduate. As long as I'm alive and the good Lord sees it, he will walk across the stage. Now if God has other plans, I can't intervene with that.

Tara has one child. They moved back to Michigan recently, and once according to my sources, they are not active in school. Now let's not write them off yet but the odds are not looking to good. Satan does not have any kids. There is a God. And Peanut did not have any at the time of his passing.

Now let's tally up the score.

Nine kids with three that graduated, and at least two with equivalents. From those nine kids, we have fourteen nieces and nephews. And among those seven will not graduate, and the rest are either too young or currently in school.

Think about this for a second. Here we are the middle three kids, Fran, me, and Tara. We are the only ones to graduate, and the only ones with only one child. Wouldn't that be even stranger if our three kids graduated?

I have forgot what was even being discussed before this school thing crossed my mind.

Now where was I?

Oh ok we were talking about what has been going on since you left us momma.

Let me catch you up to date until the last year of two-thousand.

Can you believe Tara has gotten married? Yeah she finally tied the knot with someone. I don't know too much about him but he looks like a looser to me. It was around November of two-thousand when she got married.

I have gotten in trouble too many times expressing my opinion about someone, but I call it as I see it.

Now here's a joker that wears damn tight jeans with cowboy boots and a big silver buckle.

Looking like one of them original negro cowboys.

Come here boy a bale that cotton.

I didn't want to tell you but your mother passed away at the end of September two thousand and one..

It seems so strange that the two of you lived across the street from each other passing away less than six months apart.

Now I have lost my mother and grandmother in the same year. You, your mother, father, some sisters and brothers are gone.

On dad side his mother and father are gone. So now all is left is him.

Who would have thought at age thirty two through the lineage of both sides, I would have only my father left.

And I try to see him as much as I can. Even after putting aside the drinking, cursing, smoking, drugs, and whatever else fouls things they do over there, I manage to sneak a visit in here and there.

After him there will be no more.

Moms, your sisters and brothers that are gone, I don't know if they were even sixty years old.

Should we look forward to an early departure?

The New Year has arrived, and just like the same as all the other years, you wish for a more prosperous year.

Two-thousand and one was ok up until April 7th and 15th.

These are the days when we had the family get together and lost you the following week.

The first year of your death went by quick. I still drive by your old house picturing you sitting on the steps.

Satan soon after went to prison and from what the department of corrections web site states; he won't be out until two-thousand and eight. That's at least six or seven years of him being some what safe.

Now here's a hard one for you to believe moms.

Lonny got married August two-thousand and one. Well four of your kids are now married.

I don't know too much about her but if Lonny found someone that would marry him then God help them both.

Less than a month later moms, my favorite Twin Towers of New York had been attacked.

I have a surprise for you moms.

I asked Chelle to marry me and she said yes.

This still seems like a dream but at thirty-three years old, I guess it's time.

I'm moving up on the job making more money and it appears to be stable.

We are slated to get married on November 17th two-thousand and one.

I know that's Aaron's birthday, but that was coincidental and not designed.

I just wanted to hurry it up before she changes her mind.

No it won't be a big ceremony, just a nice Islamic wedding at the mosque.

No one from Michigan is coming down, because of the short notice.

Yes moms I know you are proud of me, and I will continue to make you proud.

You son is now becoming a man with great responsibilities.

No it won't be easy but I'm up for the challenge.

I'll have a great wife, as you already know from giving your approval, with great kids to bring up.

The funny thing is this was already foretold before I even knew it

Tara introduced me to Chelle in November nineteen ninety-seven.

It was around Thanksgiving and I was on my way back to Michigan.

This was also during the time I was going back and forth being undecided as to where I wanted to live.

On my way heading out the door, I'll tell you what God loves and that's the truth.

I told Tara just as plain as day tat is my future wife.

Tara just laughed it off and said "boy you are crazy, you never even seen her before."

Now here's a lady that I had never met, never seen before, and I'm making a comment like that.

I left with the thought of not coming back to Mississippi anytime soon.

Of course that didn't last long because that stint didn't last a month.

So when I came back to Mississippi December of ninety-seven, I had no thought of seeing this woman again.

I was going through some issues, and Chelle was the one that prayed for me.

I still didn't know who she was until it became clear to me she was he woman I met about a month ago.

Is this coincidental, or we were destined to meet.

To make a long story short, we became really good friends, and decided to date in August ninety-eight.

So we ended up getting married On November 17th, two thousand and one.

One year and one month after Tara got married. I guess Tara had to beat me to a set of ones.

I am one year, one month, and one day older than her. No relevance just making a statement.

So far five out of nine kids to marry so far are not bad.

Rochelle has been engaged several times, but I'm sure she'll find what she's looking for.

Satan doesn't appear to ever want to head that route.

Mike, who knows his situation down the line,

He's still in Michigan doing absolutely nothing. Well let me change that before he get mad and say I am lying. He works temporary jobs every once in a while. Guess anything to contribute to the drug habit will help.

How can you be a thirty-five year old man with no ambitions, no outlook on life, and walk around without a care in the world?

If we would have continued to hang with each other over the years, I probably would have turned out the same way.

I have always liked the finer things in life and to spend money on drugs, alcohol and gambling was not about to be the order of the day.

Walking round trying to find my next bottle to get drunk, crack rock or blunt to get high, or dollar to gamble foolishly made no sense to me.

How can addicts like this, find ways to contribute and support their habits always swear up and down they can't make ends meet?

And they really don't have a care or concern in the world.

They don't care about themselves.

They don't care about their families.

All they care about are getting the gaming industry, the liquor industry, and the illegal drug industry richer.

I'm not going to dwell on that.

Are we supposed to blame our parents for not providing as least one leg up on a future for us?

I know my parents didn't. My folks had no careers for us to try and pattern our life after.

All we knew was survival, because that's all my mother knew.

And she could only hand down to us what she knew.

My mother was not an educated woman. I think she only made it to the eighth grade if that far.

Don't know my fathers educational history, but based on where he lived and the way his parents were, it can be safe to say he at least graduated.

Last Chapter

Even though this book has been dormant since I think late two thousand and one, I will just bring everyone up to date.

It is now August two thousand and seven, and believe it or not much of what you had been reading up to now has not changed with the family.

I won't call out any names this time but hey, to each his own.

You're probably wondering why it took my so long to add to this writing.

No it wasn't that I didn't have anything to say, but this is the original contents that were supposed to head to the printing press.

I was also waiting to let everyone know how everyone turned out since the watered down version did not state it.

Well some of you may be mad with me but hey, here we go.

Starting with the oldest Aaron child and male.

He's still a preacher and has been ordained. He's even preached and giving numerous eulogies at friends and families funerals.

And I'm sure he knows there's a few things we may disagree on, he's not trying to change me and I'm not trying to change him.

We learn from each other as the way God intended for it to be. God says in the Quran I created you and made you different that you may know one another parenthetically and know one another and not be despised of one another.

And Aaron also has a good message and it's good to know after all these many years, he truly means well.

Rochelle, of course is the oldest sister and next to the oldest child.

She's still doing her thing.

We really don't talk much but hey it's been that way for years.

She's a grandmother but that don't slow her down.

Guess old habits are hard to break.

I won't get off in to the addictions, but you are free to do whatever you want to do and believe it or not, it has just soaked into my brain we will never be a loving family. You know who you are?

I'm cool with that and even if I died today, I feel my favor has been completed in at least trying to be a brother to you guys.

Lonny.

It just really not too much to say about you Lonny.

I mean you are also doing your thing and I do know you and your wife split up for several years.

Or should I say you abandoned them.

Drugs really have done a number on you and did going to prison really help you?

Mike.

Mike, Mike, Mike.

You are a sad case.

I mean here you are, was in Michigan doing absolutely nothing. You moved to Mississippi because someone was after you several years ago. Then you moved back to Michigan after you paid them, and swore on your own life you will never move back to Mississippi. Stayed there and continued to be and hang with low lives.

Now you are back in Mississippi with no ambitions in life. No outlook on life. No any sense of responsibilities.

On top of that, you are living with Rochelle and I know that's not going to last long because you are not shelling out any dollars.

You are freeloading off anyone that come your way and all of you are sucking daddy dry for his little disability check.

Yeah Mike I know those around him were and still is doing this before you came, but did you have to include yourself in that equation?

Yeah I know he's paying about five hundred a month to Rochelle for a half bedroom laundry room.

I paid two hundred a month for it but I guess inflation went up drastically over the ten years since I was there.

Well he has a nice home in north Jackson, but because of someone else's lies and greed, he doesn't want to live there.

He'd rather stay in Baghdad being constantly hungry where his next meal may be a bullet.

Well unfortunately Mike, this is not about daddy, this is about you.

And because you do nothing day in and day out but dope pop, then I have nothing else to say.

Fran.

My sweet dear sis Fran. My dear twin Fran.

You know something Fran. I have never really had anything bad to say about you other than when we were little.

And to this day I still have nothing bad to say about you.

You care about and love any and everyone you come into contact with.

And people love you in return.

I hate it that you try to save everyone, but guess what Fran, you can't.

I love you more today than I did yesterday.

You had the first niece to walk across the stage and graduate.

I really commend you on that.

You have done a fine job with Missie and I'm sure she will turn out to be a fine young woman.

And I am so happy you have decide to make Mississippi and Jackson in particular your home after more than 25 years.

You stayed in Michigan longer than any of us and I know it was a tough decision.

We are now assembled in Mississippi where it all started.

Moms would have loved to see this day.

Especially if she and Peanut were still alive.

Fran continue to be that sweet person and now that you are here, I'm not going to let no one, including family members take advantage of your kindness.

I love you dearly my dearest twin.

Now for you Joe.

How are you man?

This is the tenth anniversary of you being back in Mississippi.

A few major events have happened in your life since being there.

You have traveled to more places in the first few years that most people go all their lives.

I mean who can boast going to Disney World, The Bahamas, Las Vegas, Los Angeles, and even the Catalina Islands of the Coast of California.

This is in the same year.

Good thing you did meet a woman that loves to travel and be able share this with you.

You had a good job at the luxury retailers Saks Fifth Avenue Corporate office where you stayed there over eight years.

To bad you had to get laid off because of corporate down sizing, but you also know that is the nature of the business.

Well the severance package wasn't bad either they gave you. More than what some companies have been doing for employees after so many years of service.

But being there from nineteen ninety-eight until two thousand and seven you receive four promotions.

The company also sent you on business trips to numerous places such as Beverly Hills, San Diego, Santa Barbara, Palm Springs, San Francisco, and other major cities in California. They have sent you to Orlando, Miami, Tampa, Ft. Lauderdale, Palm Beach and other lovely cities in the Sunshine State. Not to mention sending you to places like Portland Oregon, Denver, Atlanta, Washington DC, Phoenix, Chicago, cities in Virginia, and other places you can't even remember.

You stayed in hotels, resorts, and other fine living arrangements sparing no expense. Rental cars, flights, and other forms of transportation were all compliments of Saks. Eating in restaurants all over with names you can barely pronounce with the tab being picked up by yours truly. Saks Incorporated.

You have also been on your own to states like Washington, Pennsylvania, Wisconsin, Texas, Alabama, Tennessee, Missouri, New Mexico, Mexico, and the list goes on.

But getting laid off was not a total loss because even before leaving you were front runner for a Senior Network Analyst position.

The only reason you did not take it was because you had already accepted a Lead Systems Administrator position with the State of Mississippi. And that was like a promotion with more money.

Your last day with Saks was March 30th 2007, and you started with the State of Mississippi on April 1st 2007. And this is no April fools.

So roughly you were unemployed for one day.

Being married was another major event that happened in your tenth anniversary being back in Mississippi.

That's working out ok but issues are nothing to run to the judge about.

I mean we have issues like kids and finances but who don't.

Being married is hard work but I have been committed to doing the right thing.

Of course you still don't drink after almost ten years and based on the past, that is a real major accomplishment. No clubs in almost ten years. Joe there's really nothing bad to say about you these last fifteen years.

Materials things have never been an issue for you. I mean you still have the finer things in life being in Mississippi that you had in Michigan. You still eat decent. This time it took a little while longer to establish some things. Lil Joe is still with you and he's not wanting for anything either. Never had in Michigan, and never have in Mississippi. You try to get him the things you never had growing up so he wouldn't have to turn to the streets to get them.

Tara.

Well, well, well.

Lady T what's going on?

Where should I start with you?

Well you are the first to make the pilgrimage from Michigan back to Mississippi.

Since you have been back you have obviously done well for yourself.

Opening your own business, as owner and director of something you love to do.

And that is providing education for children.

Must pay well if you are able to buy a home, and have multiple vehicles.

You dress nice and can shop and eat anywhere you want.

Satan.

Satan will be satan.

He's just been released from prison recently and I still haven't seen him.

I believe he was gone anywhere from five to seven years which is the last time I can recall seeing him.

He was at a car wash hustling and after my car was washed he walked up.

I offered to take him to Church's Chicken to get something to eat but of course he cussed me out about buying some cheap chicken. Said all that grease would kill him.

Now here's a joker that beats the streets up all day looking for drugs having the nerve to say some chicken grease will kill him.

Anyway, I went on to KFC and he was happy.

He was given the change left from the twenty dollar bill, dropped off back at the car wash, heard a few more derogatory words from him, and that was the last conversation we had.

Conclusion

In my conclusion you may still look at me in a certain way. You may even perceive me to be something other than what I am.

I have another motto which is 'I can only be what I make myself.'

I have made myself into the kind of person that has a love for all mankind.

Having the belief that all men and women are the same under the eyesight of God helps me to love myself more than ever.

Respecting all people regardless of color, religion, or even sexual orientation.

Because deep down inside, whether black, white, Indian, Mexican, or whatever color you may be, we all bow down to the one God Who's the Creator of all things, the Sender of all prophets, and the Master of the day of judgment

Whether you are Muslim, Christian, or Jewish, almighty God will still look and judge us according to how we treated ourselves, mankind, and last but not least Him.

I am a Muslim.

And for those that truly don't understand, it is simply one who submits himself to God. And Islam means peace total submission to do the will of God.

So if you want to go straight to the facts the look at the father of religion Abraham, and all the prophets. They were submitters to God, so you can call them and yourselves Muslims no matter what faith you practice.

I was watching TV one day and I heard a preacher say he could not be a Muslim because they kill innocent people and say they do it in the name of God.

What an idiot and an idiotic thing to say.

That's like me saying I could never be a Christian because the KKK kills innocent people and say they do it in the name of Christ.

What's the difference?

People it's too much hypocrisy in religion and there are extremist in every religious faith.

These people are not believers, they are brainwashed.

Let me tell you something?

God does not allow innocent people to be killed then accept the person or people responsible into paradise.

I can't speak on Christianity or Judaism, but it is a sin to commit suicide and kill others while doing it.

These people can't say they are a Muslim and carry on this way.

Islam teaches tolerance and not aggression.

Jihad means the holy struggle you go through to truly please God not holy war.

It is a struggle to live right, to do right, and to treat friends, family, and mankind right according to the way God intended for it to be. Not religion against religion to try and eradicate one for the other.

And don't act as though when we say Allah we are saying something strange or evil. Allah is the same name Muslims, Christians, and Jews use in the Middle East and numerous places outside America when referring to God.

The same as when Jehovah's Witness call him Jehovah or the Native Americans call him Kinkashala.

All referring to the one God that controls the heavens and the earth

We are all the same and the one God we worship is the same.

You may be Muslim, Christian, Jewish, Buddha, or Hindu, we can't be all.

What may be good for one may not be good for the other.

And this is the other way around.

I choose to be Muslim.

If you have never read the Quran do so.

You will find out that the media, people and the rumors associated with the negativity and portrayal of Islam are incorrect.

Being that helped me to change the way I conducted myself.

Oh I was terrible as a child, teenager, and young adult.

My behavior was learned early as a child up until early adulthood, but people still want to hang on to those days.

Why is it so easy for people to remember the bad things long ago, but can't remember the good just yesterday?

I only wanted to share a few things that plagued my mind and this helps me to be a better person.

Look at my track record the last ten or more years. It has been major progress.

And all things people can say are they remembered when you were this or that way.

Yeah trust me I remember to.

A lot of it was negative.

There has been enough time elapsed for them to compliment you on other positive accomplishments.

What you have been reading all this time are from times of despair in my life.

People that meet me in this present day and age have no idea of what I went through.

By them not seeing drink alcohol, gamble, or doing drugs they assume it has always been this way.

But this was many, many, years ago but I have to find myself defending myself to the people that know me.

Listen, let it go.

I don't let it bother me anymore so why should you.

Why am I still the subject of the day after all these years trying to walk a straight path?

I wasn't talked about this much when I wreaked havoc on society many, many years ago.

And to answer your question as to why I felt a certain way about things is because of lack of knowledge.

Remember the old saying if you know better you'll do better.'

That's me.

I know better and will continue to do better in spite or despite what you may think of me in this day and age.

Yeah it did bother me when I use to care about what people thought of me whether it was good or bad.

Then I found out they are going to talk about you either way.

Mostly bad.

People don't care if you change your life for the better because it doesn't give them the ammunition they need to justify saying bad things about you.

I use three quotes to help me get through my days and not let anything affect me.

Something was bothering me one day and I was doing my best to play it off like nothing was going on.

Now I was so good at playing things off if something bothered me that an Oscar, Emmy, and Tony awards should have been given to me.

This elderly guy looked at me and said "Joe, it's going to be alright."

I said, "Mr. Henry I am alright."

He said it again but then added "a day above ground is better than anything you can imagine."

Not only did I not fool him into believing everything was alright, he didn't buy anything else that was being said.

From that day on until now whatever bothers me I think of that quote, because a day above ground is better than anything you can imagine.

You don't believe no matter where you go in life, no matter what you do in life, and not matter what you see in life, everyday is a good day.

And if you don't believe me try missing one.

Try missing one single day and you will find out quickly how everyday is a good day.

That's why I live each day like it's my last, but I also live each day like it's going to last forever.

I don't believe in the thank God its Friday saying.

When it is Monday people are always wishing it was Friday so they can be off work or do whatever Saturday and Sunday.

You spend your whole life thinking this way and as fast as these days are going, it seems as though the weekends come even faster than the weekdays goes by.

According to stats, the average lifespan of a human being is approximately seventy to eighty years old.

Let's use the eighty years as an example for the point I'm trying to make.

If it is fifty two weeks in a year which means that the fifty two weekends equates to one hundred and four days. It's also fifty two weeks worth of weekdays that equates to two hundred and sixty days.

If you lived to be eighty years old that means you rushed twenty thousand eight hundred days, or fifty seven years of your life to enjoy eight thousand three hundred and twenty days, or twenty three years.

Go figure.

It's a verse in the Quran that states, "through difficulty comes ease, and it says it again verily through difficulty comes ease.

Yeah it gets hectic every once in a while and it feels as though you are not going to make it.

That's why look to these quotes to help me out.

So people whatever you may think of me now, or when I was doing bad things it's up to you.

I feel a favor has been completed within my self that will now allow me to finally exhale.

I have apologized to enemies, families, and those who feel they may have suffered through my reign of terror as an adolescent, youth, and young adult.

I can't let that hang over my shoulders anymore.

Family, as we continue to lose our loved ones, I can't concentrate on what you want to do out of life whether you feel it's good or detrimental to your life.

You guys can't say that even though we act barbaric at times, I haven't spent my life trying to bring us together.

And today a few of you have a decent relationship with me.

Even though we have put what's in this book behind us, we still have major issues.

As we bring new life into our immediate and extended families, they are going to be the torch carriers for this cycle of hate.

It's sad to say this, but who can deny or negate what I'm saying as untrue?

Even though I didn't and still don't, but it's becoming more apparent that 'I will have to die all alone.'

For the people that know me and have known me, thank you for seeing me for who I am today and not what I was yesterday. For the rest, thank you for reading this with an open mind, as well as an open heart as I greet you with the greetings words of peace in the Arabic language of As Salaam Alaikum.(Peace be unto you).

The Bad Part of Me

See, this is the bad part of me
I'm not liked, cause I don't want to be
You didn't like me then, so why like me now
I haven't been liked, since I was a child
All these many years, I have been unwanted
Everyday I have to be confronted
With people saying, what type of life did you enjoy
Neither, cause I was a man, before I was a boy
They still don't understand
I explain it to them the best way I can
Their brains are like brick walls
And wouldn't even break if they had a long fall
You still don't get it, to bad
Relive the life that I had
And you'll say "dam, bet"
"Joe your life was a wreck"
These past twenty years have been a dream
Cause I don't like you, we're not a team
And you don't even come up to my level
Deep inside I'm really with the devil
You don't understand see
That's the bad part of me

Tears That Don't Cry

I can tell the truth, yes I cry
My tears don't even have to tell a lie
Sometimes I will, when I really won't
Sometimes I do, when I really don't
There's nothing wrong with shedding tears
Some people haven't shed a tear for years
Crying sometimes beat out a shout
When I do, I let it all out
Tears are serious, and not done for pleasure
It really does alleviate pressure

1-26-89

The Future of Man

Living in a racist world
Can't even raise a little girl
First you die, then you live
In a place, where there's nothing to give
Though you struggle to do right
That's not good enough for life
Even though life is like a game of spades
You have them all, you have it made
I don't even have to shed a tear
Cause I know the end of the world is near
Jesse Jackson the man, Louis Farrakhan the prophet
All the racism around, I wish they would stop it
Black man will rule again, to bad I won't see it
A black president, I hope my little brother be it
So don't walk in front of me, I do not follow
Martin Luther our future, his words I'll swallow
Don't walk in back of me, I do not lead
Mandela cell dweller, I'm glad he's freed
So walk beside me, and be my friend
Then we can take it to the end

Joseph F. Henderson III

Destroy Me

I'm a person of many thoughts
my heart is money, so anything can be bought
But people treat me like a stuffed animal
I eat it all up, cause I'm a cannibal
I live for myself, and no one else
Sometimes I really do need help
If you think you can make it through life alone
Sorry to inform you, you're dead wrong
Life is something I can't handle
My heart burns just like a candle
Thought's of being here, a migraine headache
And the birth of me was just a mistake
I'll tell you what I think of me
Wishing I was dead when I may as well be
Cause I can't do a dam thing right
Even if I tried, with all my might
I talk to myself, don't even get a response
Can a person just live for once

89

My Week

Today is the beginning of tomorrow
Tomorrow is the ending of sorrow
Yesterday is a day we must not forget
Last night was a night we didn't expect
Monday is a day we all hate
Tuesday is a day to late
Wednesday is a day to sweet
Thursday is a day, past the middle of the week
Friday is a day we all love
Saturday is what the weekend is made of
Sunday. Hmmmm, I'll have to think about that one.

Joseph F. Henderson III

No Nonsense

I live for love, in exchange for the same
It hurt so bad, like no pain no gain
The way my life is, is not a gotta be
To my family, I'm a menace to society
We never loved each other, but was near
Wishing hateful things like, "wishing you wasn't here"
As for my mother, she took a lot of hell
Off me in which, I knowingly failed
The streets were my life, and still is
Won't even tell you the things I did
Forgive myself, but you wouldn't understand
If you did, but who gives a damn
Not me, I don't feel no remorse
I don't even feel guilty, of course
Will hurt anybody for a quarter
Kill a brick, and drown a drop of water
Have the will, the desire the urge
To make it, cause life ain't nothing but a four letter word
Now that's no nonsense

I'm Not Loved

How can I be loved, when I'm not even liked
To everybody, I'm not their type
Wanting to love, but I can't
No one will even give me a chance
To show them I'm a human
Instead of everyone assuming
The way my life is, is the way I'll be
Often ask the question, why me
Wished you loved me, as tight as you hugged me
Instead of saying, "Joe, why do you bug me?"
Here to help the world, black and white
But I'll have to be loved, cause this ain't right
The environments with the hearts, wondering what they think of me
Only the one's that hate, are the ones that love me
Can't keep on living like this
When it's the real world that's missed
Always isolated, only to the hateful
That's why I'm so ungrateful
But will change, only if you changed
Me being loved, may just be arranged
If I changed you, and you changed me
Then the whole world would see
That we could pull together as sisters and brothers
Cause one human being should never dis another

Joseph F. Henderson III

Signs of the For Real Times

People say that I'm impersonating a person
How could this be, when it's the whole world that's cursing
Cause it's religion against religion, black and white
You and me both know this isn't right
But we tend to go in the other direction
Instead of getting everyone up to perfection
Though we can still be taught, and not know what it mean
Drugs and money, are the powers to everything
And the government is our biggest problem
They're not our leaders, so the worries, how could we solve them
Yet their positions are to back us up
Against enemy countries, that jacks us up
And you want me to know world history
How can that be, when everything is a mystery
It's like, everybody are on their own
This it will be, until everyone is gone
Don't know what to expect or select
If it was my time to be judged, I will be a reject
But that's not likely, it's Jesus that's felt see
Wanting GOD, before the devil really get me
Everyone in this world is headed for doom
You'll know when it happens, there will be a loud boom
Meaning Jesus is here to take his people
He will not take those who are not equal
Why that is said, meaning the true ones
Not me, so I'll be a through one
It suppose to be united we stand, divided we fall
Bet everyone respond, when Jesus makes his call
You and I don't even care
Cause the smell of death is in the air

89

Joseph F. Henderson III

Real Self-Destruction

Girl being with you is a must
The more you stay away, my heart adjust
Have many pains, only very few days are left
All can be seen, is my own face of death
It’s not you, everyone is on my case
Just can’t wait for me to leave this place
Hope it’s soon, any day
Cause earth wasn’t meant for me to live on anyway
Just know you’ll be excited
As for everyone else, they will be delighted
Who’s to blame, the world or me
Guess the world, cause it never done anything for me
But made me miserable, my mind is mixed up
Headed for destruction, while you are getting fixed up
Keep on living like this, I can’t go through it
Have nothing to loose, that’s why I want to do it
End it all is what I mean, and not a dream
Think silly thoughts is my main theme
So don’t say anything, don’t need any instructions
But to solve my own ‘self-destruction’

89

I Lost

Now the time has come for me to die
Please don't cry, or ask me why
On my way to a permanent vacation
GOD will help me out of this situation
One life to live, one life to die
Look to the sky, but the ground is where I want to lie
No more pity, all my life I've worried
Beside my little brother, is where I want to be buried
My feelings for death, seem to accelerate expeditiously
No time to waste, do you pity us, or me
Heaven or hell, GOD or satan, who cares
If I'm going to hell, ok, see you there
But if I happen to come back reincarnated
Don't say "Joe, how in the hell did you make it"
Believe GOD will save every man's soul
Sixty-five and seventy, won't be considered old
Happiness and peace, for saints and sinners
In my new life, I will be a victorious winner
So little Joe, as I lay down my head
If GOD is a good GOD, then I'll be dead
Daddy loves you so dearly
Will keep a picture of you near me
Will cherish the short years we spent
Away I went, glad it's you GOD sent
So precious in my eyes, so meaningful in my heart
Sorry, please forgive me, for breaking that apart
May twenty-six, nineteen ninety-one
GOD's greatest gift to me was born
July eight, nineteen sixty-eight
That date, life is fate, now death is great
Inhale evil, then exhale hate
My heart is pumping ungratefulness, at a fast rate
Now you see why there's no desire to live

But be in a place where there's nothing to give
Look into my eyes, you'll see everything but love
Selfishness, pestilence, inequity, I'm my own judge
Day in and day out, all my thoughts are about death
You pray for happiness, I'll pray for a last breath
I can see you smiling, your wish must have come true
See I'm alive, so my guess, GOD must love you
They say if you pray, your prayers will be answered
You got your wish, guess mine was cancelled
GOD is the author of life and death
Here's my life, now figure out what's left
If a man is born, he will truly die
Everyone knows this, so when it happens, why cry
We act like GOD promised life with no death
Now we're angry with HIM, for taking someone's last breath
We curse GOD when someone is deceased
And say GOD why YOU do it, knowing HE's the AUTHOR of PEACE
The LORD works in mysterious ways, as we know
So why treat HIM like a convenient overcoat
We put HIM on, when we need HIM, we take HIM off when we don't
Praise HIM when HE's good, and when HE's not, we won't
GOD is GREAT, GOD is GOOD
Take my life, I wish YOU would
Bow my head, now I am dead
Thank you LORD, for taking this life I dread
Amen

Over & Over, Again & Again

Last night, I tried to take my life again
They say killing yourself is a sin
But as you can see, when it came down to it
Wouldn't say I was scared, just couldn't go through it
Crack and cigarettes, you're killing yourself
Why I'm wrong, when GOD is asked for help
Even though I can see my enemies killing me
LORD help him, guide him, little Joe is feeling me
You can run, but you can't hide, I'm not trying to
Just tired, I can feel it, I'm dying soon
Either by me, GOD, or an enemy
Heaven or hell, the LORD or the devil is sending me
Not shy, don't ask me why, I want to die
Won't lie, just want to try, to end it all, so little Joe don't cry
Don't worry, be happy, daddy's happy, my worries are over
The only problems, won't try to solve them, but this burden will be on your shoulder
It will be lifted soon GOD will look out for HIS children
HE's the merciful, but treat HIM wrong, HE'll kill you
In the name of ALLAH, the MERCIFUL, the BENEFICIT
HE gave me this life, owe it back to HIM, it's my biggest deficit
All that is needed in this life that's not fun
Is me and a fifth of Paul Masson
Sometimes I drink, and drink, and drink, until comatose
Dying and never waking up again, is what's dreamed of most
So see you later, whether in hell or Heaven
The zero hour is here, it's fifty-nine after eleven
LORD knows, I don't want to be alive, when you make YOUR return
So take my life now, knowing later I will burn

As you can see, I don't care if my soul be saved
GOD gave me this life, gave it back, so I paid
LORD can you help me, no I'm not asking for a lot
One last breathe, people paying respect, and a burial plot
Victory can be mine, if I died tonight
Turn out the lights now, forever, I can sleep tight
Don't wake me, don't even want to budge
The LORD will get me up, when it's time to be judged
Being trapped in hell, death is my only way out
GOD will find me guilty, beyond a reasonable doubt
The lake of fire forever, will compensate the sentence
The say Joe, change now, ask for repentance
Living in hell now, death is hell bound
Won't see Heaven, but will be buried in hell's ground
That's ok, it's the choice I had to make
Live forever in Heaven, but choose to stay in hell and bake
If the LORD hear my screams, please pull me to shore
GOD please forgive me, I don't want to burn in hell no more
Wonder if GOD make deals, I have an offer HE can't refuse
So who am I to do that, times up I loose
But wait a minute, hold up, GOD had a jump start
HE knew my life was doomed, I felt it in my heart
Sitting back trying to think, reminiscing on my life
Even as a little child, I paid a hefty price
So now little Joe is here, this foolishness should end
With him, I can see myself growing up all over again
LORD take control of my son, you can raise him better
Watch him, guide him, until I can get myself together
Don't know how long it will take, GOD is patient
The angel of death, my alias is satan
Yes, I can say I love, and believe in GOD
It's true, about wanting to die, don't that seem odd
Do I really exist, what's the purpose of being on this earth

When did this start? I have been feeling this way since birth
Years and years, I have shed so many tears
The crying almost stopped, when little Joe finally came here
GOD gave me this life, I only value death
If I had another breath, you can have it none left.

Joseph F. Henderson III

I Miss You

Peanut I know that you are deceased, but please rest in peace
From me only a nephew, sorry I couldn't give you a niece
We don't need kids growing up in this messed up world
It's easier to raise a boy, but harder to raise a girl
Kids dying, parents crying, when will it stop
I'm trying, other's relying, on this death rate to drop
Think the intoxicated, could be their own designated
Have you ever driven home drunk, and wonder how you made it
All day, everyday, can only think of death
Quiet as kept, not suicidal, just need help
Peanut tried to save ya, besides trying to raise ya
Wish you had a daughter, I would call her Daisha
But to much pride, self evident I have died
They lied, I cried, you sighed, it's sad I'm alive
Peanut why you had to leave me so soon
That's ok, I'm coming to join you, so make room
Even if we make contact, from the depths of hell
No jail or cell can hold me, only death can make me well
Hope to leave this earth, high and intoxicated
My last words would be I made it, this life, hate it
My only woman be tripping, Peanut you know that's how life goes
Death blows, LORD knows, that's what life shows
But baby please forgive me, as you have before
Have left many times, but won't leave you any more
You have stuck by my side, even when having to grieve
Don't know what came over me, to make me want to leave
What's the meaning of life, does it have any purpose
They tell me times will get better, but still feel worthless
Crying all day, dry tears are seen on my cheek
All week I can't sleep, it's hard to speak, so bury me deep

You call it depression, I call it obsession, with death
Let me answer your question, I'm not suicidal, quiet as kept
Just don't like living, it keeps getting worse
Moms had nine kids, but why you had to die first
Knowing it wasn't your fault, your killer got caught
They should have set him free, his life would have came to a halt
He's in the joint, but what's the point, his life I want
Will roll down on his ass, with a glock full of hollow points
It says thou shall not kill, I'm dead anyways
I want life to end now, death comes many ways
In my dreams many screams, Peanut we're still a team
It's not destroyed, death is in my eyes, they gleam
Joy comes with pain, and ends in despair
Don't care if life is not fair, death occur anywhere
In my bed I dread, the ground need to be fed
Sometimes I beg to be dead, just can't get ahead
How can I win if, I'm always loosing
Death is what I'm choosing, you think it's amusing
Please don't think I'm crazy, my IQ very high
My competence level exceeds all, I just want to die
Nothing can change, being in this zone
Leave me alone until I'm gone, so my life postpone
Life was fun while it lasted, and it was enough
My zero hour is here, so little Joe be tough
When you tell me you love me, pain goes through my chest
I gave you my best, so now let me get my rest.

Times Up

I live a life of sorrow, always have to beg and borrow
Wishing, I was weak enough to end it all tomorrow
Why is it the grave that's being craved
It should be easy for me to do it, I was always brave
I am strong enough, have been on this earth long enough
This time I'm right, I have been wrong enough
Living with pain, reincarnation I dread
When you die, a person can sleep forever, cause they're dead
Wish I could trade the life of my little brother
GOD didn't promise life, without having to suffer
The smell of death is in the air, I live without hope and despair
We're in the times of revelation, the zero hour is near
Materialism is my vanity, I have lost my family
You say how can it be, it seems I have no sanity
If the LORD is my SHEPPARD, how come I always want
Things that are meaningless, so I shall not flaunt
My family, friends, and females, wonder why I'm always intoxicated
GOD knows if they only knew, how much I hate it
Tell the LORD everyday, how much I want to die
HE won't grant me my wish, I often ask why
HE says "being alive is a little better, than living in hell"
But the way my life is lived on earth, I can't really tell
Living so complex, so misunderstood, often confused
Physically, mentally, and sexually abused
So many women, so little love, my body is my only advantage
One night with a woman, a bill is paid, that's how I manage
Not merciful, no passion, no remorse
I'm not happy, no, ok, feelings, I don't care about yours

People only hear me now, from my desperate cries
Man ain't truly happy, until Joe truly die
OH WHY
I'm the angel of death, the prophet of doom
Sin is you, sin is me, sentence us to doom
My heart sinks like the titanic
It's vain, but what's felt, goddamn it
But little Joe, carry on daddy's name
When you hear of the bad things, be proud, don't feel shame
Now I lay my head down to sleep
I ask the LORD my life to keep
If I should wake, before I die
I'll ask the LORD to tell me why
AMEN

Good-vs-Evil

The travesty of justice, compounds the evil
The things done, make me and the devil seem equal
It seem like GOD and the devil was playing tug-of-war
We know GOD won, but who was taking score
I'm stuck in the middle, GOD
me, satan
Debating my hating, while the love is waiting
The devil is in the cockpit, how can I fight it
I take a seat in the back, now GOD is the pilot
Satan had the nerve, to ask GOD for a challenge
Fool, never under estimate the power of GOD's talent
GOD, I may seem evil, please accept my loyalty
ALMIGHTY, your MAJESTY, MASTER, your ROYALTY
LORD take my hand, as I reach out to grab YOURS
A MAN with a DIVINE mentality, wish I could have yours
Religious by nature, but was born into sin
Didn't ask to be here, but I'm asking for my end
Good things come to those who wait
If I died in my sleep, it wouldn't be too late
Revelations are here, the end is near
LORD knows, I don't want to live to see another year
Don't know when I'll die, but GOD knows
It's soon, I feel it, in my eyes it shows
LORD please rid me of my woes and foes
And take my breath, as soon as my eyes close
Every second, every minute, every hour go by
I can't lie, I want to die, just let me try, don't ask why
Peanut, why you had to go and leave me little bro
Seems like all that's left in this world, is me and little Joe
GOD took you at an early age
I'll see you again, I know your soul was saved
This time, we will never be apart
It will be you and me again, like we were from the start
What can I say, as I lay and try to pray
Today, as little Joe play, hey, it's got to be a better way
I can't see it, my vision is blurry see

Hurry, it's not a worry, just bury me
Knowing they can only dig six feet, please make it twelve
Those extra feet, will get me closer to hell
If I shook hands with the devil, GOD would you be mad
I already did, so to dam bad
LORD, when I die, and drown in my own blood
It seems contradictory, when YOU are shown love
I have to be on good side forever
But right and wrong, are lurking in the midst together
So don't blame it on me, but regardless
The people that knows me, calls me cruel and heartless
Since my little bro passed, and left me all alone
December 11, 1995, he's gone, relocated to a different home
So rest in peace, until I can join your death
It won't be long, but while being here, I'll mourn your death
Just tell me the address, where I can find you
Don't forget, but if so, I'll remind you
Wish we could be roommates, in the same casket
Lying side by side, kicking and laughing
Having fun like we did, in the days of old
Playing ball when it was hot, trying to stay warm when it was cold
I still think about you daily, thinking and reminiscing
But playing video games, is what I'm really missing
Wanting to die bad, so I can see your face
It's been pure hell for me, I know you'll like your new place
When I'm gone, I'll move right beside you
So I can guide you, like I tried to
So little bro, I'm outta here
If you see me coming, you gotta cheer

A Sista's Nightmare

Beaten, battered, and bruised.
Mentally, physically, and sexually abused.
Yo tears drippin, while it`s 40`s brothas sippin.
The malt liquor is now his god, so he starts trippin.
No need to run, you let him exercise his manhood.
After anotha tormentful moment, he feels good.
Black power prints, indents the temple.
Near the same spot of the homemade dimple.
So now you limp away, to make it to freedom, your bed.
A two year old infant, watching blood drip from yo head.
Lying there stiff, scared to move a muscle.
More cussing is heard, you brace for another scuffle.
"Get yo lazy ass up and cook dinner" is heard from a distance.
"Oh GOD please let me die" is thought that instance.
A surge of energy burst through the body, dinner is cooked, time for him to eat.
A tired, worn out body, finds out that he's asleep.
If you wake him, he'll be mad, so you let him sleep.
If you don't wake him, he'll be mad, cause he didn't eat.
The ginsu is still sharp, the smell of death is in the air.
It's yo life or his, the zero hour is here.
On your knees with your kids, praying to GOD, hoping that you're heard.
All is left behind, nothing, disappeared without a word.

Who's to blame?

Who's to blame for all your pain.
If my being cease to exist, would you remain the same.
Tired of trying, hopelessly seeing you crying.
Once again my only way out is I see myself dying.
Putting you through a life of torment.
Never really experiencing childhood enjoyment.
Escaping misery, in exchange for living hell.
From day one, off and on, no I'm not living well.
Constantly grieving, your treatment sometimes inhumane.
Spending time felling sorrow, only death will hide the shame.
Wondering what you think of me, as these days go by.
Why it's so easy to cry, but so hard to die.
Being punished for a life that was all but great.
Your fate is from my hate, at another's sake.
Being the fourth in line, you being a gift.
For the second, no burden, no carrying on, no fifth.
Choose another alias, the cycle of Joe's must end.
Then you'll maybe treat yours like a son, not a friend.
Oh how I dread to see you this way.
This day, this May, let's have it your way.
A smile so sweet when you're happy, how lovely.
A cry so sincere, my anger emits, how ugly.
The effects sometimes gruesome, how can I do this to my first?
Lord expel me from this life, this earth, this universe.
He means well, a nice kid, all I need to see me through.
What can I do for him to approve a love that's true.
Not wanting to grow old, or be a grouch, or a miser
Son I'll get more faith, your dad will be wiser.

Made in the USA
Middletown, DE
12 February 2022